Literary Terms in Fiction and Prose

Literary Terms in Fiction and Prose

A.J. Sebastian
N.D.R. Chandra

AUTHORSPRESS

Worldwide Circulation through Authorspress Global Network
First Published 2025
by Authorspress

E-35/103, Jawahar Park
Laxmi Nagar, Delhi-110 092

e-mail: authorspress@yahoo.com

Typeset in NewCenturySchlbk by Chitra Computers

Literary Terms in Fiction & Prose
ISBN 81-7273-169-8

Printed in India at Tarun Offset, Delhi.

Preface

To appreciate Fiction it is essential that one is familiar with the tools governing them. This book is meant as a companion to students of literature who grapple with the problem of technical terms in their understanding and appreciation of the literary forms. We have consulted several authors in bringing out this handbook. We acknowledge their great contribution: J.A. Cuddon, *A Dictionary of Literary Terms*, 1977; C. Hugh Holman & William Harmon, *A Handbook of Literature*, 1986; Gerald Prince, *A Dictionary of Narratology*, 1987; Chris Baldick, *The Concise Oxford Dictionary of Literary Terms*, 1990; Lee T. Lemon, *A Glossary for the Study of English*, 1992; M.H. Abrams, *A Glossary of Literary Terms,* 2000; Joseph T. Shipley, *Dictionary of World Literary Terms*, 1993; John Peck & Martin Coyle, *Literary terms and Criticism*, 1993; Andrew Michael Roberts, *Bloomsbury Guides to English Literature : The Novel*, 1993; Richard Gill, *Mastering English Literature*, 1995; J. Pickering & J. Hoeper, *Literature*, 1990; Karl Beckson & Arthur Ganz, *A Reader's Guide to Literary Terms: A Dictionary;* Ross Murfin & S.M. Ray, *The Bedford Glossary of Critical and Literary Terms*, 1998, Goodman,W.R., *Quintessence of Literary Essays*, 2000; Wynne Davis, Marion, *Guide to English Literature*, 1989; and Booker, Peter, *Cultural Theory: A Glossary*, 1999.

We are grateful to our publishers, Authorspress, Delhi, for their keen interest in getting this work in print.

Kohima **Authors**
7 October 2003

Introduction

BEGINNINGS OF THE NOVEL

Novel is the literary form that is most popular today. It is a fictional prose narrative with a plot, characters and situations. The word *novel* is derived from the Latin *novellas* meaning 'new'. The term came to be used since the early Renaissance in the fourteenth century to depict any new story. Italian writer Giovanni Boccaccio used the term *novella* to refer to his prose narratives in the *Decameron* (1348-1353). Eventually when his tales were translated into English it was called novel.

Novel as a literary form was popular among the Greeks in the form of pastoral romances such as *Daphnis and Chloe* of the second century AD and *Aethiopica* of the third century AD. In Latin Petronius Arbiter's, the *Satyricon* of the first century AD and Lucius Apuleius's *Metamorphoses* or *The Golden Ass* of the second century AD are examples of ancient novels. In the Middle Ages there were the Old French *fabliau* which were comic tales of ordinary life in verse. Chaucer's (c1343-1400) *Canterbury Tales* can be considered as verse novel in the English tradition.

Picaresque or rogue story began to be popular in Spain in the sixteenth century with such works as *Lazarillo de Tormes* (1554) and *Guzmán de Alfarache* (1559-1604). Cervantes (1547-1616) with his satirical romance *Don Quixote de la Mancha* introduced the first great novel in Europe. John Bunyan's allegorical dream *The Pilgrim's Progress* (1678-1684) is the forerunner of the realistic novel in English.

GROWTH OF THE NOVEL IN EIGHTEENTH-NINETEENTH CENTURY BRITAIN

It is from the eighteenth century that novel began to be very popular in Britain as it dealt with social concerns. With Daniel Defoe's (1661-1731) publication of *Robinson Crusoe* in 1719, the history of the English novel begins. Along with Defoe Samuel Richardson (1689-1761), Henry Fielding (1704-1754), Tobias Smollett (1721-1771) and Laurence Sterne (1713-1768) are remarkable for their contribution towards the growth of the English novel. They introduced realism into fiction by presenting observed facts of life and attempted to describe human behaviour and surroundings as they are. They presented characters that lived in society unlike the earlier idealistic presentations.

Richardson in *Pamela* (1740) and *Clarissa* (1747-1748) introduced psychological realism through epistolary form. Fielding's concern for contemporary life made him write novels such as *Joseph Andrews, Tom Jones* and *Amelia.* Ian Watt observes in *The Rise of the Novel* "that both Richardson and Fielding saw themselves as founders of a new kind of writing, and that both viewed their work as involving a break with the old-fashioned romances...they have seen 'realism' as the defining characteristic which differentiates the work of the early eighteenth-century novelists from previous fiction."

Smollett's remarkable works are *Roderick Random* and *The Expedition of Humphry Clinker* presenting human idiosyncrasies and social criticism. Sterne is noted for his comic work *The Life and Opinions of Tristram Shandy.*

The rise of the novel is also due to certain factors such as the popular reading of the periodicals like *The Tatler* by Steele and *The Spectator* by Steele and Addison. These concerned with people in real life. There is also a shift in the reading taste of people from the serious classical texts of the past to more entertaining periodicals and novels. Novel as a genre democratised literature taking it out of the aristocracy and catering to the need of the common man.

With the ushering in of Romanticism there is a break from the neoclassical tradition of the eighteenth century. In fiction Romantic revival had its influence as there is a revival of the Romance. Horace Walpole wrote his *Castle of Otranto* (1765) introducing the Gothic romance novel saying, "I gave reign to my imagination; visions and passions choked me." In imitation of Walpole other Gothic romances were published like Clara Reeve's *Old English Baron*, Ann Radcliffe's *The Romance of the Forest*, Matthew Gregory Lewis's *The Monk*, etc.

Historical and Regional novel began in the nineteenth century with Maria Edgeworth's *Castle Rackrent* (1800). She wrote in the Irish setting with the peasant characters at the heart of it. However, in the early nineteenth century, it was Sir Walter Scott (1771-1832) who established the historical romance blending romance and realism with his erudition and humour. His 27 Waverley novels (1814-1828) cover about eight centuries with historical characters and events giving a sense of the past to the readers. Some of his popular works are *Waverly* (1814), *The Antiquary* (1816), *The Bride of Mallermoor* (1819), *Ivanhoe* (1819), *The Monastery* (1820), *The Talisman* (1825), *Castle Dangerous* (1831), etc. Historical novel being very popular, other novelists like Charles Dickens, W.M. Thackeray, Anthony Trollope, and George Eliot also attempted this genre.

The comedy of manners fiction mirroring foibles and behaviour of people was introduced by Fanny Burney (1752-1840) with her *Evelina.* Jane Austen (1775-1817) was the best in this genre with such classics as *Pride and Prejudice* (1813) and *Emma* (1816). Her achievement is noteworthy in the field of domestic fiction focusing on the dynamics of human relationships and the attainment of self-knowledge. Her genius is unchallenged in her observation and psychological interpretation of human behaviour with wit, satire and irony. She is superb in her dramatic presentation with great dialogues and excellent plot construction. She has a sympathetic understanding of her characters and turns away from questioning her society. Novel form developed further in the 19th Century characterised by realism, humour and satire. It became a channel of social criticism.

The Bronte Sisters : Charlotte Bronte (1816-1855), Emily Bronte (1818-1848), Anne Bronte (1820-1849) were unique in their distinctive achievements as novelists remarkable for their female imagination challenging the 19th century concept of womanhood.

Charles Dickens (1812-1870) has been very successful in creating his numerous characters in very sensational stories with humour and pathos. Though accused of sentimentality he is remarkable for his mission of social reforms highlighting abuses of the 19th century. As a social reformer he presents crime and violence to bring out powerfully the social abuses of the Victorian society. He is exceptional for his powerful characterization and dialogue, satirizing society and its conventions. In this he remains unconventional unlike his contemporaries Thackeray and Trollope. Some of the great novels of Dickens are *Oliver Twist* (1837), *Nicholas Nickleby* (1838-39), *Dombey and Sons* (1848), *David Copperfield* (1849-50), *Bleak House* (1852-53), *Hard Times* (1854), *A Tale of Two Cities* (1859) and *Great Expectations* (1860-61).

Among the Victorian novelists William Makepeace Thackeray (1811-1863), Anthony Trollope (1815-1882) and George Eliot (1819-1880) are considered the great realists. Thackeray's masterpiece *Vanity Fair: A Novel Without a Hero*, published in monthly numbers 1847-48, realistically pictures the contemporary upper middle class society. Trollope's great power of factual observation is seen in his great works such as *Barchester Towers, Dr. Thorne, Phineas Finn* and *The Prime Minister*.

George Eliot is characteristic in her portrayal of egoistical individuals who come in conflict with society. Her unique contribution to English fiction is that she enters into psychological analysis of her characters who think seriously of life's options. F.R. Leavis in his *The Great Tradition* finds in her works a 'Tolstoyan depth' with traditional moral sensibility. Notable among her works are *Adam Bede* (1859), *The Mill on the Floss* (1860), *Silas Marner* (1861), and *Middlemarch* (1871-2).

George Meredith (1828-1909), as a novelist has contributed to the perceptive portrayal of women and in analysing the state of mind of characters at specific moments. Popular among his works are *The Shaving of Shagpat, The Ordeal of Richard Feverel,* and *Athenaeum*.

Popular nineteenth century novels for children include Robert Louis Stevenson's *Treasure Island* and *Kidnapped*; (1840-1894) Lewis Carroll's *Alice's Adventures in Wonderland* and *Through the Looking Glass* (1832-1898).

Most of Thomas Hardy's (1840-1928) prominent novels such as *Far from the Madding Crowd* (1874), *The Return of the Native* (1878), *The Mayor of Casterbridge* (1886), *Tess of the D'Urbervilles* (1891), and *Jude the Obscure* (1895) propound his fatalistic view of man in a deterministic world. Man is a victim of 'hap' or chance leading him to tragic consequences. In a world of cruel fate Hardy sympathises with his helpless victims of destiny which made his novels appeal to the masses. Hardy's irony and pessimism made G. K. Chesterton comment on him as "a sort of village atheist brooding and blaspheming over the village idiot."

GROWTH OF THE NOVEL IN EIGHTEENTH AND NINETEENTH CENTURY AMERICA

Early writers of fiction in America are Charles Brockden Brown (1771-1810), Washington Irving (1783-1853) and James Fennimore Cooper (1789-1851). The romances of the novelist and journalist Charles Brockden Brown popularised the Gothic novel of terror with his exotic romances of suspense. He became an inspiration for Edgar Allen Poe, Herman Melville and Nathaniel Hawthorne with such works as *Wieland* (1798), *Arthur Mervyn* (1799-1800), and *Edgar Huntly* (1799). Washington Irving looked into the European past with its traditional romances and was influenced by the style of Addison, Steele and Goldsmith. His masterpieces are *Rip Van Winkle* and *The Legend of Sleepy Hollow.* James Fennimore Cooper also wrote with a sense of the American past and looked into the American myth, characters and themes. He wrote *The Pioneers* (1823), *The Last of the Mohicans* (1826), *The Prairie* (1827), *The Pathfinder* (1840), and *The Deerslayer* (1841).

American novel continued to be romantic, allegorical and mythical. Novelists William Gilmore Simms (1806-1870) and Nathaniel Hawthorne (1804-1864) wrote their romances. Simms wrote the romances of the frontier and South Carolina history. His works include *Martin Faber, Guy Rivers, The Yamassee, The Partisan, Richard Hurdis, Border Beagles, Helen Halsey*, etc.

Hawthorne set most of his stories in Puritan New England. *The Scarlet Letter* (1850) is his classical work on the Calvinistic Puritanism replete with strict codes of morality, sexual repression, sin and salvation. Hawthorne presents in all his stories the conflict between good and evil and the consequences of sin. Some of his other works are *The House of the Seven Gables* (1851), *The Blithedale Romance* (1852), *The Snow Image and Other Twice-Told Tales* (1852) and *The Marble Faun* (1860).

Herman Melville (1819-1891) has established his name as a great literary figure in America with his analysis of psychological and metaphysical themes. His major novels include *Typee* (1846), *Omoo* (1847), *Mardi* (1849), *Redburn* (1849), *White-Jacket* (1850), etc. *Moby-Dick* or *The White Whale* (1851) remains his masterpiece which is a symbolic account of man's fate within the framework of a realistic whaling voyage. He puts powerfully his thesis when Captain Ahab utters: "All visible objects are but pasteboard masks." The novel revolves around the conflict between Captain Ahab and the great white whale Moby Dick that had earlier torn off one of Ahab's legs.

Harriet Beecher Stowe's *Uncle Tom's Cabin* (1811-1896) or *Life Among the Lowly* (1851-1852) is a sentimental fiction that condemns slavery in America. She considered it inspired and 'written by God'. Her next anti-slavery novel is *Dread: A Tale of the Great Dismal Swamp*. Other works are *The Minister's Wooing*, *The Pearl of Orr's Island*, *Oldtown Folks*, etc.

Harriet Wilson (1807-1870) is the first Afro-American novelist in America who became known for her novel *Our Nig: Sketches from the Life of a Free Black, in a Two-Story White House, North, Showing that Slavery's Shadows Fall Even There* (1859). It recounts the story surrounding the marriage of a white woman with a black man.

By the end of the nineteenth century experiments were made in 'Realism' and naturalistic fiction by several writers in France and Russia such as Emile Zola (1840-1902), Balzac (1799-1850), Flaubert (1821-1880), Stendhal (1788-1842), Tolstoy (1828-1910) and Dostoevsky (1821-1881). It had its influence on writers both in Britain and America to present stories devoid of idealism and narrating them objectively (*See* Realism). Prominent American novelists in this genre include Sarah Orne Jewett, Mary Freeman, Joel Harris, and Bret Harte who wrote in the regional setting. William Dean Howells (1837-1920) is unique in his contribution to realism in American fiction with such works as *A Modern Instance, The Rise of Silas Lapham, A Hazard of New Fortunes, A Traveller from Altruria,*

Through the Eye of the Needle, An Open Eyed Conspiracy, The Landlord at Lion's Head, etc.

Mark Twain (Samuel Clemens) (1835-1910) has been acclaimed a genius in his realistic portrayal of his characters in his novels. So much so Hemingway is quoted to have said that all American literature comes from his *Adventures of Huckleberry Finn.* Some of his major works are *The Innocents Abroad* (1869), *The Adventures of Tom Sawyer* (1876),*The Prince and the Pauper* (1882), *Life on the Mississippi* (1883), *The Adventures of Huckleberry Finn* (1884), etc.

Other remarkable novels of this period of realism are William Dean Howells's in *The Rise of Silas Lapham* (1885), Edward Bellamy's *Looking* Backward (1888), Frank Norris's *The Octopus* (1901), and Theodore Dreiser's *Sister Carrie,* (1900).

Henry James's (1843-1916) realism looked to Europe for inspiration and is known for his internationalism in fiction in such novels as *The American* (1877), *Daisy Miller* (1879), *The Washington Square* (1881), *The Portrait of a Lady* (1881), *The Wings of the Dove* (1902), *The Ambassador* (1903) and *The Golden Bowl* (1904).

PERIOD OF EXPLORATION AND EXPERIMENTATION

In the twentieth century there is much Exploration and Experimentation in fiction all over Europe. The three great names are French author Marcel Proust (1871-1922), German writer Thomas Mann (1875-1955), and Irish writer James Joyce (1882-1941). Proust in *Remembrance of Things Past* (1913-1927) made an analysis of memory and past experiences and held the view that it is the task of the artist to bring out the creative energy from the unconscious. Mann's fiction explored the psychology of the artist. There is much intellectual study of characters and their thoughts. Joyce experimented in *Stream of Consciousness*. Joyce's *Ulysses* and *Finnegans Wake* were experiments in stream of consciousness and linguistics using Myth, Irish Folklore, Scholastic Philosophy and Catholicism.

Franz Kafka (1883-1924), the Jewish novelist who wrote in German, captures vividly the oppression and agony of the modern world. From his themes of loneliness, frustration, guilt and handling of grotesque and desperate situations in fiction the term "Kafkaesque" has been coined. His popular works are *Der Prozess* (*The Trial*); *Das Schloss* (*The Castle*); and *Amerika.*

Samuel Beckett (1906-1989) is an absurdist as a dramatist, novelist, and poet. He portrays a surreal world with his protagonists in anguish. He is similar to Kafka and Joyce. He is known for his novels *Molloy* (a trilogy), *Malone Dies* and *The Unnamable.*

TWENTIETH-CENTURY BRITISH NOVELS

In the twentieth century there are novelists who continue in the tradition of realism and those who made new experiments with the novel form. Realism continues in such writers as D.H. Lawrence (1885-1930), John Galsworthy (1867-1933), Arnold Bennett (1867-1931), Graham Greene (1904-1991), Iris Murdoch (1919-1999), Doris Lessing (1919-) and others. Among the experimentalists are Joseph Conrad (1857-1924), James Joyce (1882-1941), Virginia Woolf (1882-1941) and others.

Virginia Woolf like Joyce was an innovator with the stream of consciousness or interior monologue technique in the novels such as *Mrs. Dalloway* (1925), *To the Lighthouse* (1927), *The Waves* (1931), and *Between the Acts* (1941).

Joseph Conrad in his novels deals with the theme of man's struggle with good and evil. As an English Modernist he employs narrative techniques with time-sequences. *Lord Jim* (1900) is considered his best novel. Other works include the story *Heart of Darkness* (1902), *Nostromo* (1904), *Secret Agent* (1907), *Victory* (1915), etc.

D.H. Lawrence studies characters in conflict with society. He explored the Oedipus complex in his novel *Sons and Lovers* (1913). Other novels too deal with human sexuality such as *The Rainbow* (1915), *Women in Love* (1921), and *Lady Chatterley's Lover* (1928).

E. M. Forster (1879-1970) as a novelist was concerned with attitudes that disrupt relationship between people. His novels are *Where Angels Fear to Tread* (1905), *The Longest Journey* (1907), *A Room with a View* (1908), *Howards End* (1910) and *A Passage to India* (1924). In *A Passage to India* he examines the broken relationships due to clash between races and cultures.

After the Second World War postmodern tendency in fiction is to turn more attention to traditional forms and concern more with social issues.

Graham Greene has written thrillers, detective stories as well as serious novels of moral dilemma. His major novels are *Brighton Rock* (1938), *The Power and the Glory* (1940), *The Heart of the Matter* (1948), *The End of the Affair* (1951), *A Burnt-Out Case* (1961), *The Ways of Escape* (1980), etc.

Elizabeth Bowen (1899-1973) depicts the predicament and conflict of the upper middle class in her novels such as *The Hotel* (1927), *The Death of the Heart* (1949), *The Heat of the Day* (1949), *The Little Girls* (1963), and *Eva Trout, or Changing Seasons* (1968).

The tradition of the English novel of realism continues in the works of Evelyn Waugh (1903-1966), L.P. Hartley (1895-1972), C.P. Snow (1905-1980), Anthony Powell (1905-2000), R.M. Ballantyne (1825-1894), Kingsley Amis (1922-1995) and George Orwell (1903-1950).

Waugh's novels are known for their social satire and humour such as *Decline and Fall, Vile Bodies, Black Mischief, A Handful of Dust* and *Scoop*. His serious novel *Brideshead Revisited* written after his conversion to Roman Catholicism is considered the best among his works.

Like Waugh, Kingsley Amis has written social criticism coupled with humour. His satire *Lucky Jim* has been a great influence over the disillusioned 'Angry Young Men' after the Second World War. Other works are *That Uncertain Feeling*, and *Take a Girl Like You, The Green Man, Jake's Thing, The Old Devils, The Folks That Live on the Hill* (1990) and *The Russian Girl* (1992).

L.P. Hartley wrote macabre stories such as *Night Fears* (1924), *The Killing Bottle* (1932), *The Shrimp and the Anemone* (1944), *Sixth Heaven* (1946), *Eustace and Hilda* (1947), *The Boat* (1951), and *The Go-Between* (1953).

C.P. Snow examines English life in a series of his works like *Strangers and Brothers* (1940), *Time of Hope* (1949), *The Masters* (1951), *The New Men* (1954), *The Affair* (1959), *Corridors of Power* (1964), *Last Things* (1970), and *In Their Wisdom* (1974).

Anthony Powell writes with wit and humour on the upper class British society and their bohemian life. His major works include *Afternoon Men* (1931), *What's Become of Waring?* (1939), and *A Dance to the Music of Time* (1951-1975) consisting of a series of 12 novels.

R.M. Ballantyne became popular with his adventure stories projecting upright and moral heroes as in works like *The Coral Island* (1858).

George Orwell (1903-1950) is primarily known as a political writer who wrote presenting the picture of his time. As a socialist he was concerned with humanitarian issues and fought against political injustice as depicted in his novels *Animal Farm* (1945) and *Nineteen Eighty Four* (1949).

William Golding (1911-1993) is known as an allegorical writer who deals with the themes of good and evil in his novels. His major works are *The Lord of the Flies* (1954), *The Inheritors* (1955), *Pincher Martin* (1956), *The Spire* (1965), *Rites of Passage* (1980), *Close Quarters* (1987), and *Fire Down Below* (1989).

Women novelists like Muriel Spark (1918-), Doris Lessing (1919-), Iris Murdock (1919-1999), A.S. Byatt (1936-), and Margaret Drabble (1939-) have been dominant women writers in Britain making efforts to present feminine concerns through their writings.

Muriel Spark's novels are satiric comments on modern life. Her Catholic faith makes her probe deeply into the problems of good and evil like Graham Greene. Her major publications are *The Comforters* (1957), *Memento Mori* (1959), *The Ballad of Peckham Rye* (1960), *The Prime of Miss Jean Brodie (1961)*, *The Girls of Slender Means* (1963), *The Mandelbaum Gate* (1965), *The Hothouse by the East River* (1973), *Territorial Rights* (1979), *Loitering with Intent* (1981), and *The Only Problem* (1984).

Doris Lessing breaks from the traditional forms of fiction and delves into psychological analysis especially of women. Her notable works are the five-volume sequence *Children of Violence* (1952-69), *The Grass is Singing* (1950), *The Golden Notebook* (1962), *Briefing for a Descent into Hell* (1971), *The Summer Before the Dark* (1973), *The Fifth Child* (1988), *Love Again* (1996), *Walking in the Shade*(1997), and Iris Murdoch, the philosopher turned novelist, is known for her novel *Under the Net* (1954) and the philosophical work *Metaphysics As a Guide to Morals: Philosophical Reflections* (1992).

Being an academic by profession, A.S. Byatt, takes her characters from the academic circle. Her prominent novels are *Shadow of a Sun* (1964), *The Game* (1967), *Possession* (1990), *Angels and Insects* (1992), *The Matisse Stories* (1994), *Babel Tower* (1996) and *The Biographer's Tale* (2000).

Margaret Drabble, sister of A.S. Byatt, is concerned with problems faced by contemporary women. Her novels include *The Needle's Eye* (1972), *The Realms of Gold* (1975), *The Ice Age* (1977), *The Middle Ground* (1980), *The Radiant Way* (1987), *A Natural Curiosity* (1989), *The Gates of Ivory* (1991), *The Witch of Exmoor* (1996) and *The Peppered Moth* (2001).

Postmodernism in literature deals with certain absurd and disconnected writings that have emerged since 1950. Postmodern novel makes use of myth and fantasy. Writers such as Angela Carter, V.S. Naipaul, and Salman Rushdie are unique in their fictional techniques.

Angela Carter (1940-1992) in her much feminist writing makes use of magic realism and fantasy. Her prominent works are *Shadow Dance* (1965), *The Magic Toyshop* (1967), *Heroes and Villains* (1969), *Nights at the Circus* (1984), and *Wise Children* (1991).

V.S. Naipaul (1932-) is another postmodernist who writes satirically about political violence, alienation and conflict of values in society. His novels are *A House for Mr. Biswas* (1961), *In a Free State* (1971), *Guerrillas* (1975), *A Bend in the River* (1979), and *A Way in the World* (1994).

Salman Rushdie (1947-) writes in surrealist style and makes use of fantasy and magic realism in his fiction. Some of his novels are *Grimus* (1974), *Midnight's Children* (1981), *Shame* (1983), *The Satanic Verses* (1988), *The Moor's Last Sigh* (1995), and *The Ground Beneath Her Feet* (1999).

TWENTIETH-CENTURY AMERICAN NOVEL

In the twentieth century American novel came under various influences such as those of Darwin, Marx, Freud, Wars, and regionalism. These influences brought about various expressions in form and themes such as isolation, alienation, frustration, psychological expressions, search for identity and the fulfilment of the American dream, affirmation of human rights, racial prejudice, minority yearnings, women's concerns and the like.

Naturalism becomes a major factor in American literature as an expression of determinism. Naturalistic writers reject free will in man and believe that human behaviour is controlled by instinct, emotion, or social and economic factors. Man is a passive victim of natural forces. It accepts the biological determinism of Charles Darwin and the economic determinism of Karl Marx. American authors in the twentieth century sought reforms and dealt with injustices.

Upton Sinclair (1878-1968) sought social and economic reforms. Of his 90 works he is known for *The Jungle* (1906), *World's End* (1940) and *Dragon's Teeth* (1942).

Sinclair Lewis's (1885-1951) naturalistic and realistic style influenced many writers with his probing into the intellectual and spiritual sloth of the American society as depicted in his *In Main Street* (1920). Other publications are *Babbitt* (1922), *Arrowsmith* (1925), *Elmer Gantry* (1927), *Dodsworth* (1929), *It Can't Happen Here* (1935), and *Kingsblood Royal* (1947).

Theodore Dreiser (1871-1945) with his realistic treatment of sex in *Sister Carrie* (1900) caused ripples in the world of fiction. He continued his publications in this vein such as *Jennie Gerhardt* (1911), *The Financier* (1912), *The Titan* (1914), *An American Tragedy* (1925) and the posthumously published *The Bulwark and The Stoic* (1946-47).

John Dos Passos (1896-1970) through his impressionistic writing questioned the materialism and artificial life of the Americans. His post-war disillusionment is brought out in *Three Soldiers* (1921). Other works are *Manhattan Transfer* (1925), *The 42nd Parallel* (1930), *The Big Money* (1936), *Midcentury* (1961), etc.

John Steinbeck (1902-1968) with his realism coupled with romanticism deals with the dignified struggle of poor and oppressed people working on the land in novels such as *To a God Unknown* (1933), *Tortilla Flat* (1935), *In Dubious Battle* (1936), *Of Mice and Men* (1937), and *The Grapes of Wrath* (1939).

Richard Wright (1908-1960) is considered the spokesperson for the deprived blacks in America and his works portrays the racial prejudices. He wrote *The God That Failed* (1950), *Uncle*

Tom's Children (1938), *Native Son* (1940), *Black Boy* (1945), *The Outsider* (1953), *White Man, Listen!* (1957), *The Long Dream* (1958) and the like.

Willa Cather (1873-1947) and Ellen Glasgow (1874-1945) are similar in their sensibility as they wrote on women's concerns in the regional setting. Cather's works include *Alexander's Bridge* (1912), *O Pioneers!* (1913), *The Song of the Lark* (1915), *My Antonia* (1918), *One of Ours* (1922), *A Lost Lady* (1923), *Death Comes for the Archbishop* (1927), *The Professor's House* (1925), *Shadows on the Rock* (1931) and *Sapphira and the Slave Girl* (1940). Ellen Glasgow's prominent works are *The Battle Ground* (1902), *Virginia* (1913), *Barren Ground* (1925), *The Romantic Comedians* (1926), *They Stooped to Folly* (1929), *Vein of Iron* (1935), and *This Our Life* (1941).

F. Scott Fitzgerald (1896-1940) in his novels portrays vividly the desperate mood of the 1920s and the American dream in his classic novel *The Great Gatsby* (1925). His other publications are *This Side of Paradise* (1920), *The Beautiful and the Damned* (1922), *Flappers and Philosophers* (1920), *Tales of the Jazz Age* (1922), *All the Sad Young Men* (1926), *Tender Is the Night* (1934), *Taps at Reveille* (1935) and *The Last Tycoon* (1941).

Ernest Hemingway (1899-1961) had a multi-faceted career as a writer who dealt with the lost generation. His novels portray his social concerns and depict his adventurous life. Marked for his distinctive and simple style he has wielded a great influence on American writing. His most important works are *The Sun Also Rises* (1926), *To Have and Have Not* (1937), *For Whom the Bell Tolls* (1940), *Across the River and into the Trees* (1950), and *The Old Man and the Sea* (1952).

Thomas Wolfe (1900-1938) wrote with self-torment and turned autobiographical in his novels. Noted works are *Look Homeward, Angel* (1929), *Of Time and the River* (1935), *The Story of a Novel* (1936), *The Web and the Rock* (1939 posthumous) and *You Can't Go Home Again* (1940 Posthumous).

William Faulkner (1897-1962) deals with the conflict of the old and the new in his novels dealing with the Southern tradition. He created his imaginative landscape of 'Yoknapatawpha County.' His important works include *The Sound and the Fury* (1929), *As I Lay Dying* (1930), *Light in August* (1932), *Absalom, Absalom!* (1936), *The Unvanquished* (1938), *The Hamlet* (1940), *Go Down, Moses* (1942), *Intruder in the Dust* (1948), *A Fable* (1954), *The Town* (1957), *The Mansion* (1959), and *The Reivers* (1962).

Some of the other prominent novels of the period include Katherine Anne Porter's *Noon Wine* (1937), Robert Penn Warren's *All the King's Men* (1946), William Styron's *Lie Down in Darkness* (1951), Eudora Welty's *The Ponder Heart* (1954), Saul Bellow's *The Adventures of Augie March,* (1953), Bernard Malamud's *The Assistant,* (1957), Joseph Heller's *Catch-22,* (1961), Philip Roth's *Goodbye, Columbus,* (1959), Ralph Ellison's *Invisible Man* (1952), James Baldwin's *Go Tell It on the Mountain,* (1953), Kurt Vonnegut's *Slaughterhouse-Five* (1969), John Updike's the four *Rabbit* novels (1960-1990), J.D. Salinger's *Catcher in the Rye* (1951). It is to be noted that the sense of alienation was very strong in the novels of 1950s in America.

The 1960s saw the ushering in of Civil Rights Movement, Feminism and anti-war movement.

Norman Mailer (1923-) wrote in the tradition of Hemingway, using innovative styles expressing his liberal philosophy and bitterness towards society. Some of his works are *Barbary Shore* (1951), *Deer Park* (1955), *An American Dream* (1964), *The White Negro* (1958), *The Armies of the Night* (1968), *Of a Fire on the Moon* (1971), *The Executioner's Song* (1979), *Ancient Evenings* (1983), *Tough Guys Don't Dance* (1984), *Harlot's Ghost* (1991), and *An American Mystery* (1995).

Thomas Pynchon (1937-) is known for his experiments in novel form with mysterious plots and fantasies. All his stories are complicated with chaotic situations. Noted novels are *V.*

(1963), *Gravity's Rainbow* (1973), *The Crying of Lot 49* (1966) and *Vineland* (1990).

By 1970s and 1980s the American fiction focuses more on individual concerns than socio-political issues. Realism returns after the experiments of the earlier years.

John Gardner stressed ethical values in literature. In his realistic approach he made use of various techniques like flash-back, myth, and story within a story. His important works are *The Resurrection* (1966), *The Wreckage of Agathon* (1970), *The Sunlight Dialogues* (1972), *Nickel Mountain* ((1973), *October Light* (1976), *Freddy's Book* (1980), and *Mickelson's Ghosts* (1982).

Toni Morrison(1931-) celebrated the black identity in her novels with a particular emphasis on female experiences. Her major publications are *The Bluest Eye* (1970), *Sula* (1973), *Song of Solomon* (1977), *Tar Baby* (1981), *Beloved* (1987), *Jazz* (1992), *Playing in the Dark: Whiteness and the Literary Imagination* (1992), and *Paradise* (1998).

Alice Walker (1944-), in her writings presents a female perspective that concerns the poor African-American women under male domination and oppression. Her best works are *The Color Purple* (1982), *The Temple of My Familiar* (1989), *Possessing the Secr t of Joy* (1992), *Anything We Love Can Be Saved* (1977) and *The Same River Twice: Honoring the Difficult* (1997).

There is the emergence of a ' New Regionalism' in the writings of some of the novelist in recent times giving a sense of place to people who are turning more ecocentric. Works in this genre include William Kennedy's *Ironweed* (1983); Joyce Carol Oates's *Where Are You Going, Where Have You Been?* (1974), Anne Tyler's *Saint Maybe* (1991); Susan Richards Shreve's *Children of Power* (1979); Jill McCorkle's *Crash Diet* (1992); Pat Conroy's *The Prince of Tides* (1986); Jane Smiley's *A Thousand Acres* (1991); Cormac McCarthy's *The Crossing* (1994); Leslie Marmon Silko's *The Almanac of the Dead* (1991);

James Welch's *The Indian Lawyer* (1990); Thomas McGuane's *Keep the Change* (1989); Joan Didion's *Play It As It Lays* (1970); and Raymond Carver's *Where I'm Calling from* (1986).

INDIAN NOVEL IN ENGLISH

Though English is foreign for Indians, it has remained the language of education and literary expression. It was Ram Mohan Roy (1774-1833) who made a systematic campaign for the introduction of English-medium education. Indian writers in English have made remarkable contribution to fiction. It has become to some extent a medium of presenting Indian culture and thoughts to the world.

The first Indian novel in English is Bankim Chandra Chatterjee's (1774-1833) *Rajmohan's Wife* which appeared in the serial form in *Indian Field* in 1864. He remained supreme in his romantic, historical and humorous portrayal of characters. By then there was a growing educated middle class reading public in India to appreciate the writings in English in India. Later Bankim published *Anandamath* (1882).

Next in line is Lal Behari Day, who became a Christian, who published *Govinda Samanta: Bengal Peasant Life* in 1874 portraying a peasant's life. It also depicts the social life in the villages in Bengal during that time.

Other works during this period are Raj Lakshmi Devi's *The Hindu Wife* (1876), Toru Dutt's (1856-77) *Bijoy Chand* (1888), Khetrapal Chakravarti's *Sarada and Hingana* (1895).

Krupabai Sathianathan (1862-94) who became a Christian wrote with autobiographical strain *Kamala: A Story of Hindu Life* (1894) and *Saguna: Story of Native Christian Life* (1895). Shevanthi Bai wrote *Ratnabai* advocating education of women. Swarnakumari Goshal (1855-1932) wrote romantic novels like *The Fatal Garland* and *An Indian Love Story*.

Rajam Iyer wrote *True Greatness of the Vasudeva Sastri.* Madhaviah pictures his traditional society in works such as *Thillai Govindan, Satyananda,* and *Clarinda.*

Behramji Malabari made a mark as a journalist and social reformer trying to bridge the gap between cultures both Eastern and Western. His major works are *Gujarat and Gujaratis* (1882) and *The Indian Eye on English Life* (1893).

S.M. Mitra wrote on East-West relationship in *Hindupore: A Peep Behind the Indian Unrest* (1909). Sarat Kumar Ghosh wrote *The Prince of Destiny* (1909) also on East-West theme.

Though Indian novel in English got a beginning in the above mentioned writers, it is from the 1920s with the Gandhian movement and rising nationalism that the novel form began to progress further. K.S. Venkataramani published his novels *Murugan the Tiller* (1927) and *Kandan the Patriot* (1932) presenting the Gandhian thoughts concerning Satyagraha and political and economic freedom.

The three great Indian novelists who emerged in the 1930s are Mulk Raj Anand (1905-), Raja Rao (1909-) and R.K. Narayan (1907-2001). Novels began to be written in English from 1930s by Mulk Raj Anand, R.K. Narayan and Raja Rao. For some of these novelists fiction became an end in itself.

Mulk Raj Anand (1905-) was influenced by his British education which had an impact on his writing. He depicts his socialist vision honestly and realistically. His major novels are *Coolie* (1933), *Untouchable* (1935), *The Village* (1939), *Across the Black waters* (1940), *The Sword and the Sickle* (1942), *Two Leaves and a Bud* (1951), *Seven Summers* (1951), *The Private Life of an Indian Prince* (1953), *The Woman and the Cow* (1960) etc. Anand proves himself a political writer with a mission to reform society. He has his sympathy for the deprived which is central to his major novels: *Coolie, Untouchable* and *The Woman and the Cow..*

Though Raja Rao (1909-) has written only a few novels and short stories, he portrays better the pulse of India than the other contemporary novelists. His master-pieces are *Kanthapura* (1938), *The Cow of the Barricades and Other Stories* (1947), *The Serpent and the Rope* (1960), *The Cat and Shakespeare* (1965) *The Policeman and the Rose and other Stories* (1978). Raja Rao differs from Mulk Raj Anand who is politically committed and R.K.Narayan who is poetic and metaphysical. *Kanthapura* (1938) focuses on the intensity of Indian life and the Gandhian struggle for freedom. *The Serpent and the Rope* (1960) is considered his spiritual autobiography. *The Cat and Shakespeare* (1965) is set in the background of the famine of 1942, is a philosophical comedy.

R.K.Narayan is a novelist who projects 'Malgudi' as the locale for most of his stories. He has a keen eye for the comic as observed in the life around him. In his writing there is a distinctive blend of western techniques and eastern materials. His sensibility is purely Indian. His first novel, *Swami and Friends* (1935), was based on his experiences as a village school teacher. *The English Teacher* (1945) and *The Vendor of Sweets* (1967) also present humorous and well crafted picture of daily life in a fictitious southern Indian town. Narayan's other novels include *Waiting for the Mahatma* (1955), *The Guide* (1958), *The Man-Eater of Malgudi* (1961), and *A Tiger for Malgudi* (1983). *A Horse and Two Goats* (1970), *Malgudi Days* (1982), and *Grandmother's Tale* (1994) are collections of Narayan's short stories and contain simple, yet insightful, character portrayals. He also revived the classic Indian epics *The Ramayana* (1972) and *The Mahabharata* (1978), condensing the lengthy works and setting them in modern surroundings.

His novels are comedies of sadness and also lighted with subtle mockery of self and others. He is very realistic and writes chiefly about the Indian middle class, the class he understands best as he belongs to it. R.K. Narayan portrays an eternal India. He peoples his novels with caricatures rather than characters. His Malgudi epitomises millions of Indian towns. His genius lies in pinpointing the comedy that life is.

Nirad Choudhuri has contributed his share with his *Autobiography of an Unknown Indian* (1951) and *A Passage to England* (1959) depicting beautifully the clash of two civilisations.

Govind Desani wrote *All About H. Hatter* (1948) which is an experimental and irregular work like those of James Joyce. M. Ananthanarayanan's *The Silver Pilgrimage* (1961) is a mixture of fantasy and reality. Khwaja Ahmad Abbas's *Inquilab* (1955) brings out powerfully the freedom struggle in India. Similar in theme is Venu Chitale's *In Transit* (1950).

Bhabani Bhattacharya writes with first-hand human situations and dipicts the struggle of people for social justice. His novels are *So Many Hungers* (1947), *Music for Mohini* (1952), *He Who Rides a Tiger* (1954), *A Goddess Named Gold* (1960) and *Shadow from Ladakh* (1966).

Anita Desai (1937-) makes colourful studies of Indian life portrayed through her characters struggling to fulfil their dreams. Her publications are *Cry, the Peacock* (1963), *Games at Twilight and Other Stories* (1978), *The Village by the Sea* (1982), *Clear Light of Day* (1980), *In Custody* (1984), and *Journey to Ithaca* (1995).

Sudhin N. Ghose is able to present the Indian sensibility to a great extent in his novels though he lived for many years in England. His major works are *And Gazelles Leaping* (1949), *Cradle of the Clouds* (1951), *The Vermilion Boat* (1953) and *The Flame of the Forest* (1955).

K. Nagarajan gives South Indian picture of the 1930s and the various socio-political and religious conflicts in his novels like *Athawar House* (1939) and *Chronicles of Kedaram* (1961). Though popular as a Milton critic, B. Rajan also published novels such as *The Dark Dancer* (1959), and *Too Long in the West* (1961).

Manohar Malgonkar writes about the Indian Independence struggle and the aftermath of partition. His novels are *Distant*

Drum (1960), *Combat of Shadows* (1962), *The Princes* (1963), and *A Bend in the Ganges* (1964).

Chaman Nahal is quite an outstanding novelist of the 1970s with his novels *My True Faces* (1973), *Azadi* (1975), *Into Another Dawn* (1977), *The English Queens* (1979) and *The Crown and the Loincloth* (1981).

Ruth Prawer Jhabvala, a German by birth and married into an Indian family, writes witty novel of manners with trans-cultural elements. She observes vividly the Indian scene and characters but remains Western in her outlook. Her works include Booker Prize winner *Heat and Dust* (1975), *To Whom She Will* (1955), *Esmond in India* (1958), *The Householder* (1960), *A Backward Place* (1963), *In Search of Love and Beauty* (1983), and *Shards of Memory* (1995).

Arun Joshi, though a management consultant by training and profession, has deeply absorbed the spirit of *Bhagavad Gita* and Mahatma Gandhi and writes his novels with Indian thought. His novels include *The Foreigner* (1971), *The Strange Case of Billy Biswas* (1971), *The Apprentice* (1974), and *The Last Labyrinth* (1981).

Kamala Markandaya deals with several themes such as poverty and hunger, conflicts in family and society, the struggle for self realization and the like. Her prominent novels are *Nectar in a Sieve* (1954), *Some Inner Fury* (1955), *A Silence of Desire* (1960), *Possession* (1963), *A Handful of Rice* (1966), *The Coffee Dams* (1969), *The Nowhere Man* (1972), *Two Virgins* (1974), and *The Golden Honeycomb* (1977).

Khushwant Singh as a realist attempts to present things objectively in a world of political hypocrisy and religious fanaticism. His prominent works are *Train to Pakistan* (1956), *I Shall not Hear the Nightingale* (1959), and *Delhi* (1989).

Nayantara Sahgal in her novels is concerned with human relationships and human values. Her novels include *A Time to be Happy* (1958), *This Time of Morning* (1969), *Storm in Chandigarh* (1969), *The Day in Shadow* (1971), and *A Situation in New Delhi* (1977).

Kamala Das, besides writing poetry, wrote novels dealing with female quest for identity such as *A Doll for the Child Prostitute* (1961) and *Alphabet of Lust* (1980).

Vikram Seth is exceptional in his depicting the everyday life of people everywhere in his novels *The Golden Gate* (1981), *A Suitable Boy* (1993), and *An Equal Music* (2000).

V.S. Naipaul and Salman Rushdie, though listed in the British fiction scenario, have been great writers of Indian origin and their writing is deeply rooted in Indian sensibilities.

Arundhati Roy bagged the coveted Booker Prize for her first novel *The God of Small Things* in 1997 presented in the backdrop of south India.

Other novelists who have come into the Indian scene include Sashi Tharoor, Amitav Ghosh, Upamanyu Chatterjee, Vikram Chandra, Shobha De, Shashi Deshpande, Dina Mehta, Allan Sealy, Firdaus Kanga, Farrukh Dhondy, Shiv K. Kumar, B.S. Gidwani, Ranga Rao, Raj Gill, Balraj Khanna, Deepak Chopra, Ginu Kamani, Rohinton Mistry, Jhumpa Lahiri, Kiran Desai, Ruchira Mukerjee and others.

Indian novel in English has come of age today and it has been receiving global recognition. As for instance, in the year 1997, Arundhati Roy received Booker Prize for her novel *The God of Small Things*. Jhumpa Lahiri in 2000 made headlines winning the Pulitzer Prize for fiction for her short stories *The Interpreter of Maladies*. Over and above all these, V.S. Naipaul receiving the Nobel Prize for literature in 2001 was a splendid boost for Indian novel in English.

FUTURE OF NOVEL

Among the various literary forms it is the novel that has the largest publication and readership world-over. With the growth of film and television, novels have found better scope as many of them are adapted for films and television serials.

As electronic publishing is becoming more and more popular eventually novels will be available to readers electronically and through the internet. Despite the revolutions in information technology, the printed novel form will continue to stay. Today, more than ever, a wide variety of novels are written and published on forms ranging from adventure stories to cyberpunk and hypertext fiction.

A

Abridged edition is a compendium of a larger work. It is the compressed or condensed version of a literary work that gives its central ideas. Often a lengthy literary work or all the works of an author are published in abridged form, e.g., abridged versions of works published by *Readers' Digest*. Abridged editions of novels and plays are often brought out for school-teaching purposes.

Absent narrator is a device employed in behaviourist narratives in which an impersonal narrator portrays events without having recourse to a narrating self. Hemingway in his short story "Hills Like White Elephants" applies the technique of the absent narrator, presenting subtly the depth of the relationship between an American and a girl. They have no names and they are on a journey at the railway station where the girl observes great beauty in the dry hills that look like white elephants.

Adaptation is re-casting of a work such as a novel or a play for cinema or television, eg., Henry James's novel *Washington Square* has been filmed as *The Heiress;* Bernard Shaw's play *Pigmalion* has been adapted into a musical film *My Fair Lady*.

Addisonian is a term applied to refer to the unruffled and humorous prose style of Joseph Addison (1672-1719) in his essays. His language is marked by its musical quality as well as simplicity. Dr. Johnson in his *Life* (1781) is full of praises for the style of Addison and referred to it as "the model of the middle style; on grave subjects not formal, on light occasions not grovelling." Addison himself claimed to have "brought philosophy out of closets and libraries, schools and colleges, to dwell in clubs and assemblies, at tea-tables and coffee houses," in tune with the middle-class sensibilities, e.g., "There is no place in town which I so much love to frequent as the Royal Exchange. It gives me a secret satisfaction, and, in some measure, gratifies my vanity, as I am an Englishman, to see so rich an assembly of countrymen and foreigners consulting together upon the private business of mankind, and making this metropolis a kind of emporium for the whole earth. I must confess I look upon high-change to be a great council, in which all considerable nations have their representatives. Factors in the trading world are what ambassadors are in the politic world; they negotiate affairs, conclude treaties, and maintain a good correspondence between those wealthy societies of men that are divided from one another by seas and oceans, or live on the different extremities of a continent" (From *Spectator*, No.69, May 19, 1711).

Advance mention is a device by which a character, a thing or a situation is presented in the beginning of a novel or story in a casual manner. Later, the character, the thing or the incident gets due importance as the story unfolds.

Advance notice is a technique employed by a writer by which he or she mentions something in a passing manner which will be narrated at length at a later part of the story. For example, "There was great commotion in the locality due to the death of my child in a road accident; I shall speak of it at a later time."

Adventure novel is built around exciting and dangerous action. Some of them fall into the category of mystery stories, e.g., R.L. Stevenson's *Treasure Island* (1883), Rider Haggard's *King Solomon's Mines* (1885), Hammond Innes's *Atlantic*

Fury (1962), Alistair MacLean's *The Guns of Navarone* (1957), Fletcher Knebel's *Seven Days in May,* (1962), Lawrence Block's *The Thief Who Couldn't Sleep,* (1966), Jack Higgins's *The Eagle Has Landed,* (1975) and, Tom Clancy's *The Hunt for Red October* (1984).

Advertisement (ad) is a form of communication intended to promote the sale of product or service, to influence public opinion, to advance a particular cause to gain political support or to elicit some other responses desired by the advertiser. It is a kind of mass selling when direct efficient person-to-person selling is impractical or impossible. Strictly speaking advertising should be differentiated from propaganda and publicity. Advertising can consist of notices in the classified advertisement columns of newspapers or flashy presentation in newspapers, magazines, billboards, mail, radio, television and internet. It has become a worldwide industry with heavy investment. The characteristics of advertisement are: (i) catching attention (ii) stimulating interest (iii) arousing desire (iv) supplying convincing detail (v) motivating action and so on. The ideological functions of advertising are (i) building images (ii) building relations and (iii) building consumers. Advertising employs language with various linguistic devices such as (i) coinage of new words (ii) alliteration (iii) use of vocabulary in unusual contexts (iv) pun (v) parallelism (vi) slogan (vii) disjunctive grammar (viii) rhyme and the like.

Aesopic fables are associated with Aesop (6th century BC), a native of Asia Minor to whom Greek fables are attributed. According to some traditions he is a legendary figure. Based on folklore, the fables aim to exhort and amuse with animals, men, gods and inanimate things presented in them. Aesopic fables to some extent drew strength from the Babylonian and Assyrian traditions. The fables were transmitted orally until in the third century AD. Babrius compiled them into verse form. Phaedrus in the first century AD translated some fables into Latin. In the fourteenth century they were introduced into the west by Maximus Planudes. Later Erasmus with his Latin edition in 1513 made them popular.

Aesthetic or **psychic distance** refers to the degree of emotional and psychological involvement of a reader in a work. The aesthetic distance is great when the reader is least involved in the action or the fate of the characters in the work. If the reader is influenced emotionally or psychologically by the action or characters in the work, the aesthetic distance is the least. The ideal aesthetic distance according to many theorists is when the reader is able to establish an involvement that is deep yet with sufficient degree of detachment that allows tranquil recollection of the aesthetic and thematic quality of the work

Aesthetics is the philosophy of art which studies beauty as an end in itself in art, music and literature. There are two major approaches to aesthetics: the philosophical and the psychological. The philosophical approach is through deductive reasoning to establish the nature of art and beauty as well as their relations to truth and goodness. The psychological approach stresses the study of the process of creation in the artist and of appreciation in the beholder.

Agrarian movement is a 'back to nature' movement in the 1920s and 1930s especially in the Southern USA, propounded by writers such as Sherwood Anderson, Allen Tate, Donald Davidson, J.C. Ransom, J.G. Fletcher and others. It is associated with the 'Regionalism' which hailed virtues and values of the rural life in contrast to the rapid industrialisation in the cities. Their publications such as *The Fugitive* (1922-25), *I'll Take My Stand* (1930), *Culture in the South* (1934), etc., revolted against the barbarism of science and technology. Sherwood Anderson in his short stories *Winesburg, Ohio* (1919) highlighted the simple lives of rural folks in the background of rapid industrialisation.

Allegory literally means *other reading.* It is a way of interpreting a narrative or a text to extract a more general, or a less literal meaning from it. Allegory in fiction can be on abstract themes, political and historical themes in the form of dream visions, parables, fables and the like. Bunyan's *The Pilgrim's Progress* is a moral allegory on man's salvation in the form of a prose narration. It depicts the journey of humanity to the divine and the Pilgrim who flees the city of Destruction represents all men. Hence, it is a literary device by which people, objects or events in prose or verse are presented symbolically giving a meaning other than the one actually described. "As I walked through the wilderness of this world, I lighted on a certain place where was a den, and I laid me down in that place to sleep: and as I slept I dreamed a dream. I dreamed, and beheld I saw a man clothed with rags, standing in a certain place, with his face from his own house, a book in his hands, and a great burden upon his back. I looked and saw him open the book and read therein; and as he read, he wept, and trembled; and not being able longer to contain, he brake out with a lamentable cry, saying, what shall I do?" (From *The Pilgrim's Progress*). In the Middle Ages allegory was associated with the interpretation of the Biblical *Old Testament* in relation to the *New Testament*. Allegory is often used to convey a moral lesson. The main technique used is personification by which abstract qualities are presented in human form. To this genre belongs allegorical lyric poetry, allegorical drama and allegorical narrative. The allegorical sensibility prevailed in the Christian literature of the Middle Ages in Morality Plays and Dream Visions, e.g., Dante's *Divina Commedia*, medieval morality play *Everyman,* Langland's *Piers Plowman*, Spenser's *The Faerie Queene*. Allegory is used in twentieth century 'Expressionist Drama' and 'Theatre of the Absurd'. Novelists like George Orwell in his *Animal Farm* (1945) makes use of a beast fable to present a political and social satire in an allegorical manner.

Alternation is a narrative device by which narrative sequences are made to alternate with each other, e.g., "I was well; my brother was sick. But I was found to be with cancer; my brother recovered and was discharged from hospital. I was desperate; my brother was well."

Alliteration is repetition of initial consonant in successive words or initial sounds of several words which marks the stressed syllables in a line of poetry or prose. For example: '***B***ear to ***b***attle or ***w***ield in ***w***ar' (*Beowulf*). The technique is used for emphasis and to give oratorial effect. Often several words which are not next to each other are alliterated in a sentence for artistic purpose. It is unrhymed with dactilic four stress lines. As a rule two words beginning with the same letter in the first half and one or two in the second. It is found in Germanic languages like Old English(Anglo-Saxon), Old Norse and continued into the fourteenth century, e.g., the epic *Beowulf*. Spenser used it decoratively or to link adjective and noun, verb and object, e.g., "Much daunted with that dint, her sense was dazed." Modern poets use it with modifications and it has become less systematic and more musical. In prose alliteration is also used for rhetorical effect, e.g., "It is he (Death) that puts into a man all the wisdom of the world without speaking a word" (From Sir Walter Raleigh's *A History of the World*).

Ambiguity means multiple meaning or different interpretation of an idea. William Empson in *Seven Types of Ambiguity* (1930) justifies ambiguity as a poetic technique.

Margaret, are you grieving
Over Goldengrove unleafing?
Ah! The heart grows older
It will come to such sights colder
By and by, nor spare a sigh
Tho' world of wanwood leafmeal lie;
And you *will* weep and know why.

('Spring and Fall' G.M. Hopkins)

Ordinarily, the last line in the poem above means, in the future, she will know the reason for a sorrow that is now only a blind grief. But by placing an accent mark on '*will*' it ceases to be merely an auxiliary verb and becomes the present tense of the verb 'to will'. She persists in weeping and demands the reason for the falling of leaves and her grief. William Empson uses the term to refer not to carelessness that produces two or more meanings where a single one is intended, but to the richness of poetic speech which can be brought about by "any verbal nuance, however slight, which gives room for alternative reactions to the same piece of language." For the purpose of classification Empson groups these ambiguities into seven categories: (1) A word or syntax can be effective in several ways at once. (2) Two or more meanings may make up the single meaning of the writer. (3) In pun two ideas can be given simultaneously. (4) Different meanings can combine to make clear a complicated state of mind in the writer. (5) An image or figure may lie half way between two ideas. (6) The reader may be forced to invent interpretations because the things said are contradictory. (7) Two meanings may be contradictory and show a fundamental division in the author's mind.

American renaissance is often referred to as the American literary revival prior to the Civil War which may be considered a delayed Romanticism. F.O. Matthiessen in his *American Renaissance* (1941) refers to the works of R.W. Emerson, H.D. Thoreau, Melville, Hawthorne and Whitman. Emerson's Transcendentalism is the basic Philosophical tenet of the movement (*See* Transcendentalism).

Amplification is a rhetorical device by which emphasis is given to language, e.g., "But indeed, at that time, putting to death was a recipe much in vogue with all trades and professions, and not least of all with Tellson's. Death is Nature's remedy for all things. And why not Legislatures? Accordingly, the forger was put to Death; the utterer of a bad note was put to Death; the unlawful opener of a letter was put to death; the purloiner of forty shillings and sixpence was put to death; the holder of a horse at Tellson's door, who made off with it, was put to Death; the coiner of a bad shilling was put to Death" (*From* Dickens's *A Tale of Two Cities*).

Anachronism is setting a person, thing, or event not in its historical perspective, for instance, the use of modern day costumes while staging a play of Shakespeare. Some playwrights and novelists have tried to experiment with anachronism to create the 'Alienation-effect', setting the past in the present, e.g., Mark Twain's in *A Connecticut Yankee in King Arthur's Court* presents the story of a Yankee knocked down in a fight, who dreams of being imprisoned in King Arthur's court. He proves himself to be a hero applying nineteenth century technological devices to win war and improve the lot of the people.

Anachrony is a device by which events are presented in a different manner from their chronological order. The device employs techniques of going back to the past through *flash-back, analepsis* and *retrospection*; going forward to the future through *flash-forward, prolepsis* and *anticipation*. Often the story begins *in medias res* (in the middle of things) and goes back to the beginning.

Analogical is something that has a mystical interpretation having morally sublime ideals. For example, the *Old Testament* of the *Bible* has undergone interpretations in the literal, allegorical, moral and analogical sense. Of these the analogical exegesis gives an idealistic interpretation in the context of the eschatological end of everything.

Analepsis is a kind of retrospection or flashback by which certain past information is narrated in the course of a story being told *in medias res*. It can provide background information in an effective manner. It is a term employed by Gerard Genette referring to the account of an event prior to the narrative in question (*see* Prolepsis).

Analogy is an association of similarity between two or more things. The comparison is usually imaginative between two essentially unlike things which none the less share one or more common features. They are presented in the form of extended simile. For example, an analogy between the human eyes and a camera can be presented. In logic, analogy is the name of an inductive form of argument which affirms that if two or more things are similar in some cases, then it is possible that they will be similar in other cases. For instance, if one student was good in sports and passed well in the examinations, another student who is good at sports may also pass well in his examinations. Analogies can be used Theologically, Historically, Scientifically and Philosophically, e.g., "Let me make use of illustration. In the combination of colours, very different results are produced by a difference in their selection and juxtapostition: red, green, and white. Change their shades, according to the contrast to which they are submitted. And, in like manner, the drift and meaning of a branch of knowledge varies with the company in which it is introduced to the student" (From Newman's, *The Scope and Nature of University Education*).

Analytic author is like the omniscient narrator who can interpret everything that happens in a story, e.g., William Thackeray's *Vanity Fair.* "While the present century was in its teens, and on one sun-shiny morning in June, there drove up to the great iron gate of Miss Pinkerton's academy for young ladies, on Chiswick Mall, a large family coach, with two fat horses in blazing harness, driven by a fat coachman in a three-cornered hat and wig, at the rate of four miles an hour. A black servant, who reposed on the box beside the fat coachman, uncurled his bandy legs as soon as the equipage drew up opposite Miss Pinkerton's shining brass plate, and as he pulled the bell, at least a score of young heads were seen peering out of the narrow windows of the stately old brick house. Nay, the acute observer might have recognised the little red nose of good-natured Miss Jemima Pinkerton herself, rising over some geranium-pots in the window of the lady's own drawing-room" (*see* Omniscient narrator).

Anaphora is a rhetorical figure associated with the method of repetition by which the same word or phrase is repeated at the beginning of lines or sentences. It is found in Dickens, Whitman and others, e.g., Dickens begins *A Tale of Two Cities* with such a rhetorical figure: " It was the best of times, it was the worst of times, it was the age of wisdom, it was the age of foolishness, it was the epoch of belief, it was the epoch of incredulity, it was the season of Light, it was the season of Darkness, it was the spring of hope, it was the winter of despair, we had everything before us, we had nothing before us, we were all going direct to Heaven, we were all going direct the other way...."

Antagonist is the major character that opposes the protagonist or the hero of a fiction, a narrative or a drama. He sets the conflict in motion. The antagonist is often the villain who represents negative values in the theme developed, e.g., Satan is the antagonist in Milton's *Paradise Lost*; King Claudius is the antagonist in Shakespeare's *Hamlet*; Sergeant Troy is the antagonist in Hardy's *Far from the Madding Crowd*. Sometimes the antagonist can be in the form of a few persons, natural forces as well as the split personality of the protagonist.

Anticlimax is an abrupt and deliberate descent from the sublime to the ridiculous, when the action is about to reach its climax. This brings about the reduction of tension. This device is employed to provide humour and surprise. In a comedy the performer intentionally speaks of something serious and unexpectedly climaxes it with something insignificant, e.g., "Because one person dropped a cigarette end, these houses were burned to the ground, a collection of irreplaceable books and curios was destroyed, four people lost their lives and Mrs. Robinson's washing was spoilt by the smoke."

Anti-hero / anti-heroine is a protagonist who lacks traditional heroic qualities such as valour, honesty, generosity, goodness and the like. He/she is often found in drama and narratives.

He/she is a failure and a victim of circumstances; a misfit and a drop-out. He/ she has negative attributes that are contrary to that of the hero/heroine. He/she is not the same as the antagonist, e.g., Kingsley Amis in *Lucky Jim* presents the disagreeable character of James Dixon who belongs to a social group that has come up by hard work and is radical in his views. Other anti-heroes include Arthur Miller's protagonist Willy Lowman in the *Death of a Salesman*; John Osborne's Jimmy Porter in *Look Back in Anger*; Leopold Bloom in James Joyce's *Ulysses*. "Leopold Bloom (for it is he) stands silent, with bowed head before those young guileless eyes. What a brute he had been! At it again? A fair unsullied soul had called to him and, wretch that he was, how had he answered ? An utter cad he had been. He of all men!" (from *Ulysses*).

Anti-narrative is a device used by writers who question the very nature of narrative convention in their writing. Samuel Beckett in his *Molloy* (1951) employs anti-narrative method. Beckett does away with all the traditional form of contemporary fiction and directs his attention to consciousness itself.

Anti-novel is a type of experimental novel which does not follow the traditional patterns of novel. It centres on a story being told with certain characters and the plots surrounding them. The realism and naturalism presented in such novels differ from the traditional forms. Anti-novels are replete with confusions caused by fragmentation and dislocation. The term though dates from the seventeenth century became popular with French writers such as Alain Robbe Grillet and Nathalie Sarraute in the 1950s. Others who wrote in this genre include Sterne (*Tristram Shandy*), Samuel Beckett (*Molloy*), Nabokov (*Pale Fire*), Flann O'Brien (*At Swim-Two-Birds*), Philip Toynbee (*Tea with Mrs. Goodman*), Christine Brooke-Rose (*Between*) and others. Some sort of anti-novel trend is seen in the writings of James Joyce, Virginia Woolf and Lawrence Sterne. Anti-novels are marked for their lack of proper character development, precise plots and episodes, unnecessary analysis of things, switch in time-sequences, experimentation in language and structure, etc. Such anti-novels give a collage effect with drawings and hieroglyphics.

Antithesis is a figure of speech in which contrasting and opposite statements are brought together for emphasis. It can consist of a single sentence or a pair of words or phrases. The Book of Proverbs in the *Bible* is full of antithesis. It is rhetorical device popular especially with the Augustan poets, e.g., "To err is human, to forgive divine." (Pope)

Aphorism is a concise statement of a principle. It is a pithy saying or an adage. Often it takes the form of a definition, e.g., "The highest form of vanity is the love of fame" (George Santayana). The term is similar to a proverb, maxim and apothegm. The difference consists in the fact that aphorism is attributed to an author while a proverb is anonymous. The apothegm on the other hand is more practical in stating an abstraction. "Man, being the servant and interpreter of nature, can do and understand so much and so much only as he has observed in fact or in thought of the course of nature; beyond this he neither knows anything nor can do anything" (Francis Bacon).

Apocalyptic literature is one of revelation of the future. The Book of Revelation in the *Bible* is an excellent example which is rich in allegory and continues to be the subject of different interpretations. The book is sometimes called the Apocalypse. The term 'apocalyptic' is derived from Greek 'apokaluptein' (to uncover). Apocalyptic literature concerns with uncovering and revealing something hidden. At times such literary works predict doom and concern with the end of the world and its destruction, e.g., "And there appeared a great wonder in heaven; a woman clothed with the sun, and the moon under her feet, and upon her head a crown of twelve stars: And she being with child cried, travailing in birth, and pained to be delivered. And there appeared another wonder in heaven; and behold a great red dragon, having seven heads and ten horns, and seven crowns upon his heads. And his tail drew the third part of the stars of heaven, and did cast them to the earth: and the dragon stood before the woman which was ready to be delivered, for to devour her child as soon as it was born. And she brought forth a man child, who was to rule all nations with a rod of iron: and her child was caught up unto God, and to his throne" (*Bible*, Book of Revelation 12: 1-5). The term is applied to such works as Blake's *The Book of Thel*, Edgar Allen Poe's *The Fall of the House of Usher*, H.G. Well's *The War of the Worlds*, Alan Moore's *Watchmen* and the like.

Apologue means a story or a beast fable with a moral lesson to instruct, e.g., Bunyan's *Pilgrim's Progress* (*see* Fiction).

Apology in literature is a term meaning a justification or a defence, e.g., John Henry Newman's *Apologia pro Vita Sua* (1864) was written serially in answer to Kingsley's misrepresentation of Newman's ideas. It is an exposition of his spiritual history in powerful arguments. "From the time that I became a Catholic, of course I have no further history of my religious opinions to narrate. In saying this, I do not mean to say that my mind has been idle, or that I have given up thinking on theological subjects; but that I have had no variations to record, and have had no anxiety of heart whatever. I have been in perfect peace and contentment; I never have had one doubt. I was not conscious to myself, on my conversion, of any change, intellectual or moral, wrought in my mind. I was not conscious of firmer faith in the fundamental truths of revelation, or of more self-command; I had not more fervour; but it was like coming into port after a rough sea; and my happiness on the score remains to this day without interruption" (from John Henry Newman's *Apologia Pro Vita Sua*).

Aporia is a figure of speech to presents a speaker's doubt or speculation about something, e.g., "To be or not to be" (*Hamlet*).

Apostrophe is a literary device in which words are addressed to a dead or absent person as if he were present. It could be spoken to an inanimate thing or an abstract idea. The speaker could address a particular person in the audience as well. It is employed in ode and elegy. e.g., Milton's invocation of the muses in *Lycidas,* "Begin then, sisters of the sacred well...." Rudyard Kipling writes in 'Recessional': "Judge of nations, spare us yet, / Lest we forget – lest we forget."

Arcadia is a mountainous peninsular region in Greece in the central Pelopónnisos (Peloponnesus) covering 4,419 sq km. Its scenic splendour attracts many tourists with its mountainous landscape with inland basins and the meandering Alfiós and its tributaries. The high mountainsides are coniferous while oak woodlands fill the lower elevations. In modern Greek it is Arkadhia, having a Mediterranean climate with random rainfall. Trípolis is the centre of the region's tourism. The mountain ranges are often christened "Switzerland of Greece". Greek, Roman, and Renaissance poets were captivated by the beauty of the region. According to Greek mythology, Pan, the god of nature, and the patron of shepherds, resided in Arcadia. He received the territory as a reward for his assistance to the Athenian Greeks in their battle against the Persians. Often in literature Arcadia is presented as an imaginary setting for poetry on pastoral life. Though the actual Arcadia is rough and mountainous, the landscape of the ideal Arcadia in literature is gentle and where innocent shepherds and rustic deities live. It was the Roman poet Virgil who developed the theme of simplicity of the inhabitants living in the lap of nature in his *Eclogues.* In the later literature Arcadia became an Eden-like place for innocent existence set in a classical antiquity unaffected by the care and concerns of modern life. Arcadia was widely referred to in Europe in works such as *Arcadia* (1504) of Jacopo Sannazzaro (Italian) and *The Arcadia* by Sir Philip Sidney.

It appears in the paintings of seventeenth century French artists, Nicolas Poussin and Claude Lorrain, in imitation of the pastoral, the golden age depicted in Virgil's landscape description. In the Romantic Literature, Arcadia is a powerful symbol depicting an ideal place where nature was supreme. For moderns Arcadia represents a dream of rural happiness in contrast to the tensions of urban life.

Archaism is the use of word or expression that are obsolete, old fashioned or antiquated in flavour and no longer in ordinary use. Chaucerian or Spenserian expressions are considered archaic. Sometimes a nostalgia for the past makes some writers use archaism, e.g., Keats's *The Eve of St. Agnes* in its medieval setting and expression is archaic:

His prayers he saith, this patient, holy man;
Then takes his lamp, and riseth from his knees,

The use of archaism has been a common device in poetry up to the twentieth century. Words like "saith", "riseth", "quoth", "dropt", etc., are archaically used in poetry. However, these are not used in actual speech.

Archetypal character is a character who represents a group of people that share some common features. We have such archetypal characters such as Oedipus, Macbeth, Samson and Faust. They evoke philosophical and psychological thoughts. Archetype is associated with myth criticism where symbols such as the rose and the sun appear besides themes of love and death. The setting is mythical with a paradisal garden with stock characters in search of something. Northrop Frye presents his findings in *Anatomy of Criticism* (1957). J.G. Frazer's *The Golden Bough* (1890-1915) ushered in studies in archetypal criticism in the modern period. Psychologist C.G. Jung developed his concepts of archetypes in mythology through dream analysis. He opined that ancestral memories are transmitted through 'collective unconscious' in man. Archetypal symbolism is used by writers. For example Conrad in his *Heart of Darkness* used 'blackness' symbolically for the mystery of evil, and Satanism.

Architectonics refers to the structural proportions of a work of art in its design, unity and logical sequence. This term, taken from architecture, gives the reader a comprehensive impression of finish in a piece of literature, e.g., the novels of Hardy constructed in a geometrical manner.

Argumentative prose is one in which one writes with the purpose of convincing the readers with abstract and intellectual arguments. Writers in this genre include Newman, Locke, Bernard Shaw and others.

Asyndeton is condensing expression by which connecting words like conjunctions are omitted, e.g., "The crisis, the agony, the ecstasy". The common omission is that of '*and*' as in this example, and the sequence is maintained by commas. The effect given is one of suspense.

Asyntactic occurs in verse or prose when it breaks the conventional grammatical rules.

Atmosphere means the feelings aroused by a piece of literature. It is the subjective quality that gives the tone of a work and the effect the writer has on the reader. It is the mood, tone and feelings evoked through sense perception. The mood is communicated through the attitude of the character through speech, voice modulation, actions and postures. In the hands of a dramatist the mood is made more effective by costumes, entrances and exits, lighting, sound effects and music. In fiction atmosphere is presented through description, e.g., Emily Bronte in *Wuthering Heights* brings out the atmosphere of Heathciff's dwelling thus : "Wuthering Heights is the name of Mr. Heathcliff's dwelling. 'Wuthering' being a significant provincial adjective, descriptive of the atmospheric tumult to which its station is exposed in stormy weather. Pure, bracing ventilation they must have up there at all times, indeed: one may guess the power of the north wind blowing over the edge, by the excessive slant of a few stunted firs at the end of the house; and by a range of gaunt thorns all stretching their limbs one way, as if craving alms of the sun. Happily, the architect had foresight to build it strong: the narrow windows are deeply set in the wall, and the corners defended with large jutting stones."

Atmosphere of the mind refers to the influence a writer has on the mind of the reader by which he/she is infused by the writer's thoughts and sensibilities. The phrase introduced into literature by Henry James, e.g., Chapter 42 of *The Portrait of a Lady* was considered by Henry James the best in the novel as it brings out very powerfully 'the atmosphere of the mind': "She lost herself in infinite dismay when she thought of the magnitude of his deception. It was a wonder, perhaps, in view of this, that he didn't hate her more. She remembered perfectly the first sign he had given of it – it had been like the bell that was to ring up the curtain upon the real drama of their life. He said to her one day that she had too many ideas and that she must get rid of them. He had told her that already, before their marriage; but then she had not noticed it: it had come back to her only afterwards.... She had too many ideas for herself; but that was just what one married for, to share them with someone else. One couldn't pluck them up by the roots, though of course one might suppress them, be careful not to utter them."

Attic style has clear, refined, lucid and witty expressions. Attic was an ancient Greek state known for its art and culture. There were attic (Athenian) orators in the fifth and fourth centuries BC, like Demosthenes, who were lucid and refined in their expressions.

Authorial discourse is a narrative discourse by the author who becomes an omniscient narrator, (*see* Omniscient narrator). For example, in the introductory chapter of *Tom Jones,* Henry Fielding makes an authorial discourse: "An author ought to consider himself, not as a gentleman who gives a private or eleemosynary treat, but rather as one who keeps a public ordinary, at which all persons are welcome for their money. In the former case, it is well known that the entertainer provides what fare he pleases; and though this should be very indifferent, and utterly disagreeable to the taste of his company, they must not find any fault; nay, on the contrary, good breeding forces them outwardly to approve and to commend whatever is set before them.... As we do not disdain to borrow wit or wisdom from any man who is capable of lending us either, we have condescended to take a hint from these honest victuallers, and shall prefix not only a general bill of fare to our whole entertainment, but shall likewise give the reader particular bills to every course which is to be served up in this and the ensuing volumes.... Having premised thus much, we will now detain those who like our bill of fare no longer from their diet, and shall proceed directly to serve up the first course of our history for their entertainment."

Autobiography is an account of one's life written by oneself for the public. It differs from private records such as diary jottings and journals. Autobiography differs from memoirs which are recordings of one's observations of people and events without much reference to oneself. Autobiography is marked by its introspective nature with detailed examination of one's own life, e.g., St. Augustine's *Confessions* recounts his spiritual journey centring on his statement, "You are great O Lord and greatly to be praised: great is your power and to your wisdom there is no limit. And man, who is a part of your creation, wishes to praise you.... You arouse him to take joy in praising you, for you have made us for yourself, and our heart is restless until it rests in you." Other well known autobiographies include Sir Thomas Browne's *Religio Medici* (1642), David Hume's *My Own Life* (1777), Daniel Defoe's *Robinson Crusoe* (1719), Cardinal Newman's *Apologia Pro Vita Sua* (1864), Mark

Twain's *Life on the Mississippi*, Darwin's *Life and Letters of Charles Darwin* (1887), Oscar Wilde's *De Profundis* (1905), Christopher Isherwood's *Lions and Shadows* (1938) and the like.

Autobiographical novel is a novel in which the author presents his/her life story in a fictitious manner. As Leslie Stephen wrote, "Every writer consciously or unconsciously puts himself into his novels and exhibits his own character even more distinctly than that of his heroes." John Bunyan is considered the first to attempt this genre in his homiletic narrative *Grace Abounding to the Chief of Sinners* (1666) in which recounts his spiritual history: "I could have enlarged much in this discourse, of my temptations and troubles of sin; as also of the merciful kindness and working of God with my soul. I could also have stepped into a style much higher than this in which I have here discoursed, and could have adorned all things more than here I have seemed to do, but I dare not. God did not play in convincing of me, the devil did not play in tempting of me neither did I play when I sunk as into a bottomless pit, when the pangs of hell caught hold upon me." Others who wrote with autobiographical elements include Samuel Richardson (*Pamela*), Henry Fielding (*Tom Jones*), Oliver Goldsmith (*Vicar of Wakefield*), Dickens (*David Copperfield*), George Eliot (*Adam Bede*), Maugham (*Of Human Bondage*), James Joyce (*A Portrait of the Artist as a Young Man*), Samuel Butler (*The Way of All Flesh*), and D.H. Lawrence (*Sons and Lovers*).

Automatic writing is writing done unintentionally with the movement of fingers automatically through a medium while in a trance. It is possible in a state of hypnosis or when drugged. It is done under the influence of an entity or spirit that communicates through the written word. The person writing may not be able to recognise his own handwriting with no space in between words. In some cases the person knows who is giving the message. The writer is unaware of what is being written while in trance. The writing is done at times without any order. A person can start writing backwards, from the bottom and upwards, or in mirror script. Automatic writing is found among the Dadaists and Surrealists. Psychical researchers are of the opinion that such writing comes from the subconscious of the writer through Extra Sense Perception (ESP). Psychologists and psychiatrists use it to study mental illness. André Breton and Paul Éluard are known for their literary works through automatic writing. Yeats tried it with his wife Georgie Hyde-Lees who was a medium.

Authority is the knowledge the narrator has of the events and people in the narration, e.g., Henry Fielding's *Tom Jones* (*see* Authorial discourse).

Author's intrusion is an interference by the narrator by his/her comments on the events or persons in the course of the narration. Henry Fielding in *Tom Jones* ends chapter 2 with an author's intrusion: "Reader, I think proper, before we proceed any farther together, to acquaint thee that I intend to digress, through this whole history, as often as I see occasion, of which I am myself a better judge than any pitiful critic whatever; and here I must desire all those critics to mind their own business, and not to intermeddle with affairs or works which no ways concern them; for till they produce the authority by which they are constituted judges, I shall not plead to their jurisdiction."

Autodiegetic narrative refers to a first person narrative in which the protagonist is the narrator, e.g., Charles Dickens's *Great Expectations*: "My father's family name being Pirrip, and my Christian name Philip, my infant tongue could make of both names nothing longer or more explicit than Pip. So I called myself Pip, and came to be called Pip."

Autonomous monologue is a monologue that is free of narratorial mediation and is an immediate discourse. It is opposed to the quoted monologue (*see* Quoted monologue).

Avant-garde is a French term designating innovative writing in form and method. From the late nineteenth century it is applied to writers who are dedicated to the idea of art as experiment and revolted against tradition. They were distinctly modern and through their innovations were far ahead of their contemporaries. They drew inspiration from the invention of new or unconventional techniques with new styles. Participants in the creative process can be considered members of the avant-garde. Hence we have classical avant-garde composers like Pierre Boulez, avant-garde pioneers in electronic music, avant-garde rock music, avant-garde approaches in jazz like the recording of Ornette Coleman. In the late 1950s, 1960s, and 1970s there were directors, producers, and screenwriters of avant-garde films like Michelangelo Antonioni, Ingmar Bergman, Luis Buñuel, Sergey Mikhaylovich Eisenstein, Abel Gance, etc. The avant-garde precursors of modern theatre are Antonin Artaud, Samuel Beckett, Bertolt Brecht, Jean Cocteau and Friedrich Dürrenmatt. Avant-garde painters, sculptors, architects and other artists are also in the movement which gives existence to 'Futurist sculpture', Art Nouveau and Abstract Expressionism. Novelists such as Alain Robbe-Grillet, Michel Butor, Nathalie Sarraute and others attempted in this genre.

B

Baconian Theory was mooted in mid-nineteenth century by which the plays of Shakespeare were attributed to Bacon's genius. The proponents of the theory argued that only a person of great academic background could write such profound plays. Shakespeare's obscure biography and lack of education makes them conclude that the plays could have been written by Bacon who was the most influential writer of the seventeenth century who wrote on a wide variety of topics and introduced the induction method of reasoning. Some also refer to the nonce-word 'honorificabilitudinitatibus' in *Love's Labour's Lost* (v.i). In Latin it could be interpreted as 'These plays, F. Bacon's offspring, are preserved for the world.' However, such claims have been thoroughly discredited.

Baroque is applied to queer, extravagant, superficial and highly ornamental styles in literature, art, music and architecture especially after the Renaissance in Europe from late sixteenth to eighteenth century. In Italy Baroque began as a reaction to the classical exuberance and took to present through art, religious stories in the Church and to propagate the Catholic faith during the counter-reformation. The word 'baroque' may have derived from the Portuguese *barocco* or the Spanish *barueco* referring to an uneven pearl oddly shaped rather than a spherical one. However, the word does not define exactly the style it refers to. By the end of the eighteenth century it entered the terminology of art criticism as a term applied to seventeenth century bizarre art. In England, Sir Thomas Browne and the Metaphysical poets with their conceits were considered baroque in style. To typify the spirit of the baroque the relation between the poetry of Crashaw in English and Latin, and the sculpture and architecture of Gianlorenzo Benini are compared. The prose of Sir Thomas Browne; Thomas De Quincey's prose description of his dreams in his *Confessions of an English Opium Eater* and the like belong to this genre. "For this, and all other changes in my dreams, were accompanied by deep-seated anxiety and gloomy melancholy, such as are wholly incommunicable by words. I seemed every night to descend, not metaphorically, but literally to descend, into chasms and sunless abysses, depths below depths, from which it seemed hopeless that I could ever reascend. Nor did I, by waking, feel that I had reascended. This I do not dwell upon; because the state of gloom which attended these gorgeous spectacles, amounting at least to utter darkness, as of some suicidal despondency, cannot be approached by words" (from *Confessions of an English Opium Eater*).

Beast epic is an allegorical pseudo epic in which characters are animals. Pierre de Saint-Cloud's *Roman de Renart* of the twelfth century is a prototype of beast epic inspired by Aesop's fables. It has the central character Reynard the Fox. Chaucer's 'The Nun's Priest's Tale' in *Canterbury Tales* is an adaptation of the beast epic form. Spenser wrote *Mother Hubbard's Tale* in this genre. In modern times we have Orwell's *Animal Farm* written in this tradition (*see* Beast fable and Bestiary).

Beast fable is a kind of allegory in which animals and birds talk and act like human beings and has a moral purpose. The most popular of such fables are those of Aesop (6th century BC); Chaucer's 'The Nun's Priest's Tale' in *Canterbury Tales* and the like (*see* Beast epic). The story of the 'Nun's Priest's Tale' centres on Chauntecleer, a rooster who is challenged by the fox to sing and is almost killed (*see* Aesopic fables).

Beat generation is a group of American writers in the 1950s under the leadership of Allen Ginsberg (1926-1997). They sought an ecstatic state through drug, sex and Zen mysticism. Their unorthodox works and way of life reflected an estrangement from contemporary society. They grew beards, wore blue jeans and sandals. Jack Kerouac (1922-1969), with the publication of his novel *On the Road* (1957), became popular in representing the movement. He considered it basically a religious generation seeking beatific experience. 'Beatific' is abbreviated as 'beat'. Kerouac was the first to use the term Beat Generation and gives a somewhat loose account of the Beat experience in his *On the Road* (1957) and a sequel to it in *Big Sur* (1962). His novel *The Dharma Bums* (1958) recounts how self-fulfilment can be attained through Zen Buddhism. The writings of Jack Kerouac, Allen Ginsberg, William S. Burroughs, Gregory Corso and Lawrence Ferlinghetti were signs of social protest. Gingsberg's poem *Howl* (1956) is a major work of the beat generation that represents the disillusionment of the movement with modern society's materialism and militarism. The movement was centred in San Francisco, California, and Greenwich Village, New York City, and they concerned themselves with poetry readings and jazz performances. William Burroughs's novels are of visionary types consisting of social satire such as *Junky* (1953), *Naked Lunch* (1959), *The Soft Machine* (1961), *The Ticket That Exploded* (1962), *Nova Express* (1964), *The Wild Boys* (1971), *Exterminator!* (1973), *Port of Saints* (1975), *Cities of the Red Night* (1981), *Place of Dead Roads* (1984), *Queer* (1985), and *The Western Lands* (1987).

Belles-lettres means 'fine writing' in French. It is an imaginative light writing, distinct from the philosophical or scientific works. In the modern times the term is applied to elegant creative writing which is not scholarly, e.g., Lewis Caroll's *Alice in Wonderland.*

Bestseller is a term that came into prominence since the 1920s to refer to a book that has sold most number of copies in a country than any other work, e.g., Charles Dickens's *Pickwick Papers*, Margaret Mitchell's *Gone with the Wind*.

Bestiary is a type of book in prose or verse very popular in the Middle Ages, describing all the animals in creation and tracing their human traits. These tales were used as Christian allegories for moral and religious instruction. Bestiary tales inspired the animal symbolism used by medieval architects, painters, and sculptors. Among the modern writers of such tales we find Lewis Carroll, James Thurber, and Jorge Luis Borges. George Orwell's *Animal Farm* is a modern form of bestiary in which the wise boar calls the meeting of the animals in the farm and calls for a revolt against Mr. Jones: "Man is the only real enemy we have. Remove Man from the scene, and the root cause of hunger and overwork is abolished for ever. Man is the only creature that consumes without producing. He does not give milk, he does not lay eggs, he is too weak to pull the plough, he cannot run fast enough to catch rabbits. Yet he is lord of all the animals."

Bildungsroman is a German term to refer to 'Formation Novel' or 'Apprenticeship Novel' which usually is autobiographical and concerns the growth and development of the hero from childhood to adulthood. According to critics Goethe's *Wilhelm Meister's Apprenticeship* (1796) is a prototype of this genre. Others who wrote in this tradition include Charles Dickens (*David Copperfield*), Charlotte Bronte (*Jane Eyre*), Somerset Maugham (*Of Human Bondage*), James Joyce (*A Portrait of the Artist as a Young Man*), Samuel Butler's *The Way of All Flesh*, D.H. Lawrence's *Sons and Lovers*, Doris Lessing (*Children of Violence*), Saul Bellow (*The Adventures of Augie March*) and Ralph Ellison (*Invisible Man*). When the novel concerns itself with the story of the hero's development as an artist it is called "Kunstlerroman" ('Artist Novel') such as James Joyce's *A Portrait of an Artist as a Young Man*.

Biography is the written historical account of a person's life with reference to his, character, personality, achievements, and milieu. It is to be distinguished from memoirs and autobiography, e.g., James Boswell's *Life of Samuel Johnson*, Lytton Strachey's *Eminent Victorians* (*see* Autobiography, Memoirs).

Black humour refers to gloomy and grotesque comical elements found in some anti-novels and absurd drama. Humorously such writers present the helplessness of man in the face of death and suffering. Beckett employs black humour in his novels as, for example, *Molloy* concludes: "Then I went back into the house and wrote, It is midnight. The rain is beating on the windows. It was not midnight. It was not raining." Joseph Heller's *Catch-22* is another novel replete with black humour (*see* Antinovel).

Blue book was a cheap, shocking thriller published by the end of the eighteenth century with blue covers. There were several such sentimental thrillers popular among the masses entertaining them with horror stories and romances like the dime novel (*see* Dime novel).

Bodice-ripper is a form of romance that is centred on sexual excitement and ravishment, e.g., Kathleen Winsor's *Forever Amber* (1944).

Bohemian is a term that refers to someone fully committed to literary or imaginative art and does not care for social conventions. The term was introduced into English by W.M. Thackeray in his *The Newcomers*. A bohemian prefers to live his life free from encumbrances. Bohemian means a native of Bohemia which is a historical region of central Europe forming roughly the Westernmost two-thirds of what is now the Czech Republic. In the fifteenth century gypsies were supposed to have come from this region. They were persons of loose habits. Later, any person who set aside social conventions were considered bohemian.

Bombast is verbose and exaggerated language with bombastic words. It is derived from 'cotton stuffing' depicting the hollowness of such high-sounding expressions. Thus the term means inflated language. Elizabethan Tragedy especially Senecan plays are known for bombasts.

As are the elements, such are the heavens,
Even from the moon unto the empyreal orb,
Mutually folded in each other's spheres,
And jointly move upon one axle-tree,
Whose termine is termed the world's wide pole.

(*Doctor Faustus* : Marlowe)

Bovarysme refers to a kind of daydreaming in which one lives in a world of one's own imagination. The term is derived from French novelist Gustave Flaubert's novel *Madame Bovary* in which he presents the adulteries and suicide of a doctor's wife. Jane Austen's character Catherine Morland in *Northanger Abbey* is a character living in a world of dreams.

Bowdlerise is the practice of expunging certain passages of indecent nature consisting of sexual references which can be of embarrassing nature in the presence of women and children. It is a practice introduced by Thomas Bowdler (1754-1824). Hence there began bowdlerised editions of literary works such as *Gulliver's Travels*, *Moby Dick* and the like meant especially for children.

British Academy was founded in 1901 to represent in the Royal Society 'Literary science', namely, the science of language, political sciences, history, antiquity, law and philosophy.

British Council was established in 1934 to promote understanding of Britain overseas with cultural and educational exchanges. It maintains contact with academics overseas with library facilities.

Brook Farm is a cooperative community established in 1841 in West Roxbury, USA by the leaders of transcendentalism.

The wqs farm was directed by the American critic and social reformer George Ripley. It consisted of the Brook Farm Institute of Agriculture and Education set-up and the members shared equally the work and profits. Many literary and religious leaders were associated with it—Amos Bronson Alcott, Ralph Waldo Emerson, Margaret Fuller, Nathaniel Hawthorne and Theodore Parker. The farm was one of the headquarters of the Fourierist movement in the United States (1845 to 1849). The Brook Farm community published a weekly newspaper entitled the *Harbinger* for some time. The community was abandoned in 1847 after the central building was ravaged by fire in 1846. Hawthorne took the Brook Farm as the setting of his novel *The Blithedale Romance* (1852).

Burlesque is a term derived from Italian *burla* meaning "mockery" with comic and ridiculous effect. A burlesque can be satiric and can have two forms: (i) as a mock epic in which a trivial subject is treated in an exalted manner as Alexander Pope in *The Rape of the Lock;* (ii) and as a parody in which a serious subject is treated as a trifle as Cervantes in *Don Quixote*. Burlesque should not be confused with farce and parody. Parody is a mocking imitation of a particular work or of the style of a writer; while farce is written to excite laughter. The earliest use of burlesque was in the Greek mock epic poem *The Battle of the Frogs and the Mice*. Aristophanes and Euripides employed it in drama. In England burlesque began with Geoffrey Chaucer. French comic playwrights Paul Scarron and Molière excelled in its use. Samuel Butler's *Hudibras* is an excellent mock epic poem. In the modern times the *Nonsense Novels* (1911) of the Canadian author Stephen Leacock is an example. In the USA. burlesque is considered a kind of theatrical production popular between the two World Wars. American burlesque began in the late nineteenth century with minstrel show and vaudeville. In twentieth century it took the form of ribald comedy and striptease in which a female performer strips herself on stage. Of the many strippers who achieved fame,

Gypsy Rose Lee was the most prominent. Interest in burlesque declined as films became popular.

Byronic hero is a character type in Lord Byron's works such as *Childe Harold's Pilgrimage* and *Don Juan*, who rebels against conventional morality and suffers from complexes of self-love, guilt, pride and desolation. He is a cynic and pessimist who sees nothing good in life. Macaulay described such a hero as "a man proud, moody, cynical, with defiances on his brow, and misery in his heart, a scorner of his kind, implacable in revenge, yet capable of deep and strong affection." Emily Bronte's Heathcliff in *Wuthering Heights* is such a Byronic Hero.

C

Cacophany is the discordant and dissonant combination of sounds which is the opposite of euphony. It is marked by tongue-twisters deliberately used by writers to criticise literary works.

Let twenty pass, and stone the twenty-first,
Loving not, hating not, just choosing so.
Say, the first straggler that boasts purple spots
Shall join the file, one pincer twisted off.

(*Caliban upon Setbos*: Robert Browning)

Cabbala derives from Hebrew *qabbalah*', a Jewish tradition of the mystical interpretation of scriptures (9th to 13th centuries) in contrast to rational explication. It believed in emanations of '*sephiroth*' entering into relations with the finite. This tradition also believed in the number value of each letter of the biblical texts which have hidden meanings. A trace of it is found in reference to the beast in *Revelations* 13:18.

Cadence is the inner tune or natural rhythm of language by rhythmical rise and fall of speech effected by stressed and unstressed syllables or the inflection of accent. It is found in verse and prose and found in a writer which indicates his 'voice' in linking words, phrases and sentences. Cadence supports the meaning as sense and sound are inseparable from each other. It is also a term used in music that communicates a feeling of rest at the end of a composition.

Calvinist refers to the French religious reformer John Calvin (1509-64) who taught the doctrine of Scripture as the only rule of faith. He denied free will in fallen man and God's absolute predestination of every man before creation, to salvation or damnation. Milton was influenced by strict Calvinism but later rejected absolute predestination.

Campus novel is a comical or satirical novel set in the background of a University campus depicting its comical elements, e.g., Kingsley Amis's *Lucky Jim*, David Lodge's *Changing Place,* John Barth's *Giles Goat-Boy* and the like.

Canon refers to the books of the *Bible* accepted by the Church as inspired since the fourth century. Those books that are not included in the canon are classified as *apocryphal.* Canon hence means recognised works by an authority as authentic. In literature the term canon is applied to mean the collection of an author's literary works, e.g., the Shakespearean Canon comprises 37 plays by the playwright. In case of doubt regarding authorship of a work, it is classified under *apocryphal writings.*

Caricature is the likeness of anything so exaggerated or distorted as to appear ridiculous. In it physical features as well as mental characteristics are comically exaggerated, e.g., in Shakespeare, Falstaff's large belly is caricatured as belonging to creatures who live and change. Novelists such as Fielding, Smollet, Dickens and Thackeray used caricatures in their works. Thackeray's caricature of Sir Pitt Crawley in *Vanity Fair* reads: "Among the most respected of the names beginning in C, which the *Court Guide* contained in the year 18-, was that of Crawley, Sir Pitt Baronet, Great Gaunt Street, and Queen's Crawley Hants. This honourable name had figured constantly also in the Parliamentary list for many years, in conjunction with that of a number of other worthy gentlemen who sat in turns for the borough."

Carnival is a feast traditionally observed in the Church before the liturgical season of Lent (a period of 40 days from Ash Wednesday to Easter observed which is a time of fasting in commemoration of the 40 days of Christ's fast in the wilderness). Carnival means 'saying goodbye' to meat. During the carnival festivities people indulge in merrymaking, feasting and amusements with fair-like entertainment. The term was used by Bakhtin to describe a kind of festive language that challenges social order.

Carlylean is a term referring to the prose style of Thomas Carlyle (1795-1881) distinct for its irregular sentences with striking figures. "The latest Gospel in this world is, know thy work and do it. 'Know thyself': long enough has that poor 'self' of thine tormented thee, thou wilt never get to 'know' it, I believe! Think it not thy business, this of knowing thyself; thou art an unknowable individual: know what thou canst work at; and work at it, like a Hercules! That will be thy better plan" (from *Past and Present*).

Carnivalisation is a theory developed by the Russian formalist critic Bakhtin. According to him, in popular carnival there is a mingling of the sacred with the profane and the noble with the ridiculous. In it there is a reversal of the order of things and situations. The marginalised gets prominence and expresses the repressed. According to Bakhtin Carnivalisation is a means of displaying otherness. By it the serious and the sacred are ridiculed.

Catalyser is a term used to refer to the narrative unit that is secondary to the nuclei. It fills in the space in between and belongs to the domain of the discourse. Nucleus on the other hand belongs to the domain of the text as a narrative unit which is a key unit of the plot.

Catholicism (Roman) in English literature was a strong force till Henry VIII separated from the Catholic Christendom and authority of the Pope by the Act of Supremacy in 1534. The Counter Reformation after the Council of Trent (1545-1563) began a strong defence of the Catholic position against the onslaughts of Protestantism of the sixteenth century. Some Catholic poets of the seventeenth century include Richard Crashaw and Alexander Pope. The Oxford movement or Tractarian movement was an intellectual movement within the Church of England in the nineteenth century led by Newman. Eventually Newman became a Catholic and explained the reasons in his *Apologia Pro Vita Sua.* G.M. Hopkins is another Anglican who came over to the Catholic faith under the influence of Newman. There is a Metaphysical revival in the religious poetry of some of the Catholic contemporaries of Hopkins, namely, Coventry Patmore, Francis Thompson, and Alice Meynell. Since the seventeenth century there was hardly any important English religious verse. There is a link thus established by the poets with the religious verse tradition of the past. The elements of the Metaphysical tradition suited these poets to express their philosophical and religious thoughts. Patmore fused thought and passion in his religious verse. Alice Meynell is noted for her logical arguments, metaphysical wit and dramatic elements besides her intense thought and feeling. Francis Thompson is able to couple the concrete with the spiritual. They all refer to very intense personal religious experience. But none of these poets were able to make an impact on their society or influence poetry in general. It is only Hopkins who is successful in his effort to usher in a new era of Religious poetry after the seventeenth century. From the time of Reformation there was a school of thought that remained close to Roman Catholic traditions known as the Anglo Catholicism. T.S. Eliot belonged to this school of thought and claimed to be "Royalist in politics, Anglo-Catholic in religion and classicist in literature." Roman Catholicism is presented in the works of Graham Greene, Evelyn Waugh, Anthony Burgess, David Lodge and Muriel Spark.

Cenacle, meaning 'supper room' in French, refers to a coterie of writers and intellectuals who gathered around a leading personality for discussions and intellectual pursuits. It was considered a kind of hero-worship ushered in by the spirit of Romanticism. The first such meeting was held at the salon of Charles Nodier (1780-1844), and the second at the residence of Victor Hugo.

Censorship was practised in the English theatre during the time of Henry VIII when Lord Chamberlaine was appointed to check heresy and sedition presented in drama. Later, Licensing Acts were promulgated under James I in 1713 and 1737. The Theatre Act came into effect in 1843 giving licences to theatres and plays for public performance. The 1968 Theatre Act abolished Lord Chamberlaine's power to censor tests. The 1959 Obscene Publications Act controls writers, directors and the media.

Chapbook is a small booklet containing ballads, fairy tales, religious legends, romances, biographies, witchcraft, accounts of travel, crime and strange events. Chapbooks were sold by pedlars called 'chapmen' from the sixteenth to early nineteenth century. These booklets mirrored the attitudes of the time.

Character is the person in a narrative or dramatic work or his/her personality. Aristotle in his *Poetics* considered character that aspect of the plot from which the action arises. In chapter VI of *Poetics* he argues that Plot is more important than Character. It looks as though there is an antithesis between character and plot. But it is not so in reality as character is formed by plot. Speaking about characters he demands that they be 'good' (ch.XV). Good means ethically good. The goodness he requires is the moral purpose which is inseparably linked to the goodness of the whole action. In Chapter XV of *Poetics* Aristotle discusses that character should be 'good', 'appropriate', 'like reality' and 'consistent'. It looks as though there is a sharp antithesis between 'character and plot' or 'character and action'. But in reality they are not opposed but inseparable. In each individual, character is formed by action. By 'tragedies without character', Aristotle meant plays in which personages go through a change of fortune. Probably a change from happiness to misery, rather than the opposite in which they suffer and act. Characters can be major or minor depending on the textual prominence; dynamic (when there is change) or static (when there is no change); flat (simple) and round (complex).

Characterisation is the process by which a person is represented in narratives or drama. Through it the narrator or the dramatist communicates with the audience. E.M. Forster in *Aspects of the Novel* (1927) distinguishes between 'flat' and 'round' characters (*see* Flat character, Round character). Characterisation can be *direct* (when the narrator presents clearly the character traits) or *indirect* (when the reader/ audience gets to know character traits from the actions, thoughts and emotions of the character).

Children's books were not common until the nineteenth century except a few didactic works for instruction and training in good manners. Few books that appealed to them included Aesop's *Fables*, Bunyan's *Pilgrim's Progress* (1678), Defoe's *Robinson Crusoe* (1719), Swift's *Gulliver's Travels* (1726), etc. It was John Newbery (1713-67) who began the publication of specifically children's books with his *A Little Pretty Pocket-Book* (1744) and *The History of Little Goody Two-Shoes* (1765). With the ushering in of the Romantic Period more and more children's books began to appear influenced by the concept of Rousseau's ideas on education. Eventually there is a steady growth in books meant for children such as Thomas Day's *Merton and Sandford* (1783-9), Sarah Trimmer's *Fabulous Histories* (1786), Maria Edgeworth's *Moral Tales* (1801), William Rosecoe's *The Butterfly's Ball and the Grasshopper's Feast* (1807), Grimm's *Fairy Tales* (1823), Lane's version of the *Arabian Nights* (1839-41), Thackeray's *The Rose and the Ring* (1855), Lewis Carroll's *Alice's Adventures in Wonderland* (1865), Anna Sewell's *Black Beauty* (1877), Stevenson's *Treasure Island* (1883),

Kipling's *Jungle Book* (1894-95), Mark Twaine's *Adventures of Tom Sawyer* (1876), Potter's *Peter Rabbit* (1902), Lofting's *Dr. Dolittle* (1920), A.A. Milne's *Winnie the Pooh* (1926) and others. Since the 1950s there has been an increase in the publication of books for children. Some known writers include Alan Garner, Rosemary Sutcliff, Leon Garfield, Nina Bawden, Walter Farley, Dr. Seuss, Sandburg, Mary Ellen Chase, E.B. White and others.

Chivalric or Medieval Romance was prevalent in the Medieval Europe from the twelfth century. It described the adventures undertaken by a chivalric knight and celebrated courtly love, honour and loyalty. Medieval romances can be divided into: Roman classical stories; French romances on Charlemagne; British romances on King Arthur and his court, e.g., *Sir Gawain and the Green Knight*, Malory's prose romance *Le Morte D' Arthur* (1485). "And when Sir Mordred saw King Arthur he ran unto him with his sword drawn in his hand, and there King Arthur smote Sir Mordred under the shield with a foin of his spear, throughout the body more than a fathom. And when Sir Mordred felt that he had his death's wound, he thrust himself with the might that he had up to the burr of King Arthur's spear, and right so he smote his father, King Arthur, with his sword held in both his hands, upon the side of his head, that the sword pierced the helmet and the tay of the brain And therewith Mordred dashed down stark dead to the earth" (From *Morte D'Arthur*).

Chronicle is a bare record of events in order of time. It could be of national or of universal nature. If chronicled events are considered year by year they are called *Annals.* Chronicles in England began under King Alfred in the ninth century known as *The Anglo Saxon Chronicle* consisting of legends and facts. Other chronicles include Geoffrey of Monmouth's *The History of the Kings of Britain* (c. 1136) in Latin, recording the legends of King Arthur and other legendary British history; Raphael Hollinshed's *Chronicles of England, Scotland, and Ireland*, which Shakespeare and other dramatists used in their chronicle plays. Chronicle novels are written based on chronicles (*see* Saga).

Chronological order is maintained in the course of a narration when events are presented in their chronological order (*see* order), e.g., Daniel Defoe in *Robinson Crusoe* maintains a chronological order of events (*see* Order of plot).

Circumlocution is roundabout reference to something, e.g., *The son of my mother's brother* is circumlocution for *my cousin.*

Classic is referred to a literary work of recognition. It is a term used mainly to refer to a period of creative work. In its strict sense *classic* denotes any ancient Greek or Roman literary work of the highest quality like the works of the Greek dramatist Sophocles and the Roman poet Virgil. In its broad sense the term is applied to anything accepted as a model of excellence in its cultural relevance and value, e.g., Chaucer's *Canterbury Tales* is a classic in English literature.

Classical in the restricted sense is used to portray the art, literature, and aesthetics of the ancient Greeks and Romans. In a broad sense it refers to any style or period of creative work remarkable for its qualities that are mainly suggestive of classical Greek or Roman art, literature, and aesthetics. Among these qualities are a sense of conscious restraint in the handling of themes and a sense of rational order and proportion in forms.

Classicism means the imitation of the style and aesthetic principles of ancient Greek and Roman classical art and literature. It also refers to the adoption of such principles in music today. The late seventeenth and early eighteenth centuries were the most important periods when classicism prevailed in Western thought. The term *neoclassicism* is often used in referring to revivals of classicism.

Cliché is a French word meaning 'a stereotype block'. It is applied to a stock expression or phrase which by constant usage has become lifeless and old-fashioned, e.g., *my better* *half, all and sundry, flesh and blood.* Cliches are at times used for emotional and dramatic effect.

Climax is the turning point in the course of a narrative or a play when it reaches crisis and resolution. Climax is often the scene of recognition and discovery, e.g., "All that most maddens and torments; all that stirs up the less of things; all truth with malice in it; all creaks the sinews and cakes the brain; all subtle demonisms of life and thought; all evil, to crazy Ahab, were visibly personified, and made practically assailable in *Moby Dick*" (*from* Melville's *Moby Dick*).

Closure is the feeling when a literary work is concluded. In Literary Criticism a closure excludes further interpretation of a work under scrutiny.

Cock-and-bull story is a dubious story similar to a *tall story* that is highly exaggerated. The phrase originated from animal fables which had animals and birds as characters. Burton in *Anatomy of Melancholy* makes reference to cock and bull stories (*see* Tall story, Beast fable).

Coda is a passage forming the completion of a piece of music, rounding it off to a satisfactory conclusion. It can be applied to a passage or piece in a story or dance sequence.

Coherence is a principle that insists on the various parts of a literary work being related to each other in a clear and logical manner. Truth of coherence has to do with the internal consistency of a piece of literature.

Coined words are those invented purposely by writers and people which are absorbed into a language in course of time. It is a literary practice that also affects language in its growth, e.g., 'inscape', 'instress' (G.M. Hopkins).

Collaboration in literature refers to a work undertaken by two or more writers. Beaumont and Fletcher wrote *Philaster* together.

Collage is derived from French meaning 'pasting things together', especially in the field of painting. In literature it consists of references, quotations and allusions taken from different sources under the influence of surrealism. T.S. Eliot, Ezra Pound and James Joyce are known to have used the device.

Collate is a comparative study of different texts or manuscripts to learn the differences between them. Such close comparative study is meant to identify the true and correct text.

Colloquialism is concerned with informal expressions used in common parlance but not in formal speech. It can be used in writing to lighten the atmosphere with comic effect. Dryden writes in his *Essay of Dramatic Poesy* : "They say the quickness of repartees in argumentative scenes receives an ornament from the verse. Now what is more unreasonable than to imagine that a man should not only listen upon the wit, but the rhyme too, upon the sudden! This nicking of him who spoke before both in sound and measure, is so great a happiness, that you must, at least suppose the persons of your play to be born poets."

Colonialism is a term that occurs frequently in the literature of the Commonwealth writers referring to the British colonisation of countries such as India, Canada, Africa and the West Indies. Writers who wrote of the oppression and hardship suffered during the colonial rule include Khwaja Ahmad Abbas (*Inquilab*), Venu Chitale (*In Transit*), K.S. Venkataramani (*Kandan the Patriot*), V.S. Naipaul (*Miguel Street*), Raja Rao (*Kanthapura*), Manohar Malgaonkar (*A Bend in the Ganges*), Kamala Markandaya (*A Handful of Rice*), Salman Rushdie (*Midnight's Children*), Chinua Achebe (*No Longer at Ease*), Ngugi (*A Grain of Wheat*) and the like.

Colophon is the symbol of the publisher placed commonly on the title page of a book to identify the publisher, e.g., 'Penguin books' have the symbol of a penguin at the bottom of the title page; 'Macmillan' has **M** printed at the bottom of the title page.

Colportage is popular literature sold by hawkers such as sensational novels, romances and the like.

Comedy of manners is primarily related to drama. The trend is found in fiction as well. In drama it is found in the Restoration drama concerned with the life of the upper classes – their moral laxity and licentiousness. Comedy of manners dealt with the artificial life of the upper classes. It was concerned with love, moral infidelity and foibles of society. It presented the habits, customs, manners, follies of gay elegant aristocracy and dealt with young nobles straining after wit. The plot is mostly made up of love intrigues, clandestine love affairs, senseless prattles, scandal-mongering, drinking and gambling. Love is an important theme in such comedies. Usually there is a pair of lovers. They are well versed in coquetry and noted for wit, sparkling dialogue and verbal fencing matches. The lovers will try to be united with each other, but others try to obstruct them. Thus the conflict is maintained. Usually lovers are simple and easily duped. There is a series of dramatic incidents and finally the conflict is resolved. For example, in Sheridan's *The School for Scandal* there are two pairs of lovers who are rewarded at the end. The villains are mildly punished. Congreve in *The Way of the World* brought the comedy of manners to perfection. Jeremy Collier in 1698 wrote on 'The Immorality and Licentiousness of English Stage', presenting the middle class reaction against it. Soon the Sentimental Comedy developed in the eighteenth century. It stood for domestic virtues and the triumph of Christian virtues and preaching to middle class audience. Goldsmith and Sheridan led the anti-sentimental movement. Sheridan's *The School for Scandal* is a very successful comedy of manners. In the Prologue Garrick speaks of its purpose – to expose the theme of scandal-mongering. He wrote, "the play had less nature than wit". It is full of wit showing absurdities. In fiction it deals with the clash between characters, their speech and behaviour in a particular social set-up. Fanny Burney was the first to write in this genre with works such as *Evelina* (1778) and *Cecilia* (1782). Jane Austen with her *Pride and Prejudice,* (1813) and *Emma* (1816) brought the genre to its perfection.

Comic novel concerns itself with arousing laughter with depiction of characters caught up in funny situations. The characters are presented as types showing certain human traits and foibles. The comic novelists make the readers laugh at the exaggerated human imperfections and follies in a satirical manner. In such a novel there is no original well constructed plot. The narration is done in a haphazard manner with no systematic progression. The language is replete with slang expressions typical of a particular class of people. Comic novel is said to have evolved with a minor writer Robert Smith Surtees (1805-1864) who began a journal, *The New Sporting Magazine,* in 1831 in collaboration with Rudolph Ackermann. Robert Smith began publishing sketches of a character he invented, named Jorrock. Eventually he wrote his novel *Jorrock's Jaunts and Jollities* (1838). In his hands Jorrocks and James Pigg became immortal comic characters in English fiction. Into this genre belongs novels of Pierce Egan, Fielding, Thackeray, Thomas Love Peacock, Charles Dickens and others. Thomas Love Peacock's *Nightmare Abbey* (1818) is a satire on contemporary literature and thoughts such as Coleridge's Transcendentalism, Byron's self-portrayal in his writings, etc. Charles Dickens's *Pickwick Papers* is considered the best in this genre. It narrates the story of the Pickwick Club founded by Samuel Pickwick with Tracy Tupman, Augustus Snodgrass and Nathaniel Winkle as members.

Comic relief is a device employed by writers by inserting some comical situations or the role of a fool. As the tragedy progresses, it relieves tension in the audience. This has a psychological effect on the audience, e.g., The episode of the drunken porter in *Macbeth;* the scene of the grave diggers in *Hamlet.* Some novelists like Malcolm Lowry employ the device in his novel *Under the Volcano* (1947), which revolves around the theme of self-destruction.

Commitment in literature denotes those writers who are committed to the propagation of their beliefs in their writings. During the Communist era it was applied to writers who made propaganda for their ideologies. In fiction novels noted names include Sartre, Doris Lessing, Guntur Grass and others. In drama Bernard Shaw, Brecht and Arnold Wesker belong to this group.

Commonplace book is an author's book containing a collection of quotations meant for reference. It is also referred to a private collection of quotes and lines of poems an individual keeps. It was a common practice in the Elizabethan times, e.g., W.H. Auden's *A Certain World.*

Commonwealth literature is a term in use since the 1940s referring to the literatures emerging from former colonies of Britain. There was also an effort to bring the capacity of the English language in West Indies, Canada, Australia, Africa, New Zealand and in the Indian subcontinent. Commonwealth writers come from different cultures and literary traditions older than the English. From the 1940s there was a tremendous growth in asserting a sense of regional identity which led to an increase in the production of national literature in English. Their language has its own variations with certain common features. Their works present their individual as well as their national and cosmopolitan voices. Their works present the landscapes of their region, their social and national interests besides themes of universal concerns. Using English as a common language, they function as a single community creating a peculiar tradition of their own. The literature of Canada, Australia and New Zealand began by the end of eighteenth century. In West Indies it began in the twentieth century.

The Indian literature in English had its beginning in the 1930s and in Africa in the 1960s. A Commonwealth writer is the writer of his region with a distinct voice in comparison with the writers of other regions and yet he belongs to the tradition of English literature. English has provided a uniform medium for commerce and education in the Commonwealth. It has given access to the resources of the West and has helped to create a national identity being a common language of communication (*see* Colonialism, Postcolonialism).

Complication is the intensification of suspense due to some forces that come in opposition to the protagonist, as the plot develops in a drama or a novel. In a five-act tragedy, usually it is the second act that presents the complication. It is known as the act of complication. According to Aristotle in his *Poetics,* "Every tragedy is in part Complication and in part Denouement. The complication consists of incidents that have taken place before the opening of the play and often some also that occur within it; the remainder form the denouement. By complication I mean everything from the beginning of the story up to the point where the hero suffers a change of fortune; by denouement, everything from the latter point to the end." Since complication develops the conflict it is also known as rising action (*see* Rising action).

Concordance is an index of words of a text alphabetically organised. It gives details of the whereabouts of the word and its occurrence in the text. Originally concordances were done on the texts of the *Bible.* Now a days they are done on a particular text of an author or on all his works. With the advent of communication revolution in the cyber age of today, very elaborate computerised concordances are available on internet.

Concrete term is a word or a phrase concerning a particular concrete thing or a person, e.g., an innocent baby : baby is concrete; its innocence is abstract. A concrete language refers directly to what we see, hear, touch, taste or smell. Most literature use concrete language and express even abstract concepts concretely through images and metaphors.

Confessional literature is a kind of autobiographical writing in which the author writes about his/her beliefs and convictions; spiritual and inner experiences, e.g., St. Augustine's *Confessions* recounts his spiritual journey centring on his statement, "You are great O! Lord and greatly to be praised: great is your power and to your wisdom there is no limit. And man, who is a part of your creation, wishes to praise you.... You arouse him to take joy in praising you, for you have made us for yourself, and our heart is restless until it rests in you." Other such works include Rousseau's *Les Confessions*; De Quincey's *Confessions of an English Opium Eater*; and James Hogg's *The Private Memoirs of Confessions of a Justified Sinner*.

Confessional novel is a kind of autobiographical fiction that has evolved inspired by the *Confessions* of St. Augustine and *The Seven Storey Mountain* (1948) of Thomas Merton. In such novels an anti-hero is presented who lives disillusioned in a vicious world. He has no choice but to accept his agony and turns inward from his rebellious nature. Novelists who have written in this genre are Dostoevsky (*Notes From the Underground, Crime and Punishment*), Sartre (*Nausea*), Camus (*The Fall*), Silvia Plath (*The Bell Jar*), Saul Bellow (*Herzog*) and others.

Confidant / Confidante (fem) is the person in whom the protagonist confides and seeks advice from and listens to. The author uses the confidant-protagonist dialogue to expose the mind of the protagonist as well as the innermost thoughts of other characters, e.g., in Henry James's *Ambassador* Maria Gostrey is the confidante of Strether.

Conflict is the opposition and struggle between two opposing forces in a plot. The conflict can be broadly divided into external or internal. In an external conflict the protagonist comes in conflict with some external force. The opposition of the two physical forces generate intense actions. Internal conflict exists when it occurs within the protagonist's own self due to internal mental struggle between opposite desires. Conflict arouses interest in a fiction or play from the suspense generated. Other types of conflict can be due to : (a) the opposition between the wills of two characters leading to the confrontation of one quality of character with another; (b) a character in confrontation with family or society; (c) the opposition between a character and the audience; (d) the struggle between a character and gods or fate. The interest aroused in the audience depends on the strength of the conflict. Conflicts arouse empathy and identification in the audience. Conflicts go through various stages such as (a) exposition, (b) complication, (c) crisis, (d) falling action, (e) resolution (*see* Exposition, Complication, Crisis, Falling action, Resolution).

Connotation is the idea associated with or suggested by a given word or phrase as opposed to its literal meaning. A word's connotation is that set of associations and emotional overtones carried by the word. Hence, connotation is the implication of something more than the denotation of it. (Denotation is that which a word denotes in its dictionary definition in contradistinction to what it connotes.) For example, *a snake* denotes a reptile. But it can connote a person of intriguing and cunning character as in Sheridan's *The School for Scandal.* Connotation of a word can imply many things according to the contexts and references. A word is only an accurate tool of communication if it conveys the same idea to both the speaker and the listener; yet the meanings of words continually change and, despite the existence of dictionaries, can only be said to mean what people think they mean. It is to be kept in mind that meanings of words also change with time.

Conte in French means tale or story. The term has been used to refer to short prose fiction that is humorous and didactic.

It is usually unrealistic in its content with allegorical and moral structure, e.g., Voltaire's philosophical romance *Zadig* (1747); La Fontaine's *Amours de Psyche et Cupidon* (1669); Johnson's *The History of Rasselas, Prince of Abyssinia* (1759) is a didactic romances in the form of an essay on the 'choice of life.' In course of time the term was applied to short story. Maupassant's stories were called *Contes*.

Contemplative prose is a genre into which belongs essays, political reflections, philosophical speculations, religious reflections and the like, e.g., Essays of Bacon, Hazlitt, Lamb, etc.

Contemporary literature is the literature written since the end of the Second World War in 1945 (*see* Postmodernism).

Content and form refer to what is presented in a literary work and how it is done. The differentiation between the two is only speculative for analysis as the two go hand in hand. There can be no content without form and vice-versa.

Context in literature means the positioning or placing of a piece of literature. It calls for the immediate neighbouring texts preceding it and following it which can give important historical, biographical, social, cultural, religious and psychological information about it. Hence, an objective interpretation of the said text or passage will depend much on its context which is spoken of as *contextualisation*.

Convention in literature is a method or style that has become an accepted form of literary expression in course of time, e.g., Pastoral elegy; Ballad tradition; use of Heroic Couplet by Dryden and Pope; Stream of Consciousness novels; Shakespearean Sonnet and the like.

Copyright is the legal right an author has over the ownership of his writing. Such copyrights are valid while he is alive and for some years after his death according to the law of the county. In England copyright is valid during the author's lifespan and 50 years after his/her death. In USA. under the

Copyright Act of 1976 which came into effect from January 1, 1978, an author's copyright for a work extends 50 years after his/her death as in England.

Corpus refers to a body of literary writing usually of the same author or related to the same subject matter.

Courtesy book deals with the training of courtiers giving them advice on social etiquette and behaviour. During the late Renaissance period the book was at times written in verse form and concerned itself with the qualities of noblemen and ladies. It originated in Italy with Castiglione's *Ill Cortegiano* and led to the writing of *The Book Named the Governor* by Sir Thomas Elyot, e.g., "It is diligently to be noted that the associating of man and woman in dancing, they both observing one number and time in their movings, was not begun without a special consideration....A man in his natural perfection is fierce, hardy, strong in opinion, covetous of glory, desirous of knowledge" (from *The Book Named the Governor: Book I*).

Counter-culture is a term that evolved in the 1960s and early 1970s in the wake of a cultural debate initiated by Roszak's *The Making of Counter Culture* (1971). It stands for the various movements in the music and drug world with networks of organisations and groups that revolted against the conservative society of the post-war world, especially in the United States. Some literary figures such as Allen Ginsberg, Robert Lowell and Norman Mailer are associated with it as well as certain groups of the women's liberation movement and civil rights organisations. Certain social movements campaigning for gay rights and environmental protection contribute to the concept of counter culture seeking social and political transformation. Noted among the works of counter-culture include Norman Mailer's *Armies of the Nights* (1968); Alice Walker's *Meridian* (1982); Richard Neville's *Play Power* (1970); Germaine Greer's *The Female Eunuch* (1970) and the like. *The Female Eunuch* is noted for its protest against the traditional morality and seeking women's rights and liberation. Greer calls for a revolutionary empowerment of women.

Crime novels are written centring on crimes committed by some-one least suspected. Agatha Christie and John Dickson Carr excelled in it (*see* Detective novel).

Crisis is a turning point in the course of a play or a novel when a decision is made. This crisis point is also referred to as the climax as the plot reaches its ultimate intensity. The term can also be attributed to a decisive and important moment in a scene or act or performance of a character. In the 'drama of crisis' a climax in the play is presented at the beginning and the protagonist is unaware of the plot, e.g., Sophocles's *Oedipus Rex*.

Critique is an assessment done on a work of literature in the form of an essay or a review.

Cut-up is a device by which a writer takes an existing text and cuts-up and reorganises to produce another piece of literature, e.g., William Seward Burroughs's novel *The Ticket That Exploded* (1962). He is known for his literary innovations through experimentation and improvisation with collage and montage.

Cycle in fiction refers to a sequence of novels or stories (*see* Roman-fleuve), e.g., Doris Lessing has her five-volume sequence *Children of Violence* (1952-1969) dealing with the autobiographical account of Martha Quest.

D

Dada is an artistic and literary movement depicting the nihilistic protest against Western culture especially against militarism during and after World War I (1914-1918). The term *dada* is a French word for hobbyhorse used by the Romanian-born poet Tristan Tzara. He began Dadaist group in 1916 with German writer Hugo Ball, the Alsatian-born artist Jean Arp, and other intellectuals living in Zürich, Switzerland. A similar revolt against conventional art began in New York led by Man Ray, Marcel Duchamp, and Francis Picabia. From 1919 the Dadaist group met in Paris and inspired the Surrealist movement. To express the negation of all current aesthetic and social values the Dadaists used unintelligible artistic and literary methods. Their manifestoes were often bewildering with the purpose of startling the public. They used innovative materials like discarded objects found in the streets in their works. The German painter Kurt Schwitters made collages of wastepaper and similar materials. French painter Marcel Duchamp exhibited as works of art ordinary commercial products like a bottle rack which he called *ready-mades.* Though the Dadaists were revolutionary in their methods, they believed in the romantic goodness of humanity. The movement declined in the 1920s, however it had an influence on modern-art movements. In the mid-1950s there was a revival of interest in Dada in New York City among several composers, writers, and artists who showed Dadaist features in their works. Dada is a forerunner of the theatre of cruelty and the theatre of the absurd. Tom Stoppard's *Travesties* (1974) is a dada comedy. The play is set in Zurich during the First World War where Lenin, Joyce and Tristan Tzara lived. It presents witty comments on Dada, Joyce's *Ulysses,* and socialist realism.

Dead metaphor is a metaphor or a cliché that has lost its figurative strength. There are hundreds of such metaphors as, for example: 'to beat about the bush', 'green with envy' and the like.

Decadence is referred to any general decadence of literary or moral standards of a period in comparison to the preceding age. However, the term came to be applied to a group of late nineteenth century French and English symbolist poets. They considered the literature of the last decade of the nineteenth century decadent, and questioned the Victorian morality, art and literature. They wanted to liberate literature from the clutches of moral and social responsibilities. Verlaine, Mallarme and Rimbaud were the prominent writers in France while in England the group included John Davidson, Arthur Symons, Ernest Dowson and Oscar Wilde.

Decolonising is a commonly used term in Postcolonial literature and theory. It is concerned with the process of liberating people from mental enslavement by the colonisers such as ideas, notions, ideologies and cultural habits.

Deconstruction is a method of analysing literature to reveal hidden ideological assumptions. It seeks to uncover multiple layers of meaning in a text, including the author's intentions and other meanings that are based on how the same language, images, or ideas have been used before. Deconstruction can be defined as a critique of the hierarchical oppositions that have structured the Western thought: inside versus outside, mind versus body, literal versus metaphorical, speech versus writing, presence versus absence, nature versus culture, form versus meaning, man versus woman, etc. Hence, it is a mode of analytical reading based on the radical assumption that the language of literature is essentially unreliable. Deconstruction analyses all possible meanings of words and phrases. It seeks the contradictions in a given text to prove that it lacks unity and coherence. The purpose is to prove that there can be no final interpretation of a text's meaning. Deconstruction calls for a process of continuous reading of a text as Christopher Norris suggests: "Deconstruction is therefore an activity of reading which remains closely tied to the text it interrogates."

Decorum in literature refers to certain propriety in the use of language. The classical writers insisted on decorum in the use of appropriate and dignified language according to the character, action and thought. The neo-classicists of the seventeenth and eighteenth centuries took care of the principle of decorum and correct taste. The Romantic revival revolted against the principle of decorum and called for a language of ordinary speech in literature as was done by Wordsworth in his Preface to *Lyrical Ballads*. Despite the two extreme viewpoints, authors such as Charles Dickens adjusted their language to the needs of the time, maintaining a balance.

Definitive edition is the final version of a text which an author wishes to be taken as his/her authoritative version.

Deism is a rationalist religious philosophy of the seventeenth and eighteenth centuries especially in England. The Deists believed that there is an inherent religious knowledge in each person or that it is accessible through the exercise of reason. This is a kind of natural religion. They denied the legitimacy of religious claims based on revelation as propounded by various churches. The most prominent seventeenth century Deists were Edward Herbert, John Toland, and Charles Blount. They believed in a rationalist religion and were fundamentally opposed to the non-rational elements in the Jewish and Christian practices. In the early eighteenth century, Anthony Collins, Thomas Chubb, and Matthew Tindal attacked the orthodoxy by disregarding miracles and Biblical truths. They established the intellectual climate of Europe in the eighteenth century and greatly influenced the English philosophers John Locke and David Hume. In France Voltaire was a proponent of Deism. Some Versions of Deism went to the extent of atheism. In America Deistic views were held by Benjamin Franklin, Thomas Jefferson, George Washington, Ethan Allen and Thomas Paine. In Europe and America it played an important role in the development of rationalist philosophy and the Deists' ideas have been absorbed by Unitarianism, Modernism, and other modern rationalist religious movements.

Demotic is the use of a simplified language pertaining to common people and distinguished from formalism, hieratic, hieroglyphics and priestly style.

Denotation is that which a word denotes in contradistinction to that which it connotes (*see* Connotation).

Denouement is derived from French meaning 'untying of the knot' and refers to the final resolution of the plot in a tragedy by which the mystery is solved. According to Aristotle in his *Poetics,* "Every tragedy is in part Complication and in part Denouement. The complication consists of incidents that have taken place before the opening of the play and often some also that occur within it; the remainder form the denouement. By complication I mean everything from the beginning of the story up to the point where the hero suffers a change of fortune; by denouement, everything from the latter point to the end" (*see* Resolution).

Desert island fiction is a literary device used by an author to set a work of fiction in an ideal world such as a remote and primitive desert island. Daniel Defoe's *Robinson Crusoe*

(1719) became a prototype of this genre. Other works that followed in this vein include J. Taylor's *The Young Islanders* (1841), R.M. Ballantyne's *The Coral Island* (1858), R.L. Stevenson's *Treasure Island* (1883), and William Golding's *Lord of the Flies* (1954). In *Robinson Crusoe* Defoe writes: "... that I enjoyed much more solitude in the middle of the greatest collection of mankind in the world, I mean, at London, while I am writing this, than ever I could say I enjoyed in eight and twenty years' confinement to a desolate island."

Detective story has a detective, solve a mystery of crime and theft through clues in a surprising manner. Such stories have elements such as a perfect crime, wrong suspects, incompetent police, an eccentric detective, the slow-witted associate of the detective who narrates the story, and the clues that lead to unpredictable climax. The problem is solved through the process of investigation and deduction by the eccentric detective. Traces of such story in English are found in Godwin's *The Adventures of Caleb Williams* (1794). The originator of this early type was the American short-story writer Edgar Allan Poe who is considered the first to invent a fictional detective, Auguste Dupin. His Dupin first appeared in *The Murders in the Rue Morgue* (1841). Poe took his inspiration from the French detective François Eugène Vidocq who was a great success in Paris at that time. In England W. Collins's *The Moonstone* (1868) was the first in the genre who created his detective character Sergeant Cuff. It was the British writer Sir Arthur Conan Doyle who created the greatest fictional detective Sherlock Holmes under the influence of Poe. He has produced four novelettes and 56 short stories with Sherlock Holmes. Other great writers of fiction in this genre are Agatha Christie (*The Murder of Roger Ackroyd*, *Murder on the Orient Express*, etc.), Chesterton (*Father Brown Stories: The Innocence of Father Brown, The Secret of Father Brown,* etc.) and others. Some well known protagonists in such fiction are Conan

Doyle's Sherlock Holmes; Dorothy Sayers' Lord Peter Wimsey; Agatha Christie's Miss Jane Marple; Raymond Chandler's Phillip Marlowe and others. In America detective fiction began to flourish since the 1950s breaking away from the classical British form and evolving crime and spy stories. Prominent writers include Elizabeth Ferrars, Ellis Peters, Michael Gilbert, H.R.F. Keating and others.

Determinism is a philosophy which advocates the belief that everything is determined by a cause over which man has no control. It does away with free will in man and has led to certain doctrines such as *fatalism* and *mechanism* (*materialistic determinism*). Determinism has been debated by Christian thinkers and certain groups, such as, the Calvinists believe in the deterministic concept of God predestining events and human actions. The concepts of predestination is found in literature as in the case with the tragic characters of Shakespeare who are victims of predestination. By the end of nineteenth century there is the development of *scientific* and *social determinism* by which everything is controlled by natural and social forces. Ibsen in his plays such as *Ghosts* explores this concept. In novelists like Emile Zola, determinism comes alive in the form of *Naturalism* in which man is under the influence of his natural environment.

Dialect is a version of a language different in grammar, vocabulary and pronunciation from other forms of the same language. A dialect which is confined to a certain area is a geographical dialect. A 'social dialect' is spoken by a specific group of people of a similar social class or education. Some dialects are written and others are only spoken. The standard literary dialect of a language often is developed from a spoken dialect that is recorded by writers of it, e.g., the Tuscan dialect used by the poets Dante Alighieri and Petrarch, dominated all other Italian dialects and became the written language of Italy. The East Midland dialect of Geoffrey Chaucer became the basis of the English language.

The English people often refer to the Americans as speaking the 'American dialect'. The Americans further contrast their spoken languages into regional dialects such as New England, Midwestern, Southern, Appalachian, black English and Bostonian.

Dialectic is a philosophical method of investigating the nature of truth by critical analysis of concepts. Formal reasoning is done through debate. Plato's *Dialogues* is the earliest example of the dialectical method in which he sought truth through discussion in the form of questions and answers. Aristotle used the term as a synonym for the science of logic. The German philosopher G. W. F. Hegel (1770-1831) applied the term *dialectic* to his philosophic system. According to him the evolution of ideas occurs through a dialectical process from 'thesis' to 'antithesis' to 'synthesis'. 'Synthesis' arises out of the conflict between 'thesis' and 'antithesis'. Karl Marx took the Hegelian concept to develop his economic determinism or materialist dialectic. He argued that society moved from feudalism to capitalism to a final synthesis in socialism. In drama the principle of *thesis-antithesis-synthesis* may operate in the relationship between characters who represent different stages of personal and social development.

Dialogue is the conversation between characters in a dramatic or narrative works such as plays, novels and stories. Dialogue helps to advance the plot. It gives a realistic impression of the characters and depict their ideas and personalities. In the course of a dialogue when a character doesn't want to listen to the other person it is called 'simultaneous monologue'. When a character converses with himself it is 'soliloquy' or 'internal dialogue'.

Diary, journal & notebook have an autobiographical quality by which a person jots down his/her intimate feelings or anecdotes that occur in life. Some important works in this category include Fielding's *Journal of a Voyage to Lisbon* (1755), Parson Woodforde's *The Diary of a Country Parson* in five volumes (1924-31), Swift's *Journal to Stella* (1766), George Eliot's *Journals* (1885), Samuel Butler's *Notebooks* (1912), Katherine Mansfield's *Journal* (1927), Arnold Bennett's *Journals* (1933-34), Somerset Maugham's *A Writer's Notebook* (1949), Graham Greene's *In Search of a Character* (1962).

Diction is the manner of speaking and the use of words used in literary works. A careful use of words make a good diction and it should be characterised by an accurate selection of words that will communicate ideas precisely. Diction can be formal, literary, colloquial, journalistic, archaic, abstract or concrete.

Didactic literature is meant to present the writer's intention to teach, guide and correct the reader. Literary works such as poems, plays and fiction appear in the form of satires and allegories with moral, social, religious, philosophical or theological instruction, e.g., Spencer's *Faerie Queene,* Pope's *Essay on Man,* Bunyan's *Pilgrim's Progress.* "Then I saw in my dream, that when they were got out of the wilderness, they presently saw a town before them, and the name of that town is Vanity; and at the town there is a fair kept, called Vanity Fair. It is kept all the year long; it beareth the name of Vanity Fair, because the town where it is kept is lighter than vanity; and also because all that is there sold or that cometh thither is vanity. As is the saying of the wise, all that cometh is vanity" (from *The Pilgrim's Progress*).

Diegesis is a term used in narrative theory. It differentiates the story from the actual narration of the events. The term can be understood better in comparison to 'mimesis'. Mimesis is representing an event which happened as realistically as possible. In a a play, for instance, the 'mimesis' would be to act a scene as it happened while 'digesis' will narrate what took place off stage in a fictional world.

Digest is a publication which consists of articles or abridged versions of books.

Digression is a deviation from the main theme of a literary work and straying into a different topic for a while and then returning to the main theme in course of time, e.g., Charles Dickens makes digressions in his novels such as *Great Expectations* by which he suddenly diverts from his narration into something irrelevant, thus breaking the trend of thought and then returning to it after a little while.

Dilettante is one who loves the fine arts in a superficial way and without serious purpose. Such a person reads and talks about literature from his casual knowledge in comparison to a serious student engaged in critical study.

Dime novel is a cheap novel published and sold for a dime in America. Dime novels consisted of the melodramatic and thriller stories that were very popular in the nineteenth century. Though they kept to conventional morality, the incidents narrated were shocking and hair-raising. Such series was begun by E.F. Beadle in 1860. By the end of the nineteenth century there were Nick Carter and Frank Merriwell series and pulp magazines that were very popular in this genre (*see* Blue book).

Discourse is usually the presentation in speech or writing the thoughts of a character in a play or narration. It could be a learned discussion or a treatise on philosophical, religious, or literary topics. The following is an example from Sir Joshua Reynold's (1723-92) discourse on *The Grand Style* in painting: "It is not easy to define in what this great style consists; nor to describe by words, the proper means of acquiring it, if the mind of the student should be at all capable of such an acquisition. Could we teach taste or genius by rules, they would be no longer taste and genius. But though there neither are, nor can be, any precise invariable rules for the exercise, or the acquisition, of these great qualities, yet we may truly say that they always operate in proportion to our attention in observing the works of nature, to our skill in selecting, and to our care in digesting, methodising, and comparing our observations. There are many beauties in our art, that seem, at first, to lie without the reach of precept, and yet may easily be reduced to practical principles...."

Discovery is when a character in a story or a play discovers the true state of things. According to Aristotle's *Poetics* it "is a change from ignorance to knowledge, and consequently either to love or to hate, in the personages destined for good or evil fortune. The finest form of Discovery is one accompanied by peripetics, such as occurs in *Oedipus*." Hence, in a tragedy discovery is the exposure of something unknown to the character which brings about a turning point in the action, e.g., Oedipus discovers that he is the killer of his own father in *Oedipus the King*. In Dickens's *Great Expectations* Pip discovers the truth of his benefactor to be Abel Magwitch, a convict, whom he had helped as a boy.

Disney cartoons began with Walt Disney's animated cartoon character Mickey Mouse. He produced cartoon series such as *Oswald the Rabbit, Steamboat Willie, Plane Crazy* and the like with Mickey Mouse as the central character. Disney began the feature-length cartoon with *Snow White and the Seven Dwarfs* (1937), *Pinocchio* (1940), *Fantasia* (1941), and *Bambi* (1942). By the 1950s and 1960s Walt Disney became a major film, television and theatre producers. The company produces books and comic strips for children featuring characters like Donald Duck and Pluto the dog. In 1955 Walt Disney opened the amusement park called Disneyland in California. Disney World opened in 1971 near Orlando, Florida, and is a major tourist attraction today.

Dissonance is the disagreement of sounds which brings in an element of discord like cacophony. It consists more of the lack of harmony than harshness of sounds, e.g., G.M.Hopkins uses it deliberately in his poems. Jonathan Swift freely used it in his writing, e.g., "I could not forbear shaking my head and smiling a little at his ignorance. And being no stranger to the art of war, I gave him a description of cannons, culverins, muskets, carabines, pistols, bullets, powder, swords, bayonets, battles, sieges, retreats, attacks, undermines, countermines, bombardments, sea-fights" (from *Gulliver's Travels*) (*see* Cacophany).

Doctrinal novel concerns itself with the propagation of a belief or doctrine. William Godwin is the first to write such a fiction with his *Things as They Are* (1794) which presents his condemnation of the miserable prison conditions in France. Other writers include Adam Smith (*Wealth of Nations*), Bentham (*A Fragment of Government*), Burke (*Reflections on the Revolution in France*), Disraeli (*Sibyl*), George Eliot (*Felix Holt*), Gorky (*Mother*), George Gissing (*The Netherworld*), A. Koestler (*Darkness at Noon*), H.G. Wells (*The Sleeper Awakes*), etc. In the following extract from Burke's *Reflections on the Revolution in France* is written in a letter intended to have been sent to a gentleman in Paris: "...Ill would our ancestors at the Revolution have deserved their fame for wisdom if they had found no security for their freedom but in rendering their government feeble in its operations, and precarious in its tenure; if they had been able to contrive no better remedy against arbitrary power than civil confusion. Let these gentlemen state who that representative public is to whom they will affirm the king, as a servant, to be responsible. It will then be time enough for me to produce to them the positive statute law which affirms that he is not."

Documentary fiction presents contemporary social problems and current news in a naturalistic manner such as sensational events, disasters or murders, e.g., Theodore Dreiser's *An American Tragedy* (1925); Graham Green's *The Quiet American* (1955), Morris West's *In the Shoes of the Fisherman* (1963), Truman Capote's *In Cold Blood* (1966); V.S. Naipaul's *In a Free State* (1971). Dreiser's *American Tragedy* shot him into fame as it introduced the new school of social realism. The novel is based on an actual murder case in New York. It recounts the story and murder of a young man who rose from extreme poverty to be a member of the worldly society.

Domesticity is a concept based on the patriarchal system in society by which males play the public roles in society. The female looks after the home where she is a faithful wife and mother. Her primary duty is to bring up her children and look after the welfare of her husband. Hence, she is an embodiment of domestic virtues of fidelity, love, patience, endurance and the like which according to the Victorians made her *an angel in the house.* Such concepts are presented in literature too like Charlotte Bronte's *Jane Eyre*, Jane Austen's *Emma* and the like.

Dramatic narrator stands between the story and the reader. Such a narrator disappears at times and the story continues further though action and dialogue. The reader is left to himself to analyse and interpret on his own. Hemingway employs the technique in his short stories like "Hills Like White Elephants", where, through the medium of dialogue, he presents two unhappy people. "The Hills across the valley of the Ebro were long and white. On this side there was no shade and no trees and the station was between two lines of rails in the sun. Close against the side of the station there was the warm shadow of the building and a curtain, made of strings of bamboo beads, hung across the open door into the bar, to keep out flies. The American and the girl with him sat at a table in the shade , outside the building. It was very hot and the express from Barcelona would come in forty minutes. It stopped at this junction for two minutes and went on to Madrid.

'What should we drink?' the girl asked. She had taken off her hat and put it on the table.
'It's pretty hot,' the man said.
'Let's drink beer.'
'Dos cervezas,' the man said into the curtain.
'Big ones?' a woman asked from the doorway.
'yes. Two big ones.'

"The woman brought two glasses of beer and two felt pads. She put the felt pads and the beer glasses on the table and looked at the man and the girl. The girl was looking off at the line of the hills. They were in white in the sun and the country was brown and dry.

'They look like white elephants,' she said.
'I've never seen one,' the man drank his beer.
'No, you wouldn't have.'

Dramatic novel is one in which there is no "hiatus between the characters and the plot" (Edwin Muir). It emphasises action and dialogue with intensive plot. It comes in contrast with the novel of character. In a dramatic novel the novelist disappears from the scene and dramatises states of consciousness of the characters. The conventional first person narrative helps the novelist in his attempt to dramatise, e.g., Jane Austine's *Pride and Prejudice*, Emily Bronte's *Wuthering Heights,* Dickens's *Great Expectations,* Hemingway's *A Farewell to Arms.* Emily Bronte describes the fight between Hindley and Heathcliff in *Wuthering Heights* very dramatically: "The charge exploded, and the knife, in springing back, closed into its owner's wrist. Heathcliff pulled it away by main force, slipping up the flesh as it passed on, and thrust it dripping into his pocket. He then took a stone, struck down the division between two windows, and sprung in. His adversary had fallen senseless with excessive pain, and the flow of blood that gushed from an artery or a large vein."

Dramatic prose is the prose used in drama. Many dramatists like Congreve, Sheridan, J.M. Synge, Ibsen, J.B. Priestley and others wrote prose dramas. The language used is of daily parlance.

Dream allegory / dream vision is a conventional narrative form of literature usually in verse form which was prevalent in the Middle Ages. The narrator in this genre falls into a reverie and dreams the various events of the story. There is allegorical element present as the narrator is guided through his vision, e.g., Dante's *Divina Commedia* (*Divine Comedy)* in which he is guided by Virgil in his visit to Hell and Purgatory and converses with his lost friends and foes. In English the form is used by Chaucer in *The Parliament of Foules*, Langland in *Piers Plowman*, Bunyan in *The Pilgrim's Progress*, and Shelley in *The Triumph of Life*, Coleridge in 'Kubla Khan'. Bunyan's *Pilgrim's Progress* begins with a dream vision: "As I walked through the wilderness of this world, I lighted on a certain place where was a den, and I laid me down in that place to sleep: and as I slept I dreamed a dream. I dreamed, and behold I saw a man clothed with rags, standing in a certain place, with his face from his own house, a book in his hand, and a great burden upon his back. I looked and saw him open the book and read therein; and as he read, he wept, and trembled; and not being able longer to contain, he brake out with a lamentable cry, saying, What shall I do?"

Dynamic characters in a drama or fiction have the capacity to change in course of time. Such characters are the protagonists in work of literature such as in Dickens's *Oliver Twist* or Twain's *Adventures of Tom Sawyer* (*see* Static characters, Flat and round characters).

Dystopia refers to an unpleasant imaginary world that is the opposite of utopia. Such a world is presented in science fiction as in the case of H.G. Wells's *The Time Machine*. In the epilogue to *The Time Machine,* Wells writes: "One cannot choose but wonder. Will he ever return? It may be that he swept back into the past, and fell among the blood-drinking, hairy savages of the Age of Unpolished Stone; into the abysses of the Cretaceous Sea; or among the grotesque saurians, the huge reptilian brutes of the Jurassic times. He may even now – if I may use the phrase – be wandering on some plesiosaurus-haunted Oolitic coral reef, or beside the lonely saline lakes of the Triassic Age."

E

Edda is two famous collections of old Icelandic literature orally transmitted after the ninth century and were written down from thirteenth century. The term Edda may be derived from the Old Norse word *edda* (great-grandmother), or from *Oddi*, a seat of culture in southern Iceland. Saemund Sigfússon and Snorri Sturluson are thought to have compiled the Eddas. The term perhaps refers to the Old Norse word *óthr* (poetry). The *Poetic Edda, Elder Edda* (9th to 12th century), is a group of more than 30 poems on the Scandinavian and Germanic gods and on human heroes. Some of these poems may possibly have been composed outside Iceland, but they were apparently first written down in the twelfth century. The *Prose Edda,* or *Younger Edda* (13th century), is the work of Snorri Sturluson. It includes tales from Scandinavian mythology and is the most important source of modern knowledge on this subject. Other sections of the *Prose Edda* form a guide to poetic diction and a metrical key. Skaldic poetry, composed between the ninth and thirteenth centuries, was written variously in honour of the nobles, in praise of love, or to satirise or commemorate current happenings.

Edition is the total number of copies of a book printed from a type set for it. An edition may have several impressions. When the original edition is modified and printed it is called the second edition and so with other subsequent editions.

Edwardian Period is the literary period between the death of Queen Victoria in 1901 and the beginning of World War I in 1914 when King Edward VII ruled England. It is often contrasted with the Victorian period. The era was known for its excitement with the new sense of freedom, but it lacked direction. The period is marked for the dramas of Shaw and the novels of Hardy, Conrad and Henry James. Despite the liberal views of the time, the writers kept alive traditional themes concerning the Empire as a source of national pride, the countryside preserving national values and the upper class having its vital role in representing English life. The period is a transition before the catastrophe of the Great War. The writers of the period include Thomas Hardy, W.B. Yeats, Alfred Noyes, Kipling, John Galsworthy, J.M. Synge, G.B. Shaw, Joseph Conrad, E.M. Forster, H.G.Wells and Henry James.

Elizabethan age is the period from 1558 to 1603 when Queen Elizabeth reigned. It was a time marked for its economic and commercial growth establishing England as a maritime power. The English nationalism was at its height. Often it is referred to as the Golden Age of English literature because of the luminaries in the literary scene like Sidney, Spenser, Marlowe, Shakespeare, Bacon and Ben Jonson. Broadly, the period is from c. 1550 to 1660 preceding the Restoration period.

Elizabethan novel is a general term applied to the prose stories written during the Elizabethan age. Though they cannot be strictly called novels, they paved the way for the development of the genre. Most of these consisted of *romances* and *picaresque stories*. The prose romance was a long story in artificial style written in the classical setting, e.g., John Lyly's *Eupheus* (1578), Robert Greene's *Pandosto* (1588) and *Menaphon* (1589), Thomas Lodge's *Rosalynde* (1590), Philip Sidney's *Arcadia* (1590) and the like. Thomas Nashe's *Unfortunate Traveller* (1594) is a prototype of the picaresque novel (*see* Romance; Picaresque novel).

Ellipsis (...) This mark stands for one or more omitted words. When the omission occurs at the end of a sentence, the ellipsis appears together with a period (....). The technique is used while quoting selected sections from a piece of literature.

Embedded means to place within. This is a literary technique used by some authors to place a narrative or a story within the framework of a main narrative or story, e.g., Chaucer in his *Canterbury Tales* places individual stories of the various pilgrims within the main story.

Emblem Book was very popular in the fifteenth to seventeenth centuries containing a collection of emblems. An emblem is made up of a motto with a picture, often engraved and a short poem presenting the main ideas of the emblem, e.g., the emblem and poem on Sir Walter Raleigh's *History of the World* (1614). The engraved title page shows an allegorical figure of History, labelled in Latin "mistress of life" and bearing aloft the globe, which remains below the eye of God. History tramples Death and Oblivion, and is attended by Experience and Truth.

Empathy is the power of entering into another's personality and experiencing in an imaginative way one's experiences. It can be also the power of entering into the spirit of something like a work of art and appreciate it fully. If an author is able to arouse empathy through his writings in the readers to enter into the personality of the characters portrayed, it will give better appreciation of the work.

Empiricism is a philosophy which believes that ideas are derived from experience. Knowledge depends on experience. Francis Bacon advocated it. It was John Locke who presented empiricism as a philosophy systematically. In contrast to empiricism is the philosophy of Rationalism as propounded by Rene Descartes, Spinoza, Leibniz. However, Immanuel Kant had tried to bridge the gap between empiricism and rationalism. American philosopher William James developed *radical empiricism.* Empiricism remained a strong influence on the British philosophy and literature.

Encomium means high commendation or eulogy. It is a literary device by which an eulogy is composed in prose or verse in praise of a hero, an idea or an event. It had its origin in the Greek tradition of singing a choral song in honour of a victorious athlete. Many odes and elegies fall into this category.

Encyclopedistes or **Encyclopedists** are the eighteenth century French writers of *Encyclopedia,* or *Systematic Dictionary of Sciences, Arts, and Trades,* commonly called the *Encyclopédie.* It was edited by Denis Diderot in Paris between 1751 and 1772 and presented the best opinions of the time in Philosophy, Politics, and Religion. The contributors included Montesquieu, Voltaire, Jean Jacques Rousseau, and Friedrich Melchior, Baron von Grimm.

Enlightenment is the intellectual movement in the seventeenth and eighteenth centuries in Europe known as the Age of Reason. The movement is marked by the writings of Jean Jacques Rousseau and the Encyclopedistes (*see* Encyclopedistes). It ushered in the French and American revolutions. Scientists and philosophers like Kant, Bacon, Descartes, Newton, Locke, David Hume and Adam Smith called for human reason to pervade in man's search for knowledge. It threw out superstitions and dogma, and called for rational and scientific enquiry. In religion it evolved Deism (*see* Deism).

Epic is a long narrative that is magnificent in theme, tone and style. Epic deals with legendary or historical events of national or universal significance. It celebrates heroic deeds and cosmically important events. Most epics deal with the exploits of heroes who have qualities that are superhuman or divine and on whose very fate depends the destiny of a tribe, nation or the whole human race. The epic has several features such as: the presentation of supernatural forces that shape the action; battles and conflicts; invocation to the Muse; statement of the theme; long lists of the protagonists involved and lofty speeches. The Greeks made a clear distinction between epic and lyric poetry. Lyric poetry expressed more personal emotion than epic poetry. Lyrics were sung while the epic was recited. Examples of epic include the ancient Greek epics by Homer, the *Iliad* and the *Odyssey*. Epics may synthesize the ideals of a great religious or cultural movement. *The Divine Comedy* (1307-1321) by Dante Alighieri expresses the faith of medieval Christianity. *The Faerie Queene* (1590-1609) by Edmund Spenser represents the spirit of the Renaissance in England. *Paradise Lost* (1667) by John Milton represents the ideals of Christian humanism. Epic verses are of two types: folk and literary epic. *Folk epics* are popular epics that developed from the orally transmitted folk poetry of tribal bards or other authors and written in course of time by anonymous poets, e.g., the Anglo-Saxon *Beowulf* (8th century), the Indian epics, the *Mahabharata* (Great Story, 300 BC-AD 300) and the *Ramayana* (Story of Rama, 3rd c. BC). Such folk epic stories are based on legends or events that occurred a long time ago. *Literary (art) epics* are the creations of known poets. They deal with the mythical or historical traditions of a nation, e.g., the *Iliad, The Odyssey, The Aeneid, The Faerie Queene* and *Paradise Lost.* In the nineteenth century the epic assumed various forms like Wordsworth's autobiographical poem *The Prelude* (1850) presenting the events of his life to explore the power of the human imagination. Walt Whitman's *Song of Myself* is a brief epic in which the first-person narrator identifies himself with all of nature and humanity. Some novels are also of epic nature such as Henry Fielding's comic epic *Tom Jones*, Melville's prose romance *Moby Dick*, James Joyce's *Ulysses* and the like.

Epigraph is an inscription especially on a building; a citation or motto at the beginning of a book or its part.

Epiphany is derived from the Greek *epiphaneia,* "appearance".

It is the feast celebrated on 6th January as the anniversary of the baptism of Christ. It also commemorates principally the revelation to the Gentiles of Jesus Christ as the Saviour, as portrayed by the coming of the Three Wise Men (*see* Matthew 2:1-12). In literature epiphany is used to mean a moment of extraordinary illumination or a sudden spiritual manifestation when one sees into the depth of things. The novelist James Joyce began his career by writing what he called 'epiphanies', i.e., sketches in which slight incidents reveal the inner truth of a character, e.g., in his *Portrait of the Artist as a Young Man* Joyce presents many epiphanies. Stephen Dedalus, the hero, finds spiritual and aesthetic fulfilment through epiphanies. He speaks of an epiphany as "a sudden spiritual manifestation".

Episode is an incident in a narrative action. It may consist of a dialogue between two characters, a particular scene or a longer action. These episodes should have a continuous flow so as to produce a single story with a beginning, middle and end. If the episodes are not woven together, the story turns out to be episodic and not a unified whole.

Episodic plot is a loosely constructed plot with a narrative that consists of a series of episodes or incidents. Such a work lacks a built-in plot, e.g., Lawrence Sterne's *A Sentimental Journey* (1768), D.H. Lawrence's *Twilight in Italy* (1916).

Epistle is a letter addressed to a friend or patron in verse or prose. These could be on philosophical themes like the *Epistles* of Horace or on romantic themes like the *Heroides* of Ovid. During the Renaissance the Ovidian form became popular with Petrarch, Aristo and other poets. It was Jonson who introduced the Horatian form of epistles into England in *The Forest* (1616). Other poets who wrote in this verse form include Vaughan, Dryden and Pope. Pope's *Moral Essays* and *An Epistle to Dr. Arbuthnot* are considered the best in the English tradition. W.H. Auden and Louis MacNeice are the modern poets who attempted this genre.

Epistolary novel is written in the form of letters. It could consist primarily of letters written by the chief character as in the case of Richardson's *Pamela* (1740), or letters written by several characters as in Smollett's *Humphry Clinker* (1771). Elements of epistolary novel are found in works such as Aldrich's *Marjorie Daw* (1873), Thornton Wilder's *The Ides of March* (1942), and Christopher Isherwood's *A Meeting by the River* (1967).

Epitaph, derived from Greek *epitaphios,* "'over or at a tomb" is a brief commemorative inscription on a tomb or a short piece of poetry or prose lauding a deceased person. Such inscription consists of a statement of the name, family, and condition of the deceased, with a prayer to some deity. Usually composed in epigrammatic form, Greek epitaphs were the first to possess literary value. Roman funerary urns gave the name, age, and office of the deceased, to which were added the name and relationship of the person who had the urn made. The epitaph was introduced to Britain by the Romans, and Latin was the language used on English tombstones until the thirteenth century, when French came into use. English began to be used at the end of the fourteenth century. During the reign of Elizabeth I, the writing of epitaphs in the form of epigrams became popular, and by the seventeenth century the epitaph had become a recognised literary device.

Epitome is the abridgment of a long work, e.g., Frazer's *Golden Bough* (1890-1915) consisting of 12 volumes was epitomised into one volume.

Eponymous is a word derived from Greek meaning 'giving name' referring to certain works of literature deriving their title from the protagonist's name, e.g., Richardson's *Pamela*, Henry Fielding's *Tom Jones*, George Eliot's *Silas Marner.*

Equivocation occurs when a word is capable of meaning two or more things. The meanings are ambiguous, e.g., *He drinks his water, waters his drink.*

Erotic literature is classification of amorous writings on love in the form of lyrics, epigrams, dramas, prose and fiction. The subject matter of such literary works consists of physical love. A distinction can be made between erotic and love poetry. Erotic poetry deals primarily with sex and sexual love; it concentrates on physical love and passion. Love poetry on the other hand primarily deals with expressions of love devoid of sexual details. Erotic poetry is found in Greek, Latin, Sanskrit and Arab literature. The English novelist John Cleland (1709-1789) is known for his epistolary erotic novel *Fanny Hill: Memoirs of a Woman of Pleasure.* American writer Henry Miller (1891-1980) wrote erotic novels like *Tropic of Cancer* (1934), *Black Spring* (1936), *Tropic of Capricorn* (1939), *The Colossus of Maroussi* (1941), *The Air-Conditioned Nightmare* (1945-1947), *Plexus* (1953), and *Nexus* (1960).

Escape literature consists of detective stories and certain musical comedies in which the protagonist appears to be escaping from life due to monotony. However, he may be in search of fulfilment in life, e.g., Gilbert and Sullivan operas which consist of social satires.

Eschatology is the branch of theology concerned with the last things. It presents the doctrine concerning life after death and the final stage of the world. The origin of this doctrine is almost as old as humanity with different concepts of immortality. Primitives believed in a life of the spirit as a sort of substance inhabiting the dead body that has to be fed. As man got more civilised the concept of the future life grew richer. He worshiped cosmic forces linked to the departed spirits. In course of time the belief in judgment after death was introduced into different cultures. According to the Hindu tradition the spirit of a dead person entered into another body and reincarnated. This brings the concept of transmigration by which a person is rewarded or punished in accordance with his previous life. This leads to a series of births and deaths and the individual can seek deliverance from the infinite wheel of existence in Nirvana. The ancient Greeks arrived at their eschatology by considering the functions of the mind as a purely spiritual essence, independent of the body, and having no beginning or end; this abstract concept of immortality led to the anticipation of a more concrete personal life after death. Similarities can be seen between the ancient Greek concepts of heaven and hell and those of Christian doctrine. Israelites believed in the Day of Yahweh that would decide the fate of the people. Although the people looked forward to it as a day of victory, prophets such as Amos, Hosea, Isaiah, Micah, Zephaniah, and Jeremiah feared that it would bring near or complete destruction. The Book of Daniel voices the hope that the kingdom of the world will be given to the saints of the Most High, the Jewish people. When Jesus Christ proclaimed the coming of the kingdom of heaven, his disciples were convinced that he would return as the Messiah upon the clouds of heaven. In Christian doctrine, eschatology has traditionally included the second advent of Christ, or Parousia, the resurrection of the dead, the last judgment, the immortality of the soul, concepts of heaven and hell, and the consummation of the kingdom of God. In the Roman Catholic Church, eschatology includes the beatific vision, purgatory, and limbo. Christianity affirms the belief in a return to the Son of God to judge the living and the dead, and in a resurrection of the just and the unjust. Islam adopted from Judaism and Christianity the doctrine of a coming judgment, a resurrection of the dead, and everlasting punishments and rewards. In the second half of the twentieth century, eschatology was equated by some theologians with the doctrine of Christian hope, including not only the events of the end of time but also the hope itself and its revolutionising influence on life in the world. The most eloquent exponent of this eschatology is the German theologian Jürgen Moltmann. In English Literature the concept of Christian eschatology is brought out in works such as *Everyman*, *Pearl*, Langland's *Piers Plowman*, Bunyan's *The Pilgrim's Progress*,

Donne's *The Holy Sonnets,* G.M. Hopkins' *The Wreck of the Deutschland,* T.S. Eliot's *Ash Wednesday* & *Ariel Poems.*

Essay is derived from French word 'essai' meaning 'attempt'. It was Michael de Montaigne who used it first by applying it to his writings as *Essais* (1580). It is a composition in prose on a particular topic. It can be of different types such as critical, historical, biographical, scientific and so on. The ancient Greek and Roman authors wrote similar compositions such as Plato's dialogues, Seneca's epistles, Plutarch's writings, Cicero's arguments, Aristotle's treatises and the like. Montaigne deals with facts and exposes ideas like his "Que sais-je?" (What do I know?). Francis Bacon is considered as one of the greatest essayists in English. In his essay "Of Studies" he writes : "Studies serve for delight, for ornament, and for ability. Their chief use for delight is in privateness and retiring; for ornament, is in discourse; and for ability, is in the judgment and disposition of business. For expert men can execute and perhaps judge of particulars, one by one, but the general counsels and the plots and marshalling of affairs come best from those that are learned. To spend too much time in studies is sloth; to use them too much for ornament is affectation; to make judgment wholly by their rules is the humour of a scholar." Other known British essayists are Addison and Steele, Dr. Johnson, Charles Lamb, William Hazlitt, Leigh Hunt, De Quincey, Coleridge, Macaulay, Carlyle, Ruskin, Matthew Arnold, Walter Pater, R.L. Stevenson, Chesterton, Belloc, E.V. Lucas, A.A. Milne, Arthur Simons, E.M. Forster, Virginia Woolf, J.B. Priestley, D.H. Lawrence, Aldous Huxley, T.S. Eliot, George Orwell, and Graham Greene. Popular American essayists are Ashington Irving, Emerson, Poe, Thoreau, John Burroughs, Christopher Morley, E.B. White, Paul Elmer More, George Santayana and others.

Euphony is the agreeable and pleasing combination of sounds easy to pronounce. It is the opposite of cacophony (*see* Cacophony).

Euphuism is the affected and bombastic literary style of John Lyly's *Euphues* (1579-80) which came into fashion in the English language. The style was highly ornate regardless of sense and with excessive use of antithesis, alliteration, repetition and allusion to historical and mythological personages. " ... For as the bee that gathereth honey out of the weed when she espieth the fair flower flieth to the sweetest; or as the kind spaniel though he hunt after birds yet forsakes them to retrieve the patridge; or as we commonly feed on beef hungerly at the first, yet seeing the quail more dainty change out diet; so I although I loved Philautus for his good properties, yet seeing Euphues to excel him I ought by nature to like him better" (from *Euphues: The Anatomy of Wit* : John Lyly).

Exegesis in literature refers to critical examination and explication of textual problems. Originally the term was applied to the study and interpretation of Biblical texts.

Exemplum is an anecdote or a short story in the form of an example to illustrate a moral lesson. It is often used in sermons and homilies as part of instruction. Collections of exemplum were prepared for sermons and meditations. In the medieval literature authors used them frequently.

Existentialism is the philosophical movement that emphasizes individual existence, freedom, and choice. It has influenced many diverse writers in the nineteenth and twentieth centuries. It emphasizes the primacy of individual existence, subjectivity, individual freedom and choice. Danish philosopher Kierkegaard (1813-1855) is considered the progenitor of the religious stream of existentialism with his concept of the highest good for the individual in finding his or her own unique vocation. He wrote in his journal, "I must find a truth that is true for me . . . the idea for which I can live or die." Jean-Paul Sartre (1905-1980) Nietzsche, Martin Heidegger (1889-1976), Karl Jaspers (1883-1969), and Gabriel Marcel (1889-1973) are important exponents of the movement. Influence of Existentialism is found in the writings of John Fowles, Iris Murdoch, Muriel Spark, William Golding, Patrick White, Joseph Conrad and others.

Expatriate writers are those writers who live for a prolonged period in a country other than their own. Some of the best known expatriate writers include Joseph Conrad, Henry James, and Ernest Hemingway.

Experimentalism in literature calls for the use of innovative methods different from the conventional ones. Experimentalism is in vogue in the modern and postmodern literature and art in the form of *avant garde* (*see* avant garde) movements calling for new forms of expressions like dada, expressionism, futurism, surrealism and vorticism.

Exposition in a drama or fiction consists of the opening part in which the major characters and plot are introduced giving sufficient background information of the preceding events and those to follow. It also sets the scenes and establishes the situation. The conflict or the potential for it is also introduced, e.g., Henry James begins his novel *Washington Square* introducing Dr. Sloper and his background: "During a portion of the first half of the present century, and more particularly during the latter part of it, there flourished and practised in the city of New York a physician who enjoyed perhaps an exceptional share of the consideration which, in the United states, has always been bestowed upon distinguished members of the medical profession.... He had married, at the age of twenty-seven, for love, a very charming girl, Miss Catherine Harrington, of New York, who, in addition to her charms, had brought him a solid dowry...."

Expressionism is a movement in the visual, literary, and performing arts to express subjective feelings and emotions rather than to depict reality objectively. It is a movement that flourished in the late nineteenth and early twentieth centuries especially in France and Germany. Expressionism depicts an emotional experience beyond the apparent and explores the recesses of the subconscious. To depict emotional experiences effectively the expressionists exaggerate with distortions and caricatures. In the twentieth century impressionists in art include Ernst Ludwig Kirchner, Erich Heckel, Karl Schmidt-Rottluff, Emil Nolde, Max Pechstein, Franz Marc, August Macke, Gabriele Münter, Heinrich Campendonk, Paul Klee, Wassily Kandinsky, Otto Dix, George Grosz, Oskar Kokoschka, Georges Rouault, Chaïm Soutine Jules Pascin, Max Weber, Mark Rothko, Willem de Kooning, Franz Kline, Jackson Pollock, Auguste Rodin, Jacob Epstein and Ernst Barlach. Expressionism in literature is found in Alfred Kubin's novels *Die Andere Seite* (*The Other Side*). He influenced Franz Kafka and other writers. Playwrights August Strindberg and Frank Wedekind had great influence on the writers such as George Kaiser, Ernst Toller, Eugene O'Neill and Elmer Rice. In fiction James Joyce, William Faulkner and Samuel Beckett are known for their expressionism. Some noteworthy expressionist works include T.S. Eliot's *The Waste Land* (1922), Elmer Rice's *The Adding Machine* (1923) and James Joyce's *Finnegans Wake* (1939).

Expurgate is removing from a text passages that are obscene or politically sensitive.

External focalisation occurs in a narrative when the readers know only the external appearance of characters and events without access to their inner psychology, e.g., Hemingway's story "Hills Like White Elephants".

External plot refers to a plot based on outside events. This is typical of the adventure stories (*see* Adventure novel).

F

Fable is derived from 'fabula' in Latin, meaning a story. It is a brief narrative in prose or verse with a moral to instruct and edify. Often the characters in fables are animals and birds. Fables had their origin in ancient Greece with those ascribed to Aesop (6th century BC) (*see* Beast fable). Sanskrit fables *Bidpai* (AD 300) is a popular Indian collection. Marie de France is considered a great contributor to this genre in the middle ages with her 102 verse fables. La Fontaine with his translations of Aesop's fables into 12 books entitled *Fables Choisies* published from 1668 is considered a master in this literary form. Those who attempted this genre include John Gay (*Fifty-one Fables in Verse,* 1727), Kipling (*Just So Stories,* 1902), James Thurber (*Fables of Our Time,* 1940), and Orwell (*Animal Farm,* 1945) (*See* Aesopic fables).

Fabulation is applied to an anti-novel which is a kind of modern comical and allegorical fiction that is in the form of a picaresque tale or romance, e.g., Robert Scholes's *The Fabulators* (1967); Durrell's *Alexandrian Quartet* (1957-60); John Barth's novels such as *The Sot-Weed Factor* (1960), a parody of eighteenth century picaresque tale on Ebenezer Cooke; *Giles Goat-Boy* (1966), an allegory of the modern world seen as a university campus (*see* Anti-novel; Black humour).

Faction refers to works that present factual things and real persons in a fictional manner. The term was used for the first time by the American writer Truman Capote in his *Cold*

Blood (1966) which recounts a cold-blooded murder. Other works in this form include the novels of Norman Mailer such as *The Armies of the Night* (1968) presenting his experiences during a pacifist march in 1967; *Of a Fire on the Moon* (1970) in the background of the lunar landings; *The Executioner's Song* (1979) on the life of Gary Gilmore, a convicted murderer.

Factories occur in fiction as industrial buildings in which people work in large numbers. Factories increased in the eighteenth century with the inventions of steam-powered machines and large industrial towns developed. It ushered in large-scale poverty of the working classes and their inhuman working conditions. The first Factory Act preventing child labour and exploitation of women came into effect in 1833; and Ten Hours Act came into force in 1847. Some of the works that exposed the factory system include Benjamin Disraeli's *Sybil*; Elizabeth Gaskell's *North and South*; and Charles Dickens's *Hard Times*. Dickens in *Hard Times* presents Industrial Revolution in an effective manner making children and women victims of it. In his introduction to the Penguin edition of *Hard Times* Professor David Craig quotes an American folksong:

Every morning just at five,
Gotta get up, dead or alive.
It's hard times in the mill, my love,
Hard times in the mill.
Every morning just at six,
Don't that old bell make you sick?
It's hard times in the mill, my love,
Hard times in the mill....
Ain't it enough to break your heart?
Have to work all day and at night it's dark.
It's hard times in the mill, my love,
Hard times in the mill.

Fairy tale is part of the folk oral tradition which is believed to have originated from the east with *The Thousand and One*

Nights or *Arabian Night's Entertainments*. The first written collections began with the German brothers Grimm *Haus-Marchen* (*Household Tales* 1812, 1815, 1822). Fairy tales are simple narratives meant to entertain children and with the purpose of instruction and edification. Freud and Jung gave a psychological interpretation to them finding universal and archetypal patterns in them. The writers who attempted fairy tales in English include Ruskin, Thackeray, Charles Kingsley and Oscar Wilde (*see* Fable).

False hero occurs in a fairy tale in which he pretends to accomplish what the hero did.

Falling action refers to a plot's sliding down from its turning point in a play or a novel. The plot eventually moves towards its conclusion as there is a dwindling in tension.

Fantastic is a term used by critics like Christine Brooke-Rose to signify certain kind of fiction in which the reader finds it difficult to distinguish between the natural and the supernatural. Many ghost stories belong to this category, e.g., in Henry James's *The Turn of the Screw* it is difficult to know if the ghosts are real or imaginative.

Fantasy is setting something in a world of imagination involving unrealistic characters and situations. Fantasy can be part of escape literature and can be satire on society. Some best known fantasies are Swift's *Gulliver's Travels* (1726); Lewis Caroll's *Alice's Adventures in Wonderland* (1865); R.L. Stevenson's *Dr. Jekyll and Mr. Hyde* (1886); Tolkien's *The Lord of the Rings* (1965). Science fiction movies such as *Star Trek*, *Beauty and the Beast* belong to this genre, (*see* Science fiction).

Fascism was a right-wing anti-communist movement which began in the 1920s and took strong roots in Italy under the leadership of Mussolini who ruled from 1922 to 1945. The movement in Germany was furthered by the National Socialist Party (1933-45) and in Spain Falangist Party that gave power to Franco. Fascists were nationalistic and anti-communistic. Some of the British and American writers who wrote with fascist influence include Ezra Pound, T.S. Eliot, D.H. Lawrence, and Wyndham Lewis.

Fashion novel is a class novel that admired the wealthy and the fashionable (*see* Silver fork novel).

Feminist criticism grew out of the feminist movement in the 1970s. It was an effort to develop a literary theory based on feminine consciousness and sensibility. Feminism champions the identity of women and their rights. It is concerned primarily with the critical examination and assessment of literary works by women and the analysis of female images portrayed by male authors. It also studies sexism, gender privilege, and the critical theories formulated by the male-dominated literary field. Thus it aimed at establishing a feminine critical tradition. Feminism can be considered a version of post-structuralism as it undertakes to deconstruct the opposition between man and woman. Elaine Showalter distinguishes 'the feminist critique' of male assumptions and procedures from 'gyno-criticism', a feminist criticism concerned with women authors and the representation of their experience as women. Women's studies as a separate subject grew popular in the 1970s in the United States and Britain. Several works of women writers were rediscovered and reprinted such as those of H. Martineau, E. B. Browning and M. Sinclair. Prominent works in this genre are Mary Ellmann's *Thinking about Women* (1968), Eva Figes's *Patriarchal Attitudes* (1970), Elizabeth Hardwick's *Seduction and Betrayal* (1974), Ellen Moers's *Literary Women* (1976), Elaine Showalter's *A Literature of Their Own* (1977), *Norton Anthology of Literature by Women: The Tradition in English* (1985), edited by Sandra M. Gilbert and Susan Gubar.

Festschrift in German means 'celebration writing' and refers to a collection of essays written in honour of an eminent scholar or writer.

Ficelle is a term used by Henry James to refer to his fictional characters in novels playing the role of a confidant through whom the readers get important information, e.g., The

Fiction is a term derived from Latin '*fictum*' meaning 'to fashion' and is applied to imaginative narrations such as novels, novellas, short stories, fables, romances and prose works. Strictly the term applies to novels and short stories. Fiction can be of different types such as satires, apologue, and novel (*see* Satire, apologue, novel).

First person narrative is a form of narration in which the story is told by someone in the first person "I" recounting everything, e.g., In Charles Dickens's *Great Expectations,* Pip the hero and narrator recounts his development: "My father's family name being Pirrip, and my Christian name Philip, my infant tongue could make of both names nothing longer or more explicit than Pip. So I called myself Pip, and came to be called Pip." In some novels the novelist invites the reader to imagine the 'I' who writes. Some novelists create the persona of the first person and the reader notices a sort of distance between the narrator and the novelist. For example, Huck is the first person narrator in Mark Twain's *The Adventures of Huckleberry Finn.* However, the author makes the reader judge for himself when there is a moral crisis in course of events. Huck, since he belongs to the slave trading community, is troubled as he is helping Jim, a slave, to escape. And yet when the slave hunters come Huck has no courage to hand over Jim and tells a lie that his family is afflicted by smallpox. In this moral crisis Mark Twain makes the reader maintain a moral distance between what Huck does and what he believes in conscience. The author makes the reader believe that Huck is wrong in his conscience pricking thoughts and what he does is right. "They went off and I got aboard the raft, feeling bad and low, because I knowed very well I had done wrong, and I see it wasn't no use for me to try to learn to do right.... Then I thought a minute, and says to myself, hold on – s'pose you'd a done right and give Jim up; would you felt better than what you do now? No, says I, I'd feel bad – I'd feel just the same way I do now...." In a first person narration the reader is able to enter into the thoughts and feelings of the narrator.

Flashback is a technique employed in fiction and film by which incidents occurred earlier are recalled. It could be done by a character recalling the past events and narrating it to another character or by dream sequences. Flashback helps a story to begin at any point of time such as *in medias res* (in the middle of things). Emily Bronte employs the technique brilliantly in her *Wuthering Heights*.

Flashforward is an anticipation of something depicted in a fiction. It is a very effective cinematic technique.

Flat and round characters are created by writers of fiction depending on the extent to which they are developed. Flat characters are type characters as they represent a particular trait or idea. These are one-dimensional characters who can be caricatured for the sake of humour. Flat characters like stock characters who recur in drama or fiction are usually minor characters. Round characters grow and change in course of time and are multidimensional possessing several qualities of mind and heart. E.M. Forster distinguishes between the two types of characters in *Aspects of the Novel* (1927). The flat character represents a type with a dominant trait and lacks depth. Such a character does not change as the story progresses. The round character on the other hand develops and changes in course of the story. Forster writes: "We may divide characters into flat and round. Flat characters were called 'humours' in the seventeenth century, and are sometimes called types, and sometimes caricatures. In their purest form, they are constructed round a single idea or quality: when there is more than one factor in them, we get the beginning of the curve towards the round. The really flat character can be expressed in one sentence such as 'I never will desert Mrs. Macawber; she doesn't, and there she is." Mrs. Macawber is a flat character in Dickens's *David Copperfield* as she is a type or caricature. Defoe's Moll Flanders is a round character.

Focal character is the character whose opinion is central to the narration in a work of fiction.

Focalisation indicates the focus of a narrative which can be internal or external. Internal focalisation sees events from the point of view of a particular focal character. External focalisation centres on the experiences of a character devoid of his/her thoughts.

Folklore is a term used for the first time by J.W. Thomas in 1846. It is applied to unwritten traditions, beliefs, myths, rituals, superstitions, legends, stories, riddles, dances and songs passed on orally from generation to generation in a particular community. These deal with the life of the community with regard to birth, marriage and death. Folklores are an essential part of literature in understanding social conventions.

Folktale is a story passed on orally from one generation to the next in a community. In course of its oral transmission the tale gets modified. Often it is based on a myth or a legend.

Form in literature refers to the structure of a work and the style employed. It can also mean the literary type into which the work can be classified such as epic, ballad, sonnet, ode, novel, drama and prose.

Folly literature was a variety of literature mostly of satires prevalent in the fifteenth to seventeenth centuries. These are called folly literature as they nonsensical and absurd. However, with the element of satire, they could expose and ridicule social follies. Noted English work in the sixteenth century is *Cocke Lorell's Bote* in which a group of trades folk take a ship and sail through England with the captain, Cocke Lorell. Erasmus wrote in praise of folly in his *Moriae Encomium* (1509). Dekker's *Gull's Hornbook* (1609) exposes foppery.

Foreshadowing is a dramatic irony by which the spectator is not fully aware of future events. However, some subtle hints are given by which the spectators can look back at past events and make some judgement. It is the technique of arranging events and information in a narrative in such a way that later events are prepared for beforehand. In a well constructed novel the very beginning may suggest the outcome. The end can be contained in the beginning giving structural and thematic unity, e.g., Graham Greene's *The Heart of the Matter*.

Form refers to the structure and shape of a work and is often understood as *genre* or *type*. Form has been redefined by New Critics based on the saying 'form equals content'. The form of a play has its various elements such as its inner form with its story and dialogue, the character relationships, motifs and tensions, e.g., the *form* of Bronte's *Wuthering Heights* is that it is a novel of love and revenge. The *inner form* of the novel consists of its tensions, love intrigues, contrast of the goodness of some of the characters compared to the wickedness of Heathcliff, etc., The *surface forms* of the novel includes its diction, imagery, grammatical form, semantic relationships, intonation, the language and the like.

Formalism is a literary movement that began in Russia in 1917 by Viktor Shklovsky. He claimed that "art is a way of experiencing the artfulness of an object; the object is not important." Hence Russian Formalism stressed that critics should concern themselves with the literariness of literature: the verbal strategies that make it literary, the foregrounding of language itself, and making strange of experience that they accomplish. Redirecting attention from authors to verbal devices, they claimed that 'the device is the only hero of literature'. For the formalists art is primarily a matter of style and technique. Thus, what the writer says may not be so important as how he says it.

Foreword is a short introduction of a work written by someone else other than the author, while preface is a written introduction by the author.

Frame story is a story within a story or a series of stories. The main story is narrated in the course of another frame story, e.g., *Arabian Nights*; Boccaccio's *Decameron* (1353); Chaucer's *Canterbury Tales* (c. 1390); Mary Shelley's *Frankenstein* (1818); Emily Bronte's *Wuthering Heights* (1847). In *Wuthering Heights* the story is narrated by Lockwood who visits his landlord Heathcliff. The narration then passes on to the housekeeper Nelly Dean.

Free association is a psychological term which has been brought into literature. By this technique an idea or word can stimulate a series of ideas or words by free association, e.g., James Joyce employs the technique in his novel *Ulysses* (*see* Stream of consciousness).

Free direct and indirect discourse are devices in fiction by which a character's thoughts or utterances are represented, e.g., Jim thought, "I will meet Jane at the party today" (Direct discourse), "Jim thought that he would meet Jane at the party that day" (indirect discourse).

Futurism is an early twentieth century *avant-garde* movement in art and literature that dropped all traditions and attempted instead to glorify contemporary life. It stressed the themes of machine and motion. The manifesto of futurism was declared by the Italian poet Filippo Tommaso Marinetti in 1909. Later the '*technical Manifesto of Futurist Painting* was signed by Italian artists Giacomo Balla, Umberto Boccioni, Carlo Carrà, Luigi Russolo, and Gino Severini. Futurism presented several successive actions of positions of a subject at the same time which looked like a series of high-speed photographs printed on a single plate, e.g., Severini's *Dynamic Hieroglyphic of the Bal Tabarin* (1912) and *Armored Train* (1915). Though the movement lasted only up to 1914, it influenced the works of the painters like Marcel Duchamp, Fernand Léger, and Robert Delauney. The futurist worship of the machine survived as a fundamental part of Fascist doctrine of Mussolini in Italy. In poetry the influence of futurism is seen in the use of putting together senseless words mechanically. In France the poetry of Guillaime Apollinaire, Dada movement and Vorticism are the outcome of Futurism. Futurism is found in science fiction or fantasy such as H.G. Wells's *The War of the Worlds* (1898), *The Time Machine* (1895); Swift's *Gulliver's Travels* (1726); Lewis Caroll's *Alice's Adventures in Wonderland* (1865); R.L. Stevenson's *Dr. Jekyll and Mr. Hyde* (1886); Tolkien's *The Lord of the Rings* (1965). Science fiction movies such as *Star Trek* belong to futuristic fiction.

G

Gazette is derived from Venetian *gazeta* meaning 'a coin of small value'. In course of time it came to mean an official newspaper. The first such gazette was the *Oxford Gazette* published in 1665.

Genre is a French word meaning 'kind' or 'class' into which works of literature can be commonly grouped into poetry, prose and drama. Sub-genres can be found in these like in poetry: epic, ballad, elegy, lyric, sonnet, etc.; in drama: tragedy and comedy; in comedy : comedy of humours; comedy of manners and the like. Fiction can be of different types such as satires, apologue, novel, etc. Genre takes into account the style, manner, form and technique employed in the literary work. Often genres overlap each other.

Gender studies is interdisciplinary in nature and began in the 1980s. It is closely linked to women's and men's studies. It explores the interrelationship and the various meanings attached to masculinity and femininity. Gender studies focus attention on the universal in literature, history and culture. Gender studies have become important in the context of the predominance of the patriarchal system in the world which exalts masculinity.

Generative poetics deals with the process of constructing texts. It is derived from the generative grammar propounded by

Noam Chomsky which examines the various rules governing a sentence in its structure. Similarly, Generative Poetics examines the rules or grammar of a text.

Genotext & phenotext are terms coined by Julia Kristeva (1941), French-Bulgarian psychoanalyst and professor of linguistics. Phenotext refers to the surface structure of a text such as grammar, syntax, diction and the like. The genotext consists of the deeper structure of a text and tries to examine the hidden and deeper meanings of language in it.

Gothic is a term originally referred to the Germanic tribe of Goths and later to things medieval, especially in its barbaric and supernatural aspects. Now the term is applied to literature dealing with the strange, mysterious and supernatural designed to invoke suspense and terror in the reader or the audience. Gothic literature invariably exploits ghosts and monsters with settings such as castles, dungeons and graveyards, giving a sinister and terrifying atmosphere.

Gothic novel is a type of mysterious and supernatural novel arousing horror and terror. It is set in the background of haunted places such as an ancient medieval castle or haunted house that is Gothic in structure. Gothic structure with its narrow spires, arches, vaults and stained glasses aroused a sense of mystery. Gothic novel began to be in vogue since the late eighteenth century with their horror narratives arousing fear, gloom and mystery. Horace Walpole's *The Castle of Otranto : A Gothic Story* (1764) is considered the first gothic novel with its story surrounding passion and bloodshed. Walpole's novel was called Gothic since it was written in his Gothic castle on a barbarous theme of the middle ages. Gothic novels include Thomas Leland's *Longsword* (1762); Clara Reeve's *The Old English Baron* (1778); William Beckford's *Vathek* (1786); Anne Radcliffe's *The Mysteries of Udolpho* (1794); Lewis's *The Monk* (1796); C.R. Maturin's *The Fatal Revenge* (1807); Mary Shelley's

Frankenstein (1818); Dickens's *Bleak House* (1853); Charlette Bronte's *Jane Eyre* (1847); Daphne du Maurier's *Rebecca* (1938); Victoria Holt's *Mistress of Mellyn* (1960); Phyllis A. Whitney's *Thunder Heights* (1960); Stephen King's *The Shining* (1977) and Anne Rice's *The Witching Hour* (1990).

Grant tour was mentioned in literature since Richard Lassels's *Voyage of Italy* (1670). Eventually many began to write on tours with guidebooks for travellers. Noted among such works are James Howell's *Instructions for Forreine Travell* (1642); Henry Logan's *Directions for such as shall travel to Rome* (1654); Thomas Nugent's *The Grand Tour containing an Exact Description of Most of the Cities, Towns and Remarkable Places of Europe* (1743); Thomas Martyn's *A Gentleman's Guide in His Tour through France* (1787) and Johann Ebel's *The Traveller's Guide through Switzerland* (1818).

Grangerise is the additions made to a book by way of illustrations and engravings. For this purpose blank pages are inserted into an edition for further illustrations, e.g., James Granger's (1723-1776) *Biographical History of England.*

Grotesque is the bizarre and exaggerated depiction of human features in fiction, drama, music and the plastic arts. In fiction it presents the absurd and the bizarre with exaggerations and distortion of the natural. It presents deformed characters that behave abnormal. Such fiction present freakish caricatures of people. Writers who wrote in this genre include Charles Dickens, Frank Norris, Nathaniel West, William Faulkner (*As I Lay Dying*), Erkine Caldwell (*Poor Fool*), Carson McCuller (*Reflections in a Golden Eye*), Flannery O'Conner and others. In drama it is a genre found in 'puppet theatre', 'Commedia dell'Arte' and the modern satirical and caricatured drama. V. Meyerhold (1874-1940) is a popular promoter of grotesque drama. He aimed to take the audience away from the usual to the unusual and bizarre in drama. Brecht employed the genre to depict alienation effect. Others who used the genre are Aleksandr Blok, Sologub and Frank Wedekind.

H

Hagiography is derived from Greek meaning 'sacred writing'. It is the study and writing on the lives of saints and martyrs. Hagiography was popular in the middle ages consisting of liturgical and literary forms. Notable writers in this genre include Eusebius of Caesarea (4th century), Theodoret (5th century), Gregory the Great (6th century), Bede (8th century). *The Roman Martyrology* (16th century), *Acta Sanctorum* (lives of saints written by the Jesuits in the 17th century), and *Sancti Benedicti* (17th century Benedictine history of saints) are remarkable contributions to hagiography. The first English hagiography was *Actes and Monuments* by John Foxe, published in English in 1563.

Handbook and manual is a small book of prayers and rituals used in the church in the medieval times. Later manuals were written for various professions such as military training.

Harlem Renaissance is the Black literature that grew in Harlem, a predominantly black area of upper Manhattan of New York in the 1920s. From 1900 Harlem had become the centre of a black literary and intellectual movement. Alain Locke's anthology *The New Negro* in 1925 is an important publication of the movement. Other writers in the movement are Jean Toomer, Langston Hughes, Countee Cullen, Jessie Redmon Fauset, James Weldon Johnson, Claude McKay, Zora Neale, Arna Bontemps, Wallace

Thurman, James Baldwin, Ralph Ellison, and LeRoi Jones. Whites who wrote about the movement include Van Vechten (*Nigger Heaven*), and Bodernheim *(Naked on Roller Skates*).

Hero or **Heroine** is the chief character or protagonist in a narrative or dramatic work. The protagonist can fall into different types. The Aristotelian tragic hero is aristocratic in origin. He is an important person in society and is a good man who falls due to a tragic flaw or error of judgement, e.g., Shakespeare's King Lear, Othello, Prince Hamlet, etc. The protagonist can be a cultural hero in legends and myths who idealises values, e.g., Achilles is the embodiment of Greek courage. The protagonist can be anti-hero who is a common man lacking heroic qualities. In modern times hero and heroine are referred to the main male and female characters.

Heteroglossia in Greek, meaning 'different tongue', is a term used by Mikhail Bakhtin to refer to the meaning of a word to be understood in its context. Bakhtin opined that novel uses more heteroglossia than poetry since it has more heterogeneous and interactive discourse. He found heteroglossia especially in a novel like that of Dostoevsky where there is no single authorial control as a range of voices and perspectives and meanings produce a polyphony. Lyric poetry in his opinion is more private and hence monoglossic. Such a narrowing down of the concept is questionable in a broad social theory of language.

Histoire is a French word used in narratology signifying story with its sequences of events reconstructed by the readers in a chronological manner which may be different from the sequence of events in the plot.

Historical novel is set in a historical context based on historical and or literary sources. It attempts to recreate historical events or personages in a fictional manner. In writing a historical novel the novelist has to be selective in presenting a limited number of characters and appropriate events. He may take liberties in selecting and eliminating historical details. The novelist often selects critical moments and individual conflicts as focus of attention. Sir Walter Scott is considered to have established this genre with his novels such as *Waverley* (1814), *Rob Roy* (1817), *Ivanhoe* (1819), and *Kenilworth* (1821). Others who wrote historical novels include W.M. Thackeray (*Barry Lyndon*); Alexander Dumas (*The Three Musketeers*); Victor Hugo (*Les Miserables*); Leo Tolstoy (*War and Peace*); J.F. Cooper (*The Last of the Mohicans*); Margaret Mitchell (*Gone with the Wind*); Boris Pasternak (*Doctor Zhivago*); Herman Wouk (*The Winds of War*) and Solzhenitsyn (*August 1914*).

Holy Grail is the sacred cup used by Jesus Christ at the Last Supper before his death. According to a legend the Grail was preserved by Joseph of Arimathea, who collected in it the blood from the body of the crucified Christ. The vessel was then brought to Britain. It had many miraculous powers like satisfying the hunger of sinless souls; striking blind the impure of heart; making dumb the disrespectful who beheld it. The Holy Grail appears in the medieval romance of Parzival who set forth to achieve knighthood at King Arthur's court. During his sojourn he reaches the castle of the Fisher King (Parzival's uncle, but unknown to him) who is the custodian of the Holy Grail and the spear that pierced the heart of Jesus. Due to his sinful life the Fisher King has been struck dumb on coming into the presence of the Holy Grail. When Parzival enters the castle he has the vision of the bleeding spear and the Holy Grail pass before the speechless king. Parzival fails to ask any questions concerning the strange behaviour. Being a pure youth, if he spoke, his uncle would have been healed. After many wanderings, Parzival returns to the Grail castle; restores the power of speech to his uncle and succeeds him as king. In another legend the Holy Grail is sought after by Sir Galahad, one of Arthur's knights. Many other knights also go in search of the Grail. The quest is realised only by Sir Bors besides Parzival and Galahad. In the fifteenth century Sir Thomas

Malory included the quest for the Holy Grail in his *Morte d'Arthur*. Tennyson brings out the Grail legend in his *Idylls of the King*. T.S. Eliot refers to the Holy Grail in *The Waste Land*.

Homeric is attributed to anything that resemble Homer's *Iliad* and the *Odyssey*.

Homily is derived from Greek meaning discourse. It is a sermon given to a congregation to admonish and edify. The earliest books of homilies were published by the Church of England in 1547 and 1563. T.S. Eliot in *Murder in the Cathedral* makes the archbishop preach such a homily: "... For whenever mass is said, we re-enact the Passion and Death of Our Lord; and on this Christmas day we do this in celebration of His Birth. So that at the same moment we rejoice in His coming for the salvation of men, and offer again to God His Body and Blood in sacrifice, oblation and satisfaction for the sins of the whole world... we celebrate at once the Birth of Our lord and His passion and death upon the cross... this is to behave in a strange fashion. For who in the world will both mourn and rejoice at once and for the same reason?...so it is only in these our Christian mysteries that we can rejoice and mourn at once for the same reason. Now think for a moment about the meaning of this word 'peace'. ...Reflect now, how Our Lord Himself spoke of Peace. He said to His disciples, 'peace I leave with you, my peace I give unto you...Not as the world gives, give I unto you'...."

Humanism in philosophy emphasizes the dignity and worth of the individual. Its basic principle is that man being rational has within himself the capacity for truth and goodness. The term is often applied to the literary and cultural movement in the fourteenth and fifteenth century Europe. The movement began with the Italian writers Dante, Boccaccio, and Petrarch who tried to discover and preserve the Greek and Roman classical works. In Italy humanism deeply influenced literature and art. It made its impact on theology and education in Germany through Johann Reuchlin and

Melanchthon. It was a major force during the Reformation. In France there was Desiderius Erasmus who introduced the movement into England. The movement was established at the University of Oxford by William Grocyn and Thomas Linacre; and at the University of Cambridge by Erasmus and John Fisher. From the universities it spread and paved the way for the great flourishing of Elizabethan literature and culture. Nineteenth century Humanism has exponents like Matthew Arnold and the 'New Humanists' in USA such as Paul More and Irving Babbitt. Arnold's humanism led to 'Liberal humanism' based on the concept of the free self-determining individual.

Hyperbole is a figure of speech using exaggeration to give a vivid impression. It is employed in bombast, e.g., "Was this the face that a thousand ships?/ And burnt the topless towers of Ilium?" (*Dr. Faustus* : Marlowe); "The blue bird carries the sky on his back." (Thoreau).

Hyperreal is a term denoting the difficulty in differentiating between the real and the fictional. At times the reproduction of the real look more realistic leading to hyperrealism. The term is attributed to French Jean Baudrillard who believed in extreme form of nihilism. He developed his theories of hyperreality in mass media. He opined that the Gulf War did not take place but was only a televised simulation of a war.

Hypertext is a term to describe documents presented by a computer. It is attributed to computer pioneer Theodor H. Nelson who developed the concept in 1965. Nowadays it is used to refer to presenting information through computer-created possibilities giving access to texts, images, sounds, and actions. Access to internet and websites give immense possibilities by which one can browse through topics of relevance. Some authors of hypertext documents can be contacted through internet for clarifications. In recent times the term 'hypermedia' is becoming popular which gives stress to the non-textual components of hypertext such as animation and video.

Hypertext fiction is an electronic mediated fiction. It is allows interaction between the reader and the text through internet access. Fiction in this genre includes Michael Joyace's *Afternoon* (1987); Judy Molloy's *Its Name was Penelope* and the like (*see* Hypertext).

Hypotactic is a mark of joining together two clauses by a connecting word, e.g., 'I am happy *because* it is sunny.' This is the opposite of *paratactic* in which the connecting word is removed giving an effect of abruptness, e.g., 'I am happy; it is sunny.'

Hysteron proteron is a figure of speech in which there is a logical reversal in the statement. What comes as a logical conclusion is set at the beginning of the statement. It uses the technique of inversion, e.g., 'The doctors have given him a few days of life; he is HIV positive.'

I

Ideology is a system of concepts and beliefs that govern our day-to-day existence. The term is attributed to the French philosopher Antoine Destutt de Tracy who strove to reform post revolutionary French society with the "science of ideas." In the writings of Karl Marx we find the modern concept of ideology. He claimed that ideologies were inventions of the ruling classes to dominate with political, social and religious ideas. In the twentieth century there emerged two modern ideologies, namely, Communism and Fascism. Other ideologies such as socialism, democracy, and conservatism have emerged that have influenced the modern world. The Cold War era of antagonism between the United States and the Soviet Union is a typical example of ideological confrontation. Today, more than ever ideological conflicts continue with the recent war in Iraq. The alliance forces led by USA and Britain claim to battle for democracy and fight against international terrorism while Saddam Hussain stands for his ideological fight for freedom of his country by whatever means available to him. In the modern world of today the ideological battle is governed by economic superiority.

Implied author is an imaginative author behind a work other than the real author which the reader implies from the type and form of writing. It is the author's second self-standing behind the scene and is responsible for its design and the values presented. Implied author is not identical with a narrator in the work. The term was used by Wayne C. Booth in *Rhetoric of Fiction* (1961) (*see* Persona).

Implied reader is to be differentiated from the actual reader. It is a hypothetical ideal reader who would understand a work of art fully in its literary and implied purpose. It is the reader's second self-shaped according to the implied author's values presented. The implied reader is to be differentiated from the narratee. The implied reader is the audience of the implied author while the narratee is the audience of the narrator.

Impressionism is a movement in painting and music that developed in late nineteenth century France in reaction to the formalism and sentimentality that characterised academic art and the eighteenth and early nineteenth century music. The impressionist movement is often considered to mark the beginning of the modern period in art and music. Impressionism in painting arose out of dissatisfaction with the classical and sentimental subjects and dry, precise techniques of paintings that were approved by the Académie des Beaux-Arts in Paris. Rejecting these standards, the impressionists preferred to paint outdoors, choosing landscapes, street scenes and figures from everyday life. Their primary object was to achieve a spontaneous, undetailed rendering of the world through careful representation of the effect of natural light on objects. The foremost impressionists included Edgar Degas, Claude Monet, Berthe Morisot, Camille Pissarro, Pierre Auguste Renoir, and Alfred Sisley. In literature impressionism refers to very personal manner of writing depicting scenes and characters as they are seen and felt by the readers. Novelists like Joseph Conrad and Virginia Woolf wrote in this genre (see Expressionism).

In medias res is a Latin phrase meaning 'into the middle of things'. It is a techniques by which a story is narrated from some exciting situation or event in the middle of it and then it returns to an earlier period. This is to draw attention of the reader and then present the various incidents using the flash back technique. Often in epics this technique is employed, e.g., R.K. Narayan begins his novel *The Guide* in the middle of the chronological order of the events in a narrative form, Raju telling his life story to Velan the villager: "Raju welcomed the intrusion—something to relieve the loneliness of the place. The man stood gazing reverentially on his face. Raju felt amused and embarrassed. 'Sit down if you like,' Raju said, to break the spell.... I am here because I have nowhere else to go. I want to be away from people who may recognise me.... I am not so great as you imagine. I am just ordinary.'" He further narrates how his life was ruined by his associations with Rosie, the temple dancer.

Indirect discourse is one in which a character's expressions are integrated into another expression by way of shifting of tenses or changing from first person to third person discourse. This comes in contrast with the direct discourse in which a character's expressions are quoted as he/she states.

Informal essay is composed without formal structure with the purpose of amusement. It is also called personal essay as it reflects the personality of the author.

Informative prose is meant to convey information as in the case of textbooks, encyclopaedias, scientific books, news articles, etc.

Interior monologue is a stream of consciousness technique by which the recording of a character's inner thoughts and impressions are made. It is an extended form of free direct thought. The focal point is internal and subjective. Masters of the technique include James Joyce, Virginia Woolf, Dorothy Richardson, and William Faulkner, e.g., James Joyce in *A Portrait of the Artist as a Young Man* writes: "He turned to the flyleaf of the geography and read what he had written there: himself, his name and where he was. *Stephen Dedalus / Class of Elements / Clongowes Wood College / Sallins / County Kildare / Ireland / Europe / The World / The Universe.* That was in his writing: and Fleming one night for a cod had written on the opposite page: *Stephen Dedalus is my name, / Ireland is my nation. / Clongowes is my dwellingplace / And heaven my expectation.* He read the verses backwards but then they were not poetry. Then he read the flyleaf from the bottom to the top till he came to his own name. That was he: and he read down the page again. What was after the universe? Nothing...."

Intertextuality refers to the relationship between the codes of a text and the codes of the audience or reader. The interpretation by actors or the audience is often coloured by their milieu and social experiences.

Intrusive narrator is the one who narrates in his own voice the events and situations of a story like an omniscient narrator. Works in this genre include Henry Fielding's *Tom Jones*; Thackeray's *Vanity Fair*; and George Eliot's *Adam Bede*, e.g., "While the present century was in its teens, and on one sunshiny morning in June, there drove up to the great iron gate of Miss Pinkerton's academy for young ladies, on Chiswick Mall, a large family coach, with two fat horses in blazing harness, driven by a fat coachman in a three-cornered hat and wig, at the rate of four miles an hour. A black servant, who reposed on the box beside the fat coachman, uncurled his bandy legs as soon as the equipage drew up opposite Miss Pinkerton's shining brass plate, and as he pulled the bell at least a score of young heads were seen peering out of the narrow windows of the stately old brick house. Nay, the acute observer might have recognized the little red nose of good-natured Miss Jemima Pinkerton herself, rising over some geranium pots in the window of that lady's own drawing-room" (From *Vanity Fair*).

Innuendo is an indirect reference to someone or something without actually saying it, e.g., "She looks *a nice girl*, and she *looks* a nice girl.

Invective is a denunciatory speech or writing. It is used in literature in the form of lampoon, satire, caricature, or philippic. Invectives are used to express contempt or dislike for a person or a class. For example Swift in *Gulliver's*

Travels makes an allegorical attack on the hypocrisy of the courts, statesmen, and political parties of his time. He also adds his personal reflections on human society as well. *Gulliver's Travels* turns at times very bitter and indecent in expressions and mocks all humankind, e.g.,"Emperor of Lilliput, delight and terror of the universe, whose dominions extend five thousand blustrugs (about twelve miles in circumference) to the extremities of the globe; monarch of all monarchs, taller than the sons of men; whose feet press down to the centre, and whose head strikes against the sun; at whose nod the princes of the earth shake their knees; pleasant as the spring, comfortable as the summer, fruitful as autumn, dreadful as winter. His most sublime Majesty proposes to the Man-Mountain, lately arrived to our celestial dominions, the following articles, which by a solemn oath he shall be obliged to perform". (from *Gulliver's Travels*).

Irony is a literary device of humorous or lightly sarcastic mode of speech in which words are used to convey a meaning contrary to their literal sense. For instance, words of praise are used as a criticism or condemnation, e.g., Jonathan Swift in his *Modest Proposal* wrote: "...that the poor people of Ireland should rid themselves of poverty by selling their children to the rich to eat." Plato in his *Republic* (4th C. BC) refers to irony as 'a glib and underhand way of taking people in'. Socrates in his *Platonic Dialogues* employs the technique. For the Roman Rhetoricians Cicero and Quintilian, 'ironia' was a rhetorical figure in which words had contrary meaning. Irony is used in the English tradition from the sixteenth century. Spenser in his *Shepherd's Calendar* (1579) calls it 'An Ironicall Sarcasmus spoken in derision.' Irony becomes a common literary device in the seventeenth and eighteenth centuries. Irony can be classified into : verbal irony, situational irony, structural irony, dramatic irony, tragic irony, cosmic irony, romantic irony, etc. *Verbal irony* is saying what one does not mean. It is saying exactly the opposite of what one says, e.g., 'Hitler was a good man'. Verbal irony is used as a hyperbole. Shakespeare uses it in

Julius Caesar : "For Brutus is an honourable man;/ So are they all, all honourable men." *Situational irony* is made by contrast between what is expected and what really happens, e.g., "He was a man who taught driving lessons and the rules of the road but didn't know driving himself." *Dramatic irony* is a kind of situational irony by which the audience is aware of a situation of a character before he is aware of it, e.g., In *Oedipus* the king announces that the evildoer who has bought about the curse on his kingdom be punished. Finally the king discovers himself to be the villain. In this case of a tragedy, the dramatic irony is called a *Tragic irony.* When a dramatic irony occurs in a comedy it is *Comic irony. Socratic irony* is derived from Socrates (469-399 BC) who employed it in his *Platonic Dialogues.* The irony consists of pretending ignorance of the other person's point of view in order to refute him in argument, e.g., "Could you explain yourself? I can't get your point." *Structural irony* is a device used by a writer who brings out a structural feature to sustain the duplicity of meaning by inventing a spokesman or a naïve narrator whose interpretation is the point of view of the writer himself. *Cosmic irony* occurs when the protagonist's life is manipulated by some cosmic powers or God or destiny, e.g., Thomas Hardy's novels present fate in the lives of the characters. Tragic situations are bought about by 'hap; or 'chance'. *Romantic irony* is created by an author who builds up an artistic illusion by his narration. Eventually he reveals that he is the creator of the illusion and manipulator of his characters and their actions, e.g. Byron in his *Don Juan* brings out several romantic ironies. Irony is presented through sarcasm, hyperbole, litotes (understatement) and satire.

ISBN(International Standard Book Number) is the number given to each book to identify it. ISBN is printed on the back of the title page along with other publication data.

ISSN (International Standard Serial Number) is the number given to each serial by title for identification. It is printed like the ISBN.

J

Jacobean is a term applied to whatever is characteristic of the period of James I of England (1603-25). It is derived from his name in Latin 'Jacobus'. The period was remarkable for outstanding English drama including those of Ben Jonson, Webster and the later plays of Shakespeare. The King James Version of the *Bible* (Authorised Version of 1611) was a landmark publication of the period.

Jeremiad is a term derived from the Hebrew prophet Jeremiah and his warnings to Jerusalem on the future destruction in 586 BC. It primarily refers to his *Lamentations* which is a collection of five poems lamenting the destruction of Jerusalem and its aftermath of ruin and exile. In spite of its mournful nature there is also a note of trust in God and hope for the future. These poems are used by the Jews in worship on the annual days of fasting and mourning, commemorating the national disaster of 586 BC. The term 'Jeremiad' has been used by authors such as Carlyle, Thoreau and D.H. Lawrence in their castigation of the evils of the time.

Jeu d'esprit in French means 'play of spirit'. It refers to a witty piece of writing in the form of epigrams or a brief comical work. Oscar Wilde excelled in this genre.

Johnsonian is a term applied to refer to the grand style of Samuel Johnson (1709-84) with its well constructed sentences with a didactic tone. He is marked for his

Latinism, e.g., "He was of a middle stature, of a thin habit of body, a long visage, coarse features, and melancholy aspect; of a grave and manly deportment, a solemn dignity of mien, but which, upon a nearer acquaintance, softened into an engaging easiness of manners. His walk was easily excited to smiles, but very seldom provoked to laughter". (on Milton from *The Lives of the Poets*).

Journal consists of the diary jottings of a person's ideas and thoughts. Often writers keep journals to take note of their reflections and impressions which they use in their works. Some writers who kept journals include Samuel Pepys, Dorothy Wordsworth, R.W. Emerson, G.M. Hopkins, Herman Melville and Virginia Woolf.

Journalism is the profession of writing for public journals. Many great writers and literary figures were journalists such as Coleridge, Southey, Hazlitt, Charles Dickens, Rudyard Kipling, Mark Twain, Bret Harte, Robert Graves, Aldous Huxley, Ernest Hemingway and Graham Greene.

Juvenilia means the works written by an author during his youth. Such works are excused for their lack of experience being immature.

K

Kailyard school is a term applied to a group of nineteenth century writers who wrote stories of Scottish such as J.J. bell, S.R. Crockett, J.M. Barrie and Ian Maclaren. Kailyard meant a 'kitchen garden' and these writers dealt with peasant life.

King's English is a term applied to the purest form of English since the sixteenth century. Reference to Queen's English is also made in the same manner.

Knickerbocker school consists of a group of New York writers in the beginning of the nineteenth century. They were grouped together not for any common literary spirit. It included Washington Irving, J.F. Cooper and W.C. Bryant. The term is derived from Washington Irving's *Knickerbocker's History of N.Y.* (1809).

Kunstlerroman is a term applied to a novel written on the development of a character from childhood to maturity, e.g., James Joyce's *A Portrait of the Artist as a Young Man;* Margaret Atwood's *Cat's Eye. A Portrait of the Artist as a Young Man* traces the development of the protagonist Stephen Dedalus from childhood, school days, adolescence, sexual adventures and guilt of student life, his destiny as a poet, patriot and unbeliever.

Kunstmarchen in German refers to written folk tales in contrast to those in the oral tradition.

L

Laconic means expressing in few words after the manner of the Laconians or the Spartans in short and epigrammatic sentences.

Lampoon is a personal satire in verse or prose ridiculing or caricaturing someone or an institution in an abusive manner. Dryden and Pope were masters of this genre in English literature.

Latinism refers to English words or expressions in imitation of Latin in structure and diction. Milton used Latinism in his writings in grammatical structure of object-subject-verb instead of the English word order of subject-verb-object.

Law of Karma asserts that an action has a chain sequence, i.e., cause and effect. The term is derived from Sanskrit meaning 'action'. In the Indian philosophy it is the totality of one's actions both good or bad. These actions are attached to the soul and are transmigrated to each new body at transmigration. The concept of Karma is found in the *Upanishads*.

Legend is a story orally transmitted from generation to generation. It is distinct from myth as they concern human beings than gods. Often stories of saints and heroes like King Arthur are the subject matter. Many legends have been written down, e.g., Old English anonymous poem *Beowulf*, the legendary story of the Geatish hero Beowulf who kills the monster Grendel and becomes the king of the Geats; Malory's *Morte D'Arthur* which narrates the exploits of the Knights of the Round Table of King Arthur. The legend of the outlaw Robin Hood has been used in fiction as in Scott's *Ivanhoe* in the character of Locksley.

Leitmotif is a German term meaning 'leading motif'. It is a literary device by which an image, symbol or phrase is frequently repeated. *Leitmotif* is a German term (*leitmotiv*) meaning 'leading motif' coined by Hans von Wolzugen in reference to a musical theme that runs through an opera. The device was used in the operas of Richard Wagner (1813-1883). Thomas Mann (1875-1955) used it as a literary device by which an image, symbol or phrase is frequently repeated in a work, associated with a particular character or situation. In drama a leitmotif gives information on the character who uses it or offers an ironic comment on the action, e.g., Graham Greene in his novels presents betrayal through this device.

Libretto in Italian means *libro* (book). It is the text of an opera or other staged musical work. The term sometimes also refers to the text of an oratorio or to a ballet scenario. In the libretto of a musical, the dialogue is called the book; and the song words, the lyrics.

Limited edition of a book consists of the few copies printed with serial numbers on it. A reprint of the bock is not made in the same form.

Limited omniscience is a device by which an author reveals the thoughts of a particular character in great details while presenting the rest of the characters only externally.

Lipogram is a kind of playful composition without using a particular alphabet. In English Ernest Wright wrote his novel *Gadsby* (1939) avoiding "*e*".

Literal means pertaining to the exact meaning of a word without embellishment and figurative or metaphorical meaning. It calls for a direct and word-for-word rendering of meanings. Literal language is opposite of a figurative language which is marked by figures of speech.

Literalism is the exact and literal interpretation of a text without any heed to any figurative sense and giving an interpretation that is merely verbal. It is very unimaginative and when done frequently can be irritating to the readers. Literalism is employed by some writers in humorous passages to counter-attack rhetorical devices unskilfully used. See the following example from Shakespeare's *The Taming of the Shrew*.

"Curtis: All ready; and therefore, I pray thee, news?

"Grumio: First, know, my horse is tired, my master and mistress fallen out.

"Curtis: How?

"Grumio: Out of their saddles into the dirt; and thereby."

Literal translation is a rendering of a language into another disregarding idiomatic expressions. This can lead to misinterpretation of texts, e.g., the English idiom "It rained cats and dogs."

Literary forgery is publishing what one has written and attributing it to someone of renown, e.g., the Ossianic controversy in the eighteenth century when James Macpherson wrote the epic *Fingal* and attributed it to Ossian (3rd century BC).

Literati is a term applied to literary men who spend time reading, writing and criticising works of literature. The term is at times applied disparagingly.

Literature is writings of a society in prose or verse. It includes all types of fiction and non-fiction writing intended for publication.

Literature of escape is a phenomenon in literature since the World Wars which ushered in books about escaping from prisoners-of-war camps. Known works in this genre are H.G. Durnford's *The Tunnellers of Holzminden*; H.E. Harvey's

Cage-birds; Eric William's *Wooden Horse*; David James's *A Prisoner's Progress;* Airey Neave's *They have their Exit*; Anthony Deane-Drummond's *Return Ticket*; Peter Medd's *The Long Walk Home* and others.

Litotes means affirmation by negation of the contrary. This is done by stating the opposite of what one intents, e.g., *I am sure we have met before = I am sure we have never met before.*

Litterateur in French means a literary man engaged in creative and critical works.

Loan words are words taken from other languages which enrich the vocabulary, e.g., Latin loan words in English like: *bonus, stimulus, memorandun, terminus*. French loan words like: *burlesque, tableau, champagne, coquette.*

Local colour refers to certain particular details of a region or environment in a narrative such as culture, local dialect, customs and traditions, mannerisms, dress and habits, landscapes and the like. Writers who used the method in their writing include Thomas Hardy, Mark Twain, Joel Chandler Harris, Sarah Orne Jewett, George Washington Cable, Thomas Nelson Page, Francis Hopkinson Smith, William Faulkner, Bret Harte, Hamlin Garland and others. Hardy describes vividly the village of Marlott in *Tess of the D'urbervilles* : "The village of Marlott lay amid the north-eastern undulations of the beautiful Vale of Blackemore or Blackmoor aforesaid, an engirdled and secluded region, for the most part untrodden as yet by tourist or landscape-painter, though within a four hours' journey from London. It is a vale whose acquaintance is best made by viewing it from the summits of the hills that surround it – except perhaps during the droughts of summer. An unguided ramble into its recesses in bad weather is apt to engender dissatisfaction with its narrow, tortuous, and miry ways" (*see* Regional novel).

Lollards were members of a religious sect in fourteenth and fifteenth centuries led by the English religious reformer John Wycliffe. Lollards held the *Bible* to be the only authentic rule of faith and exhorted the clergy to return to the simple life of the early Church. They rejected the doctrine of Transubstantiation, Confession, and the use of images in worship.

Loose and organic plots are found in fiction. A novel of loose plot consists of a number of disconnected episodes with no logical unity, e.g., Dickens's *Pickwick Papers* with several disconnected episodes. Samuel Pickwick is the only connecting link in the novel who is the general chairman of the Pickwick Club. In such a novel, the novelist does not have a clear chalked out outline of the story. He/she allows it to develop in course of time as Anthonly Trollope says, "When I sit down to write a novel, I do not at all know, and I do not very much care, how it is to end." *Robinson Crusoe, Vanity Fair,* etc., are examples of this genre. On the other hand an organic plot has structural unity. In such a novel different episodes are closely knit so as to form an organic whole. The episodes are linked to each other in such a manner that they are essential for the coherent development of the plot, e.g., Jane Austen's *Pride and Prejudice.* All the episodes in the novel lead to the final union of Elizabeth and Darcy. W.L. Cross writes: "The marriage of Elizabeth to Darcy is not merely a possible solution of the plot, it is as inevitable as the conclusion of a properly constructed syllogism or geometrical demonstration."

Lost generation refers to a generation of writers in between the First World War and the Depression who were disillusioned by their traditional upbringing in a puritanical society. The term was used for the first time by Gertrude Stein who called them 'a lost generation'. Ernest Hemingway used the phrase in his *The Sun Also Rises*. It came to be applied to the expatriate writers of America in the 1920s and 1930s who resided especially in Paris such as Ernest Hemingway, F. Scott Fitzgerald, William Carlos Williams, Thornton Wilder, Hart Crane, Archibald MacLeish and others.

M

Mabinogion is a collection of Welsh prose tales, composed between eleventh and thirteenth centuries based on oral tradition. These comprise Welsh mythology, folklore and present the Arthurian legend. The English translation was made in 1838-39 by Lady Charlotte Elizabeth Guest. The name *Mabinogion* is derived from the four stories that begin the collection, "The Four Branches of the Mabinogi" on the life of Prince Gwri or Pryderi. The collection ends with three Arthurian romances.

Magic realism is a device used in fiction by which the writer mingles realistic treatment of a subject with supernatural and bizarre elements. There is excellent weaving of realism, fairy tales, myths and fantasy in such works. The device evolved as a postmodernist trend in the 1940s especially in Latin America, e.g., Gabriel Garcia Marquez's *Cien Anos de soledad (One Hundred Years in Solitude* 1967*)*, Isabel Allende's *La Casa de los espiritus (The House of the Spirits*, 1982), Laura Esquivel's *Como Agua para chocolate* (*Like Water for Chocolate*, 1989). Gabriel Garcia Marquez, Colombian novelist and Nobel laureate, excelled in the use of the device in his novels such as *One Hundred Years of Solitude* which is an epic story of a Colombian family. The theme of incest is realistically presented by which two close relatives are married and a child is born with a pig's tail. Others who attempted the genre include Jorge Luis Borges,

Alejo Carpentier, Margaret Atwood, Margaret Drabble, William Golding, John Irving, Bernard Malamud, Toni Morrison, Iris Murdoch, John Updike, John Fowles, Angela Carter and Salman Rushdie.

Main narrator is the one who introduces the whole narrative and is responsible for it, e.g., Pip in Dickens's *Great Expectations* is the main narrator. The novel concludes with his union with Estella: "I took her hand in mine, and we went out of the ruined place; and, as the morning mists had risen long ago when I first left the forge, so, the evening mists were rising now, and in all the broad expanse of tranquil light they showed to me, I saw no shadow of another parting from her."

Mannerist literature is written in an exaggerated and superficial style with the idiosyncratic style of the author, e.g., The style of John Lyly and some of the seventeenth century metaphysical poets. Among the modern writers James Joyce's *Ulysses* belongs to this genre. Mannerist style is ornate with difficult and old syntax, and far-fetched imagery. Mannerism is derived from Italian art of 1520-1600, during the period between the High Renaissance and the Baroque style. Artists such as Tintoretto, El Greco, Bronzino and Vasari developed mannerist art. Michaelangelo and Raphael were mannerist in their art towards the end of their career. These artists laid more stress on intellectual preconceptions than visual perception, e.g., "Life those chaps out there must have, stuck in the same spot. Irish Lights board. Penance for their sins. Coastguards too. Rocket and breeches buoy and lifeboat. Day we went out for the pleasure cruise in the Erin's King, throwing them the sack of old papers. Bears in the zoo. Filthy trip. Drunkards out to shake up their livers. Puking overboard to feed the herrings. Nausea. And the women, fear of God in their faces" (from *Ulysses*).

Marginalised refers to the neglected of exploited. With the growth of the modern literary theories such as Feminism, Post-colonialism, Post-structuralism, etc., the term has received theoretical overtones. It refers to those identities that have suffered under privileged classes, colonialism and racial prejudices.

Marxist criticism is a kind of historical criticism based on the economic theory of Karl Marx and interpreted by various Communist spokesmen. It is based on the economic conflict between the social classes. According to the Marxist critical thought, those who control the economics of society control its mind and culture. Marx and Engels did not develop a systematic aesthetic theory. However, we find Marxist aesthetics in the writings of Trotsky, Gramsci, Louis Althusser, Lucien Goldmann and Gyorgy Lukacs. Lukacs developed his concept of 'critical realism'. Christopher Caudwell is considered the first important English Marxist critic who wrote *Illusion and Reality* (1937) and *Studies in a Dying Culture* (1938). In these works he defined the Marxist theory of art and inspired the writers of the thirties to commit themselves to the culture of revolutionary proletariat. Raymond Williams presented his Marxist concept of the relationship between literature and society in his books *Culture and Society 1780 - 1950* (1958), *The Long Revolution* (1961), Modern *Tragedy* (1966), and *The Country and the City* (1973). Other modern Marxist critics include F.O. Matthiessen and George Lucas.

Masochism is a term derived from the name of the Austrian novelist Leopold von Sacher-Masoch who presented several characters in his writings who derived sexual pleasure from self-laceration and whipping. In psychoanalysis the term has a wider connotation. It is applied to anyone being dominated by others and succumbing to humiliation and punishment inflicted upon them. The opposite tendency is sadism by which a person inflicts pain on others and derives sexual satisfaction from it (*see* Sadism).

Maxim or **apothegm** is a concise and memorable statement or aphorism giving practical counsel, e.g., "A little learning is a dangerous thing" (Pope); "Remember that time is money" (Benjamin Franklin).

Medievalism is a term in literature referring to the imitation of the arts and manners of Europe in the middle ages (8th to 15th century). Medievalism is characterised by the use of archaism, religious faith and chivalry. In the late eighteenth and nineteenth centuries there was a growing interest in the medieval, e.g., Keats's *The Eve of St. Agnes* (1820), Walter Scott's *Ivanhoe*(1819).

Medievalist is a person doing scholarly studies in medieval history, art or culture.

Memoir novel is written in the form of memoirs of the writer with autobiographical elements in it. It included diary jottings and journals kept by the author. It can be semi-autobiographical or fully fictional in nature. Sometimes the author turns out to be merely an editor of someone else's memoirs. This genre began in the seventeenth century France and Daniel Defoe excelled in it in England with his *Robinson Crusoe* (1719) and *Moll Flanders* (1722). Other such works include Smollett's *Roderick Random,* Goldsmith's *The Vicar of Wakefield,* Mackenzie's *The Man of Feeling,* Dickens's *David Copperfield,* Melville's *Moby-Dick* and Charlotte Bronte's *Jane Eyre,* e.g., in *Moll Flanders* Defoe lets his protagonist begin her memoirs with autobiographical elements: "My true name is so well known in the records or registers at Newgate, and in the Old Bailey, and there are some things of such consequence still depending there, relating to my particular conduct, that is not to be expected I should set my name or the account of my family to this work; perhaps, after my death, it may be better known; at present it would not be proper, no, not though a general pardon should be issued, even without exceptions and reserve of persons or crimes."

Metafiction is a term applied to fictional writing which questions the relationship between reality and fiction. It intentionally draws attention to itself as a linguistic construct. Metafiction speaks about itself. Such writers concern themselves with the nature of fictional composition and make humorous comments on them, e.g., Sterne's *Tristram Shandy* (1760-7), John Fowles's *The French Lieutenant's Woman* (1969) (*see* Reflexive novel).

Metonymy is the use of a word or phrase for another to which it is closely associated. In some cases the effect is used for the cause or the abstract for the concrete, and similar constructions, e.g., "He was a voracious reader of Shakespeare", (*Works of Shakespeare*) "My mother kept a good table" (gave good food).

Minority discourse refers to the study of the literatures of ethnic minorities in the United States in the recent past. The main effort has been to revive and promote the study of Black, Latino, Asian American and native American writing. There is a great awareness to strengthen the cultural identity of particular groups and linking it to a tradition of writing. Cultural diversity and multiculturalism ought to be celebrated. Attempts are made: to generate theories of minority discourse; to develop concepts for the analysis of specific cultural traditions; to use a position of marginality to expose the assumptions of majority discourse; and to intervene in its theoretical debate.

Modernism is a term applied to several tendencies in the arts prominent in the first half of the twentieth century. It comes directly after the Victorian age in 1887. The First World War gave a new direction to literature and the real new poetry began by 1914. It ended an era of idealism and filled people with bitterness and despair. The literature of this period was deeply influenced by the psychology of Freud and the anthropology of Sir J. Frazer's *Golden Bough*. Emphasis was given to the irrational and the unconscious in man. The age was one of experimentalism and *avantgarde* trends as it rejected traditional Victorian forms in literature. Delving into the 'stream of consciousness' in human mind was an essential feature of the time. The aesthetic vision of modernism broke with the immediate past traditions. The various modernist movements include Symbolism, Expressionism, Imagism, Vorticism, Futurism, Surrealism, Dada and the like. Modernism came as a reaction to Realism and Naturalism undermining the Representationalism (Mimesis) associated with those movements. The stream of consciousness novel is a good example to modernism. Some of the prominent modernist novelists include James Joyce, Virginia Woolf, Franz Kafka, Conrad, Marcel Proust, and William Faulkner.

Monologic narrative is one in which the narrator's knowledge and views are the ultimate authority in the world depicted. It has a unifying voice throughout the narrative, e.g., Dickens in his *A Tale of Two Cities* narrates: "A wonderful fact to reflect upon, that every human creature is constituted to be that profound secret and mystery to every other. A solemn consideration, when I enter a great city by night, that every one of those darkly clustered houses encloses its own secret; that every room in every one of them encloses its own secret; that every beating heart in the hundreds of thousands of breasts there, is, in some of its imaginings, a secret to the heart nearest it! Something of the awfulness, even of Death itself, is referable to this. No more can I turn the leaves of this dear book that I loved, and vainly hope in time to read it all...."

Motif is a concept, image or event which recurs as a theme. It is a synonym for leitmotif (*see* leitmotif), e.g., the passage of time is a recurrent theme in Shakespeare's Sonnet sequence. In folklore common motives are found, e.g., in Malory's *Le Morte d' Arthur* the theme of the quest for the sword occurs as a motif : " 'I command,' said the Archbishop, 'that ye keep yourselves within your church and pray unto God still; that no man touch the sword till the high mass be all done.' When all masses were done all the lords went to behold the stone and the sword...." In Western music motif is a short melodic or rhythmic segment of a theme that repeats throughout a composition. Although a motif is often repeated in a slightly varied or elaborated way, it carries a recognizable form throughout the composition.

Multiple narration is a narrative technique employed by some novelists who mix primary, secondary and tertiary narrations. Emily Bronte in her novel *Wuthering Heights* employs the device effectively. Practically the entire novel is narrated by the primary narrator Lockwood who is an extern and a tenant of Heathcliff. Later certain incidents are narrated by Nelly Dean who is the secondary narrator. The novelist still makes use of tertiary narrators such as some of the characters in the novel like Cathy, Heathcliff and Isabella. Such narrations make the readers get to know different points of view before coming to a final conclusion. Mary Shelly employs multiple narration technique in her *Frankenstein* in a very complex manner.

Mythology is the study and interpretation of ancient folk beliefs and traditional stories of gods and heroes in a particular culture. These present in symbolic language the origin of a culture often in supernatural terms. Usually they describe the origin of the world, creation of man and the origin of customs and practices of people, and mysteries of life and death. Myths have been associated with religion, gods and supernatural themes. It can be a source of information of a particular culture and its mythical past. Myth is to be distinguished from legends as they contain deeper universal religious phenomena and traditions though with no historical basis. Legends on the other hand deal more with human existence. Sometimes myth is considered synonymous with plot. Novels based on myths include Herman Melville's *Moby Dick*, James Joyce's *Ulysses* and D.H. Lawrence's *The Plumed Serpent*. James Joyce's *Ulysses* is inspired by Homer's Odysseus story in Greek mythology. Odysseus (Ulysses) is the ruler of Ithaca and was one of the Greek heroes who fought in the Trojan War. Homer narrates the adventures of Odysseus before he returns home. Joyce in his novel takes the various characters from the myth and recounts the wanderings of the main characters Stephen Dedalus, Leopold Bloom and Molly through the streets of Dublin on 16 June 1904. Leopold Bloom represents Odysseus, Molly stands for Penelope and Stephen represents Telemachus.

Mythopoeia refers to the making of myths by writers who base themselves on a framework of myths. This myth making is an elaboration of a story by an individual or a community which often leads to a dramatic form. For example, the stories of the Trojan war or Biblical stories were transformed into plays. Such mythopoeia is seen in G.B. Shaw's *Pygmalion*; T.S. Eliot's *The Family Reunion* and *The Elder Statesman*; Eugene O' Neill's *Morning Becomes Electra,* etc. The term in a wider sense, is applied to any writing based on old myths.

N

Narratee is the imaginary person, the narrator addresses, in the course of a narration. The naratees are not to be confused with the readers or the implied authors though they are not easily identifiable, e.g., in Browning's 'Last Duchess', the Duke of Ferrara speaks to the narratee who is the envoy of the Count of Tyrol.

Narrative is the process of telling a story or sequence of events. It can be fictional or real written in either prose or verse. It includes epic, romance, ballad, novel, short story, biography, travelogue and the like.

Narrative prose is the most popular form in the prose genre. It consists of narrating a story either real or fictional with exciting details. Most novels are written in this genre, e.g., Hardy's *Far from the Madding Crowd*, Dickens's *Great Expectations* and the like.

Narratology studies the nature, form and modalities of a narrative. The term has been used since 1960 by Russian formalists and French Structuralists to analyse a narrative.

Narrator is the one who narrates the story and it is coloured by his outlook which the reader perceives. He is to be distinguished from the real author, the perceived author and the narratee. A narrator who is directly involved in the story is called the first person narrator, e.g., in Browning's 'Last Duchess', the Duke of Ferrara speaks out "That's my last

Duchess painted on the wall...." The narrator who is outside the story is third person narrator, e.g., Lockwood is the narrator of the story in Emily Bronte's *Wuthering Heights*. The narrator who stands outside and observes the inner thoughts of the characters is omniscient narrator. The narrator is very useful in presenting very complex materials in course of a historical novel involving timespan. The narrator provides necessary information to the audience and creates the scene and atmosphere, (*see* Historical novel).

Naturalism in literature calls for an objective and empirical presentation of human beings. It differs from realism. Naturalistic writers reject free will in man and believe that human behaviour is controlled by instinct, emotion, or social and economic factors. Man is a passive victim of natural forces. It accepts the biological determinism of Charles Darwin and the economic determinism of Karl Marx. Naturalists refused to idealise experience as all human experiences are subject to natural law. Naturalism was first noticed in the nineteenth century French authors Edmond Louis Antoine de Goncourt, Jules Alfred Huot de Goncourt, and Emile Zola. Zola tried to apply methods of scientific observation to the depiction of pathological human character. In his essay "The Experimental Novel" (1880) he examines his theory of literary naturalism. His influence has been remarkable in plays and novels of the century. American novelist Frank Norris deals with naturalism in his novel *McTeague* (1899). Other naturalistic writers include Sherwood Anderson, John Dos Passos, Tolstoy, Gorki, Theodore Dreiser, James T. Farrell, George Moore, Stephen Crane, George Gissing and others.

Negritude is a black cultural movement began in 1932 in Paris which influenced many black writers in the French-speaking world. They sought to uphold traditional African values and resisted the attempt of the whites to absorb the blacks into the white man's world. The leaders were Leopold Sedar Senghor and Aime Cesaire.

Nemesis means retributive justice often referred to in the case of tragic heroes. 'Nemesis' is the Greek goddess of retribution who punishes erring humans.

Neoclassicism known by various names, 'Augustan Age', 'Age of Reason' or 'The Enlightenment' is a movement in literature which imitated the great classical authors of the ancient Greece and Rome. Aristotle's *Poetics* (4th century BC) and Horace's *Ars Poetica* (c.20BC) became the dominant literary influences on the writers of the period with the principles of decorum and instruction. They took up to the Aristotelian unities of time, place and action. This resurgence began with the French literature in the seventeenth century and deeply influenced the English literary scene from 1660 to 1780. Neoclassicism stood for reason, judgement, decorum, correctness and argumentation. They used Heroic couplet form in poetry. The neoclassical beliefs generated a definite vision of man and mankind. Man and his activities were the main subject matter of poetry. They frequently used satire to correct excessive folly, stupidity and corruption which threatened maintenance of good moral order and literary discipline. Alexander Pope wrote, "Order is Heaven's first law." Hence, the neoclassicists were obliged to instruct as well as to please through their works. The period is called classical as it was a revolt against the Romantic exuberance of the Elizabethan period that preceded it. However, they lacked the genius of the Elizabethans and turned to the great classical writers for guidance and inspiration. The period also coincided with the restoration of Charles II in 1660 when the puritan government collapsed. The period, marked by the French influence of Moliere, is evident in the Restoration Comedy of Manners. In tragedy the neoclassicists imitated the French and the Latin forms and produced the heroic play. The authors devised many rules and issued the injunction "be correct". Dr. Johnson applied to Dryden the term "Augustan" saying that "Dryden did to English literature what Augustus did to Rome, which he found brick and left marble." The neoclassical poetry became excessively a town poetry showing no interest in the landscapes and country people. They distrusted emotions and turned to good sense and reason. Important literary figures of this period are Dryden (1631-1700), Swift (1667-1745) Addison (1672-1719), Steele (1672-1729), Pope (1688-1744), Fielding (1707-1754), Johnson (1709-1784), and Goldsmith (1730-1774).

Neoplatonism is a philosophical and religious system founded by Plotinus (AD 205-270) which blends Platonic ideas and oriental mysticism. It sets aside the over-emphasis of Plato on rationalism and ideas, and stressed more on the intuitive and mystical pursuits of truth. They believed in the hierarchy of the spiritual levels of the individual soul in its communion with the Eternal. Neoplatonism in literature stressed the theory of love based on the concept that earthly beauty is the image of the absolute beauty. It believes in the existence of invisible airy creatures. Art and nature in their view are the copy of the super-sensuous reality.

New directions is an experiment in new prose and poetry, begun by James Laughlin IV in 1936. It was meant to present new ideas through an annual publication. Those who contributed to the annual include such names as Kenneth Burke, Cummings, Henry Miller, Wallace Stevens and the like. New Directions became eventually a publishing house which began publishing the works of authors entitled *New Directions Reader.*

New England Renaissance refers to the cultural awakening in America in the mid-nineteenth century led by Unitarianism and Transcendentalism (*see* Transcendentalism).

Nom de plume meaning 'pen-name' in French is a term used in English to refer to a fictitious name employed by a writer to keep his/her anonymity. It was meant to keep the name of the author secret. In the nineteenth century since women writers were not given due credit, some wrote with male pen names. Prominent writers who used *nom de plume* include

O. Henry (William Sidney Porter), George Eliot (Mary Ann Cross), Stendhal (Mary Henri Boyle), and Mark Twain (Samuel Langhorne Clemens).

Nonsense literature is written with no logic in it such as nursery rhymes and some folk tales written to amuse children. It became popular in the Victorian period when there was a great deal of mental restlessness, e.g., Lewis Carroll's *Alice's Adventures in Wonderland* which narrates the dream of Alice who follows a White Rabbit into its rabbit-hole and to a wonderland where she meets characters such as the Duchess and Cheshire Cat, the Mad Hatter and March Hare, the King and Queen of Hearts and others.

Nouveau roman meaning 'new novel' is a French literary movement in the 1950s propounded by Nathalie Sarraute, Claude Simon, Michel Butor, Robert Pinget and Alain Robbe-Grillet. They revolted against the mimetic element in literature which is purely imitation of life. They challenged the conventional forms of plot, character, and narration in the novel and called for depersonalisation and presentation of things with an individual version and vision of things. In drama the theatre of Absurd has this new trend.

Novel is derived from Latin 'novellus' and Italian 'novella' meaning 'a little new thing'. It was Giovanni Boccaccio who applied the term 'novella' to his prose narratives in *Decameron* (1348-53). When these tales were translated into English the term 'novel' came to be applied. In its wider sense it is applied to an extended prose fiction. In its growth and evolution the novel has absorbed various elements from prose writings such as essays, letters, memoirs, histories, tracts, travel sketches and so on. In novels there is more of a private relationship between the author and the reader through its anecdotal narrative presenting something new which has made it popular unlike other forms of literature. In fact, today literature can widely be classified into 'fictional' and 'non-fictional'. Novel is a kind of prose narration or story with characters, plot, incidents and situations with a great deal of realism in its presentation. With regard to its length it should be longer than a short story. In modern times it is expected to be over 60,000 words so as to publish it as an independent volume. Miguel de Cervantes Saavedra (1547-1616), the Spanish writer, is considered the first to write a novel in the west with his *Don Quixote de la Mancha.* It is written in the form of a chivalric burlesque presenting the adventures of Don Quixote, a poor gentleman of La Mancha, who by his inordinate reading of romances imagines himself going on adventures with his old horse Rosinante and in the company of the rustic squire Sancho Panza. Later works such as *La princess de Clèves* (1678) by Madame de la Fayette and *The Pilgrim's Progress* (1678-1684) by John Bunyan are noteworthy works in the genre. During the eighteenth century there is a growing popularity of the novel as the novelists wrote on people and society. Prominent English authors of the eighteenth century are Daniel Defoe, Samuel Richardson, Henry Fielding, Tobias Smollett, and Laurence Sterne who were pioneers in establishing the tradition of the novel. Their popular works include Defoe's *Robinson Crusoe* (1719), a desert island romance surrounding a shipwrecked Crusoe; Richardson's *Pamela* (1740) establishing the epistolary novel tradition in the form of letters and journals; Fielding's *Tom Jones* (1749), a comic epic presenting social types of the age; Smollett's *The Adventures of Roderick Random* (1748), episodic in form and based on his own experience as a naval officer; Sterne's *The Life and Opinions of Tristram Shandy* (1760-67) an eccentric masterpiece full of interruptions and digressions which is the precursor of the stream-of-consciousness novel in the twentieth century. Several new trends are seen in the eighteenth century in the form of 'didactic novel', 'gothic novel', and 'comedy of manners'. In the 'didactic novel' authors intent to present their theories and concepts to teach and instruct. For example, French philosopher Jean Jacques Rousseau wrote his *Emile* (1762) in which he propounds his theory of educating a child in the surrounding of nature to develop his independent character uncorrupted by civilisation. William Godwin's *Caleb Williams* (1794) is a didactic novel presenting the tyrannical power exercised by the powerful over the less privileged in society, (*see* Didactic novel). The 'Gothic novel' is a type of mysterious and supernatural novel arousing horror and terror. It is set in the background of haunted places such as an ancient medieval castle or haunted house that is gothic in structure. Horace Walpole's *The Castle of Otranto : A Gothic Story* (1764) is considered the first gothic novel with its story surrounding passion and bloodshed (*see* Gothic novel). 'The comedy of manners' is found in fiction mirroring society and behaviour of individuals. Jane Austen excelled in this genre with her *Pride and Prejudice (* 1813) and *Emma* (1816) (*see* Comedy of manners). Nineteenth century witnessed the growth of the English novel. Sir Walter Scott's Waverley novels (1814-1828), full of historical elements, established the tradition of 'historical novel' as a genre (*see* Historical novel). The age saw prolific output of fiction from Charles Dickens, William Makepeace Thackeray, Anthony Trollope, and George Eliot. These writers make their powerful attack on the social evils of the Victorian society. Dickens fills his novels with injustices and inequalities between the rich and the poor. Important novels of the period include Dickens's *Oliver Twist* (1838), *David Copperfield* (1850), *Bleak House* (1853), *Hard Times* (1854), *Great Expectations* (1861); Thackeray's *Barry Lyndon* (1844), *Vanity Fair* (1847-8), *The Newcomers* (1854-5); Trollope's *The Warden* ((1855), *Barchester Towers,* (1857), *Doctor Thorne* (1858); George Eliot's *Adam Bede* (1859), *The Mill on the Floss* (1860), *Silas Marner* (1861), *Middlemarch* (1871-2); Emily Bronte's *Wuthering Heights* (1847); Charlotte Bronte's *Jane Eyre;* George Meredith's *The Ordeal of Richard Feverel* (1859), *and The Egoist* (1879). Towards the end of the nineteenth century Thomas Hardy became very prominent in England with his novels of character and environment with works such as *Under the Greenwood Tree* (1872), *Far form the Madding Crowd* (1874), *The Return of the Native*

(1878), *The Mayor of Casterbridge* (1886), *Tess of the D'Urbervilles* (1891) and *Jude the Obscure* (1895). R.L. Stevenson wrote several novels during this period like *Treasure Island* (1883) and *Kidnapped* (1886). Prominent novels in the United States since the middle of the nineteenth century include works such as Nathaniel Hawthorne's *The Scarlet Letter* (1850); Herman Melville's *Moby Dick* (1851); Mark Twain's *The Adventures of Huckleberry Finn* (1884); William Dean Howells's *The Rise of Silas Lapham* (1885). Frank Norris's *The Octopus* (1901), and Theodore Dreiser's *Sister Carrie* (1900). In the twentieth century novels turn more psychological and philosophical with writers such as James Joyce, e.g., Joyce's *Ulysses* (1922) deals with the events of a single day in Dublin presented with stream-of-consciousness technique. D.H. Lawrence presented vividly the Oedipus complex in *Sons and Lovers* (1913) with autobiographical elements in it. Other noteworthy novels include Joseph Conrad's *Lord Jim* (1900); Virginia Woolf's *To the Lighthouse* (1927); E.M. Forster's *A Passage to India* (1924); Evelyn Waugh's *A Handful of Dust* (1934); Joyce Cary's *The Horse's Mouth* (1944); Kingsley Amis's *Lucky Jim* (1954); Iris Murdoch's *A Severed Head* (1961); Graham Greene's *The Power and the Glory* (1940), etc. Other novelists of the modern times include names such as James Aldridge, Lawrence Durrell, Angus Wilson, William Golding, William Sansom, John Wain, Muriel Spark, John Braine, Brooke-Rose, Anthony Burgess, V.S. Naipaul, and Margaret Drabble. Prominent American novelists of the twentieth century are Upton Sinclair (*The Jungle,* 1906); Theodore Dreiser (*An American Tragedy,* 1925); John Dos Passos (*U.S.A.,* collected in 1938); James T. Farrell (*Studs Lonigan: A Trilogy,* 1935); John Steinbeck (*The Grapes of Wrath,* 1939); Richard Wright (*Native Son,* 1940); F. Scott Fitzgerald (*The Great Gatsby* 1925); Ernest Hemingway (*The Sun Also Rises,* 1926); Thomas Wolfe (*Look Homeward, Angel,* 1929), Nathaniel West (*The Day of the Locust,* 1939); William Faulkner (*The Sound and the Fury,* 1929);

Katherine Anne Porter (*Noon Wine,* 1937); Robert Penn Warren (*All the King's Men,* 1946); William Styron (*Lie Down in Darkness,* 1951); Eudora Welty (*The Ponder Heart,* 1954); Norman Mailer (*The Naked and the Dead,* 1948); Saul Bellow (*The Adventures of Augie March,* 1953); Bernard Malamud (*The Assistant,* 1957); Joseph Heller (*Catch-22,* 1961); Philip Roth (*Goodbye, Columbus,* 1959); Ralph Ellison (*Invisible Man,* 1952); James Baldwin (*Go Tell It on the Mountain,* 1953); Nathaniel West (*Miss Lonelyhearts,* 1933); Thomas Pynchon (*V.*, 1963); John Barth (*Giles Goat-Boy,* 1966) Kurt Vonnegut, Jr. (*Slaughterhouse-Five,* 1969); John Updike (the four *Rabbit* novels, 1960-1990); Joyce Carol Oates (*A Garden of Earthly Delights,* 1967); Toni Morrison (*Song of Solomon,* 1977), etc. Indian and Commonwealth novels have made a mark in English literature. Popular Indian novels include Mulk Raj Anand's *Coolie* (1933), *Untouchable* (19350; R.K. Narayan's *Swamy and Friends* (1935), *The Guide* (1959); Raja Rao's *Kanthapura* (1938), *The Serpent and the Rope* (1960) and the like. Other popular Indian novelists are G.V. Desani, M. Ananthanarayanan, Bhabani Bhattacharya, Manohar Malgonkar, Anita Desai, Khushwant Singh, Arun Joshi, Kamala Markandaya, Nayantara Sahgal, Salman Rushdie, Vikram Seth, Sashi Tharoor, Amitav Gosh, Vikram Chandra, Shobha De, Rohinton Mistry, Arundhati Roy, Manjula Padmanabhan, Kiran Desai, and Jhumpa Lahiri. Some of the Commonwealth novelists are Chinua Achebe, Wole Soyinka, James Ngugi, Cyprian Ekwensi, Alan Paton, Joseph Furphy, Patrick White, Henry Kingsley, Jane Mander Katherine Mansfield, Frank Sargeson, Morley Callaghan, Hugh MacLennan and others (*see* Introduction to the book).

Novel in verse refers to fiction written in verse. It is not a clearly defined genre. Some examples include Arthur Hugh Clough's *Amours de Voyage* (1858), a short epistolary novel; David Jone's *In Parenthesis* recounts the First World War in verse and prose; Vikram Seth's *The Golden Gate* (1986) is a novel in sonnet form.

Novel of manners is similar to the comedy of manners. It refers to novels that deal with customs, practices and idiosyncrasies of a particular society in a comical and satirical manner. Novelists in this genre include Henry Fielding, Jane Austen and Henry James.

Novel of sensibility is a form of novel that presented social sensibility since the middle of the eighteenth century (*see* Sentimental novel).

Novel of the soil is a sociological novel which depicts man's struggle against the forces of nature. Works in this genre include D.H. Lawrence's *The Rainbow* (1915), Ellen Glasgow's *Barren Ground* (1925), John Steinbeck's *Grapes of Wrath* (1939), Patrick White's *The Tree of Man* (1956), and Kamala Markandaya's *Nectar in a Sieve*. Kamala Markandaya in *Nectar in a Sieve* depicts rural India with the struggle and tragedy of the Indian peasants, Rukmani and her husband Nathan. They are victims of nature as their crops fail due to drought or flood.

Novelette is a work of fiction longer than a short story and shorter than a novel, e.g., Hemingway's *The Old Man and the Sea.*

Novella is a short fictional prose narrative which can be moral, satiric and usually realistic. It is longer than a short story and shorter than a novel. Originally the term is derived from Italian 'novella' and French 'nouvelle' referring to short tales since fourteenth century such as Boccacio's *Decameron* (1471) and Tomassa Guardati's *Novellino* (1467). Chaucer's *Canterbury Tales* is considered a series of novellas. In the modern context novella is a long short story, e.g., Joseph Conrad's *Heart of Darkness;* Henry James's *The Aspern Papers*. Hemingway's *The Old Man and the Sea* is considered a parable-novella.

Novelle refers to a German prose narrative shorter than a novel with a single incident that is strange yet factual.

O

Objective correlative is a term coined by T.S. Eliot to explain how emotions can best be expressed in poetry and drama. In his essay "Hamlet and His Problem" he says that emotion cannot directly be transmitted from the poet to the reader but has to be objectified into something suggestive of it. In this way the object evokes the same emotion in the reader. "The emotion and the object should become indissolubly one within the structure of the poem or the drama, so that the one spontaneously evokes the other." According to him *Hamlet* has been an artistic failure as Hamlet's complex emotions have not been properly objectified. In his opinion, "The only way of expressing emotion in the form of art is by finding an 'objective correlative'; in other words, a set of objects, a situation, a chain of events which shall be the formula of the particular emotion; such that when the external facts, which must terminate the sensory experience, as given, the emotion is immediately evoked." Eliot give the example of Lady Macbeth's sleep walk as an example of objective correlative. It communicates her state of mind by "a skilful accumulation of imagined sensory impressions; the words of Macbeth on hearing his wife's death strikes us as if, given the sequence of events, these words were automatically released by the last event in the series. The artistic 'inevitability' lies in this complete adequacy of the external to the emotion." The term describes poetry that is pure image.

Objectivity is the quality of presenting characters and plot in a literary work free from one's personal sentiments. It comes in contrast to subjectivity in which personal opinion of the author is of prime importance. Henry James is very objective in his novels keeping the aesthetic distance from the characters and situations. Ernest Hemingway is known for presenting objectively his characters and plots. In *The Old Man and the Sea* he presents objectively his old man Santiago, a certain Gregorio Fuentes who was a Cuban fisherman and friend of Hemingway. While describing the old man Hemingway presents it very objectively: "The old man was thin and gaunt with deep wrinkles in the back of his neck....The blotches ran well down the sides of his face and his hands had the deep-creased scars from handling heavy fish on the cords. But none of these scars were fresh. They were as old as erosions in a fishless desert. Everything about him was old except his eyes and that were the same colour as the sea and were cheerful and undefeated." This Hemingway's old man died on January 13, 2002 at the ripe old age of 104 at Cojimar, Cuba (*see* Subjectivity).

Occupatio is a literary device by which an author pretends to pass something casually thereby giving emphasis to it. Chaucer repeatedly used this technique in his *Canterbury Tales*.

Oratory refers to the art of public speaking which was taught in classical rhetoric.

Oeuvre in French means 'work' and is used to refer to all the works of an author.

Objective narrative (*see* Objectivity).

Officialese refers to pompous and circumlocutory language used in official circles by bureaucrats, politicians and officials. Such a language uses jargons and technical terms to a great extent. The term was first used by Sir Ernest Gowers in his *Plain Words* (1948).

Omnipresent narrator is a narrator who is present in scenes and events at different places at the same time. Such a narrator need not be omniscient.

Omniscient narrator is a narrator who is all knowing. It is a common device in third person narratives by which the narrator presents external events and internal thoughts and emotions of all the characters. Such a narrator is Godlike in being able to present simultaneously events taking place at different times and places. He/she is able to interpret events, actions and thoughts and turn the theme of the story to his/her point of view. The technique is used by writers such as Fielding in *Tom Jones*, Thackeray in *Vanity Fair*, George Eliot in *Adam Bede*, and Dickens in *A Tale of Two Cities*.

Omnibus edition is a one volume edition containing all the works of an author.

Onomatopoeia is the imitation of natural sounds by words, e.g., "the *bubbling* water", "the *cackling* hen", "the *hissing* snake", and "the *grinding* mill." The actual sounds of the words suggest their meaning, e.g., "The bees are buzzing and humming with great zest: the doves are cooing; and the children chatter as they clatter downstairs to come and dabble in the cool stream." Tennyson employs the device in *The Charge of the Light Brigade*—Cannon in front of them Volley' and thunder'd.

Oral tradition or **Word of mouth** is passing on from generation to generation personal and cultural history through songs, chants, proverbs and stories.

Op. cit. is the abbreviation of the Latin phrase *opere citato* meaning 'in the work cited'. It is used to refer to references previously referred to.

Organic form is a term used in literature in contrast to the mechanical. It refer to 'life and growth'. It is based on Coleridge's conception of imagination and fancy. The term organic is used for literary works that continue to evolve due to their vitality. Like a living organism a work grows from a seminal concept. For example, Shakespeare as a dramatist followed the organic form in his works while Racine followed strict rules in his works. Again a 'farce' is mechanical as it is fixed and conventional in form.

Oral literature consists of literature passed on from generation to generation by word of mouth. It is common among less literate cultures and ethnic groups. Such literature consists of folktales, ballads, and proverbs. These are transmitted by memorising through repetition with traditional phrases. In course of time some of these get written down as, for example, the early version of *Iliad* existed in oral tradition.

Order of plot refers to the manner in which events or episodes occur in a plot. In some plots there is perfect chronological progression of episode or events leading one to the other. This is often the case with short stories, while in a novel due to its lengthy nature the chronological order can easily be broken with more flexible and loose stringing of events or episodes. Some novelists break the chronological sequence for greater emphasis like Hemingway who begins some stories in the middle of things. Flashback is a device used by novelists to break chronological progression (*see* flashback).

Originality is the quality an author possesses by which he/she introduces spontaneously novelty and innovations in his/her writing based on some organic principle. However, according to T.S. Eliot "that which is absolutely original is absolutely bad." He held the view that every writer is dependent on the past traditions. Originality consists of reshaping of the materials held in common and bringing these into relation with something new in the writer's own time. In *Tradition and the Individual Talent,* he writes : " ... the historical sense involves a perception, not only of the pastness of the past, but of its presence; the historical sense compels a man to write not merely with his own generation in his bones.... No poet, no artist of any art, has his complete meaning alone.

His significance, his appreciation is the appreciation of the relation to the dead poets and artists. You cannot value him alone; you must set him, for contrast and comparison, among the dead...what happens when a new work of art is created is something that happens simultaneously to all the works of art which preceded it..." Originality according to Scott "consists in the mode of treating a subject."

Oxford movement or **Tractarian movement** is an intellectual movement within the Church of England in the nineteenth century led by Newman, Keble, Pusey and Froude. They ushered in a fresh thinking in England and gave vitality to the English Church through their influence over the Romantic poetry. The Church needed to be made more aware of the need for integrating theology and poetry. Newman was trying to collect the fragments of the world, the man, the religion and the arts, rendered so by the tides of Science, Rationalism, Scepticism and Secularism. He tried to unify the fragments both religiously and aesthetically as he was convinced of the relationship between art and religion. Keble too formulated his views on poetry as something noble as it is inspired by God. He was able to show that Romantic poets helped bring about a Christian religious revival, stressing the sacramental unity of the world. Both Keble and Newman found close relationship between art and religion. Newman wrote about poetry leading man through a kind of contemplative experience.

The Oxford Movement came as a reaction to the insipid and superficial religious teaching and literature of the previous age. The basic force behind the movement was of aesthetic and religious nature. But for them art was subservient to religion. Poetry, for them, is one of the available means at the disposal of man to reach out to God in prayer. For Newman, Protestantism had become very unpoetical in spirit. There was absolutely no imagination in matters of revelation. Newman had an aesthetic view of religion and the Catholic Church. The movement began in 1833 to restore the authority of the Catholicity of the English Church. Newman had become a Roman Catholic in 1845. To counter the onslaught of Roman Catholicism, the High Churchmen (Anglo-Catholics) gathered around Dr. Pusey in defence of the Anglican 'middle way'.

Oxymoron is a combination of two seemingly contradictory words forming often into a pithy paradox, e.g., 'dead alive', 'loving hate', 'waking sleep', 'fair storms', freezing fires,' "Feather of lead, bright smoke, cold fire, sick health" (*Romeo and Juliet* : Shakespeare). Though Oxymoron is usually used in poetry, it is also employed in prose.

P

Palilogy is a rhetorical device by which a word or phrases are repeated for emphasis.

Palimpsest is a method of manuscript writing common in the Middle ages before paper became common. By this device writing was done on a surface after erasing the earlier manuscript. The term is applied to literary works with different layers of meaning.

Pamphlet is a word derived from a Latin poem *Pamphilus seu de Amore* of the twelfth century. It is an unbound but stitched booklet of about 5,000 to 10,000 words written on a particular topic like a treatise or a tract. Usually a pamphlet is written on a controversial subject of the day such as political, religious or polemical topics. It became popular during the Reformation as well as the sixteenth century. The first political pamphlet in England is J. Knox's *First Blast of the Trumpet against the Monstrous Regiment of Women* (1588). Prominent English writers of this genre include Sir Thomas More, Tyndale, Dekker, Milton and Swift.

Panoramic method is a method in fiction by which the author is able to have an omniscient view of things.

Parable is a short moralistic narrative with characters that are usually human beings. It is a dramatic allegory which invites the audience to set the story in comparison with another set of events. The parables of Jesus in the New testament are often set to parable plays such as : the parables of the Good Samaritan, Prodigal Son, Sower, Pearl, Lamp, Lost Coin, Mustard Seed and the like. The parable of the mustard seed reads: "The kingdom of heaven is like to a grain of mustard seed, which a man took, and sowed in his field: Which indeed is the least of all seeds: but when it is grown, it is the greatest among herbs, and becometh a tree, so that the birds of the air come and lodge in the branches thereof" (Mt:14:31-32). John Steinbeck's *The Pearl* (1948) is a prose parable of about a Mexican fisherman who gets a pearl and brings misery and evil to his family. Hemingway's *The Old Man and the Sea* (1952) is considered a parable of human courage and struggle with the natural forces as depicted in the courage and endurance of Santiago who battles with a great catch of a Marlin after 84 unlucky days.

Paradox is that which is apparently absurd and self-contradictory but is essentially true. Just as a pun is a form of ambiguity that plays on words, a paradox plays on ideas. Paradoxes have been known since the time of the Greek philosopher Zeno (5th century BC). Many paradoxes are based on false premises. Semantic paradox is based on the structure of language and is used as a rhetorical device. They are unexpected and initially inexplicable. Paradoxes call for efforts at understanding and if the effort is successful it is delightful to the reader. Paradoxes call for the reader's intellectual participation in the creation of a literary meaning. In general, a paradox involves a contradiction between the physical or material meaning of words and their spiritual, emotional, or supernatural connotation. In drama, paradox can have a serious or comic effect. For example, Brecht in his *Mother Courage* uses paradoxes to give alienation effect. Mother Courage explains her own name paradoxically: "They call me Mother Courage cause I was afraid I'd be ruined." American critic Cleanth Brooks explores the uses of paradoxes in his *The Well Wrought Urn* (1947). He was inspired by the writings of T.S. Eliot on the metaphysical poets and their use of paradoxes. Eliot's

Murder in the Cathedral and *The Cocktail Party* are excellent in presenting paradoxical situations. Both these plays present the paradox of Christian suffering and salvation. G.K. Chesterton is excellent in his use of paradoxes in arousing humour in his writings, e.g., "Truth makes the greatest libel" (Hazlitt "On Wit and Humour"); "Nothing is so much to be feared as fear. Atheism may comparatively be popular with God himself" (Thoreau).

Paragraph is a unit of a piece of writing consisting of a short passage which conveys a particular point in the composition.

Paralipomena is a Greek word signifying 'things omitted'. It refers to items left out from the main body of a work but included in the appendix.

Parallelism is a device in literature by which a balance in structure and sense is maintained among sentences or phrases which as placed beside one another. It is found especially in poetry of the oral tradition and incantatory prose. Among those who used it in their works include Langland, D.H. Lawrence, Walt Whitman and T.S. Eliot. Hebrew poetry uses the device as in the following example from the Book of Isaiah 41:17-18.

"When the poor and needy seek water, and there is none, and their tongue faileth for thirst, I the Lord will hear them, I the God of Israel will not forsake them."

"I will open rivers in high places, and fountains in the midst of the valleys: I will make the wilderness a pool of water, and the dry land springs of water."

Parody is a burlesque in comic imitation of a literary work. By it a composition ridicules another by imitating and exaggerating its content, structure and style. It is a kind of satirical mimicry. A parody has to have close resemblance to the original and distorts it creatively. In a parody a light theme is treated in the style of a serious work, e.g., Cervantes' *Don Quixote* is a parody of the chivalric romances of his time. Chaucer in "The Nun's Priest's Tale" parodies Master Reynard the fox in the widow's barnyard by describing it in a very lofty language and comparing it to the fall of Troy. In English those who have written parody include Alexander Pope, Jonathan Swift, William Thackeray, James Joyce, Max Beerbohm, and Ogden Nash. In drama parody began with the satyr play and old comedy. Aristophanes's *Frogs* (405 BC) is a parody of the style of Aeschylus and Euripides. Shakespeare parodied some of the writers of his time in his *Love's Labour's Lost.*

Passim is a Latin word used to mean 'everywhere or throughout' and is used in footnotes for materials occurring at several places.

Pastiche derived from Italian meaning 'paste' refers to a kind of literary imitation by which passages or phrases from different authors, sources or from several works of an author is put together. Such a presentation of fragments put together and creates the effect of a parody.

Pastoral is linked to poetry, drama, comedy or fiction that share the conventional pastoral background of shepherds in their rural life. Pastoral convention depicts the innocence of shepherds in their rural world. Following a specific literary convention, pastoral poems can be found as love lyrics, dramatic works and elegies. Classical pastoral poetry originated from the folk songs and ceremonies that honoured the pastoral gods. The first pastoral poems were the *Idylls* written by the Greek poet Theocritus in the third century BC. Later in the second century BC Bion and Moschus wrote pastoral poems. Virgil wrote his *Bucolics* (37 BC) in Latin in imitation of Theocritus. Petrarch (1304-74) and Giovanni Boccaccio (1313-75) wrote eclogues (short pastoral poems) in Latin. These were dialogues between simple shepherds in rustic surroundings expressing moral or philosophical viewpoints. Politian (1454-94) wrote *Orfeo,* one of the earliest dramatic pastorals in Italian. In England Edmund Spenser wrote *The Shepheardes Calendar* in 12 pastoral eclogues

(1579). This was a model in England and the pastoral spirit influenced other forms of English literature. In drama pastoral spirit is found in *The Arraignment of Paris* (1581?) by George Peele and *Sad Shepherd* (1641) by Ben Jonson. *Arcadia* (1590) of Sir Philip Sidney is a pastoral romance. Lodge, Greene, Thomas Campion, Robert Herrick, Andrew Marvell and others wrote pastoral lyrics, songs and madrigals. William Shakespeare also used the pastoral convention in *As You Like It* (1600). Moschus (150 BC) wrote his pastoral elegy *Lament for Bion*. This influenced Milton's pastoral elegy *Lycidas* (1637), Shelley's *Adonais* (1821) and Arnold's *Thyrsis* (1866). William Empson in *Some Versions of Pastoral* refers to pastoral as any work associated with simple life such as that of a child, a shepherd or a working man. Hence, the term is applied to fiction as well like the proletarian novel. The Wessex novels of Thomas Hardy are pastoral in nature showing his love and observation of the natural world. In *The Mayor of Casterbridge* he observes: "When Elizabeth Jane opened the hinged casement next morning the mellow air brought in the feel of imminent autumn almost as distinctly as if she had been in the remotest hamlet. Casterbridge was the complement of the rural life around; not in its urban opposite. Bees and butterflies in the cornfields at the top of the town, who desired to get to the meads at the bottom, took no circuitous course, but flew straight down High Street without any apparent consciousness that they were traversing strange latitudes. And in autumn airy spheres of thistledown floated into the same street, lodged upon the shop fronts, blew into drains, and innumerable tawny and yellow leaves skimmed along the pavement, and stole through people's doorways into their passages with a hesitating scratch on the floor, like the skirt of timid visitors."

Patavinity refers to a provincial style of dialect in writing. The word is derived from Patavium, the birthplace of the historian Livy who used provincial expressions in his writings.

Pataphysics is a mock philosophical system of Alfred Jarry (1873-1907) known as the Science of Imaginary Solutions. It was a metaphysics of nonsense devoid of any reason. In his novel *Gestes et Opinions du Docteur Faustroll* he presented a parody of logic, language and learning. His absurd philosophy is considered main source of the Theatre of the Absurd.

Pathos is a Greek term signifying 'feeling' or 'suffering' and is used to signify the suffering of the protagonist in classical tragedy due to certain forces out of his control. This evokes feeling of pity in the reader or the spectator, e.g., In *Prometheus Unbound*, Aeschylus presents the suffering of Prometheus who is punished for defending humans. He is chained on a rock and agonises in pain. This arouses pity and compassion in the audience which is a quality of the drama. Hegel distinguished between 'objective' and 'subjective' pathos. Objective pathos aimed at activity while subjective pathos led to passivity.

Pathopoeia is derived from Greek meaning 'arousing feeling.' It refers to any passage or scene that arouses the feelings of the audience or reader.

Pause is a device used in prose fiction to allow some reflection on the part of the reader. In poetry it is marked by *caesura* and in drama it is marked by silence.

Periods of English Literature is classified differently by historians. Given below is a general division for easy reference.

650 to 1066	: Old English or Anglo-Saxon Period
1066 to 1400	: Middle English Period
1350 to 1450	: Age of Chaucer
1450 to 1550	: Chaucer to Spenser
1500 to 1660	: In general is called the Renaissance comprising different ages according to the reigning monarchs or major literary figures.

1550 to 1600		Elizabethan age or Age of Spenser
1600 to 1625		Jacobean age or Age of Shakespeare
1625 to 1649		Caroline age or Age of Milton (1625-60)
1649 to 1660		Commonwealth Puritan period
1660 to 1798	:	Neoclassical period
1660 to 1700		The Restoration or Age of Dryden
1700 to 1745		The Augustan Age or Age of Pope
1745 to 1798		The Age of Transition or Age of Johnson
1798 to 1832	:	Romanticism
1832 to 1901	:	The Victorian Period
1901 to 1914	:	The Edwardian Period
1901 to 1936	:	The Georgian Period
1914 to 1950	:	Modern Period
1950 -	:	Postmodern Period

Penny dreadful is a term to indicate cheap novels worth a penny and with sensational appeal. Such popular novels dealt with crime or adventures. These consisted of the melodramatic and thriller stories that were very popular in the nineteenth century. Though they kept to conventional morality, the incidents narrated were shocking and hair-raising with vulgar expressions. It is like the dime novels in America (*see* Dime novel).

Pensee is derived from French meaning 'thought'. In literature it refers to a thought put into writing which can be either in the form of a maxim or a lengthier exposition of a few pages. The most noted writer of pensee is Blaise Pascal (1623-62) who is known for his posthumously published *Pensees* (1670) in defence of Christianity. There are about a thousand of his *Pensees*, e.g., "Had Cleopatra's nose been shorter, the whole history of the world would have been different" (*Pensees*, 2, 162); "The heart has its reasons which reason does not know" (*Pensees*, 4, 277). Those who wrote pensees in English include Ben Jonson, George Savile, Marques of Halifax, T.E. Hulme and Cyril Connolly.

Pentateuch in Greek means 'containing five books' and is applied to the first five books of the *Holy Bible,* namely, *Genesis, Exodus, Leviticus, Numbers and Deuteronomy.* Genesis means 'origin' and it recounts the creation of the universe, the origin of mankind, sin of mankind and its consequences. *Genesis* opens thus: "In the beginning God created the heaven and the earth. And the earth was without form, and void; and darkness was upon the face of the deep. And the Spirit of God moved upon the face of the waters. And God said, Let there be light: and there was light" (*Genesis* 1:1-3). Exodus means 'departure' and describes the story of the people of Israel and their departure from Egypt. It deals with their journey to Mount Sinai and God's covenant with them. *Leviticus* is a book of regulations concerning worship and religious ceremonies. The book of *Numbers* is the story of the people of Israel of about 40 years from the time they left Mount Sinai until the time they reached the promised land. The book of *Deuteronomy* consists of the exhortations of Moses after their journey in the wilderness before entering the land of Canaan.

Period is a term used in the history of literature for a convenient and arbitrary division of historical times. We may thus distinguish different periods of English literature such as Ranaissance, Restoration, Augustan, Romantic, Victorian, Modern, Postmodern, etc. Each period is marked by its specific characteristics such as Renaissance is known for creative arts; Augustan for its neoclassical styles; Romantic with its stress on emotions and imagination and the like (*see* Periods of English literature)

Periodical is a journal or magazine published at regular intervals. It could be a weekly, fortnightly, monthly or quarterly. It had its origin from the mid-seventeenth century. The *Mercurius Librarius* (1668-1711) was the first periodical. The *Athenian Mercury* (1690-97) and the *Gentleman's Journal* (1692-94) followed in this genre and were forerunners of the *Spectator* (1711-12). Addison and Steele established *Tatler* (1709-11), the *Spectator* (1711-12) and the *Guardian* (1713). Other well known periodicals include *Gentleman's Magazine* (1731-1907), *Analytical Review* (1788-990, *Blackwood's Magazine* (1817-1980), *London Magazine* (1820-90, *Bentley's Miscellany* (1837-69), *Monthly Review* (1900-7), *London Mercury* (1919-39). The *Scots* (1739-1817), *The Oxford* (1768-82), *The European* (1782-1826), *The Museum* (1746-7), the *Monthly Review* (1749-1845), the *Critical Review* (1756-1817), *London Review* (1775-80), the *British Critic* (1793-1843), *Edinburgh Review* (1802-1929), the *Quarterly Review* (1809-1967). Noted nineteenth century periodicals are *London Quarterly Review, London Magazine, Dublin University Magazine, The Athenaeum, Saturday Review, Fraser's Magazine, The Cornhill Magazine, The Examiner, The Speaker, Truth Week-End Review, New Statesman, New Age, Times Literary Supplement, T.P.'s Weekly, G.K.'s Weekly, Horizon, Encounter,* etc.

Periphrasis is derived from Greek meaning 'roundabout speech' and refers to circumlocution by which something is said in a roundabout manner having recourse to several long words instead of simple and direct expressions, e.g., The penultimate month of the year = November; the fair sex = women; one's better half = wife, etc. Periphrasis is used in verbose and pompous expressions by politicians, lawyers, officials and others. Such expressions occur due to slack thinking or are used for comic effect. At times periphrasis is the result of propriety and poetic decorum.

Peroration is the concluding section of an oration or a written argument. It recapitulates the main ideas contained in the oration of arguments to impress the audience or the readers. It was a literary device used by Greek and Roman orators as well as some statesmen and writers in the eighteenth and nineteenth centuries such as Macaulay, Samuel Johnson and Edward Gibbon. For example, Samuel Johnson concludes his section on Dryden and Pope in *The Lives of the Poets* : "Of genius, that power which constitutes a poet; that quality without which judgment is cold, and knowledge is inert; that energy which collects, combines, amplifies, and animates; the superiority must, with some hesitation, be allowed to Dryden. It is not to be inferred that of this poetical vigour Pope had only a little, because Dryden had more; for every other writer since Milton must give place to Pope; and even of Dryden it must be said, that, if he has brighter paragraphs, he has not better poems. Dryden's performances were always hasty, either excited by some external occasion, or extorted by domestic necessity; he composed without consideration, and published without correction.... If the flights of Dryden therefore are higher, Pope continues longer on the wing. If of Dryden's fire the blaze is brighter, of Pope's the heat is more regular and constant. Dryden often surpasses expectation, and Pope never falls below it. Dryden is read with frequent astonishment, and Pope with perpetual delight."

Persona is derived from Latin meaning 'mask' and refers to a character in a poem, drama or fictional narrative who has a masked identity. It is the creation of the author through whom he speaks in the narrative. It should not be mistaken for the writer as he or she can make use of many personas in a work. Such a persona can be the narrator or the "I" in a first person narration. Personas give unity to a work. Examples: Milton's first person narrator in *Paradise Lost*; the narrator in Pope's *Epistle to Dr. Arbuthnot*; the Duke in Browning's "My Last Duchess"; the narrator in Salinger's *The Catcher in the Rye*; narrator in Fielding's *Tom Jones*; Gulliver in Swift's *Gulliver's Travels*; the narrator in Virginia Woolf's *Orlando*; Lockwood who narrates the story in Emily Bronte's *Wuthering Heights,* etc. There is a distinction between fictional characters as in Browning's "Last Duchess" or Swift's *Gulliver's Travels* and narrators closer to the author in Pope's *Epistle to Dr. Arbuthnot* or Pip in Dickens's *Great Expectations.* However, many modern critics are of the view that any speaker in a literary work may be considered persona. Pip narrates his story in *Great Expectations*: "My father's family name being Pirrip, and my Christian name Philip, my infant tongue could make of both names nothing longer or more explicit than Pip. So I called myself Pip, and came to be called Pip" (*see* Implied author).

Personal essay is a prose composition which presents an author's personal ideas and expressions. It is informal and is written in a familiar, humorous form.

Personification is a figure of speech in which inanimate objects or abstract ideas as represented as living beings.

How soon hath Time, the subtle thief of youth,
Stolen on his wing my three and twentieth year!

(Milton)

Personifications are used in common speech as well as in prose writing, e.g., "But the iniquity of oblivion blindly scattereth her poppy, and deals with the memory of men without distinction to merit perpetuity" (From Sir Thomas Browne's *Urn Burial*).

Philippic is a term associated with Demosthenes's (384-322 BC), one of the greatest orators of ancient Greece, who prepared powerful speeches against the Macedonian kings Philip II whom he saw as a threat to Greek city-states. In his orations known as *philippics* he made denunciations of Philip of Macedonia (382-336 BC) warning the Athenians about the Macedonian menace to their freedom. His First *Philippic* reads: " [1] If the question before us were a new one, men of Athens, I should have waited until most of the regular speakers had delivered their opinions, and if satisfied with any of their proposals, I should have remained silent, but if not satisfied, I should then have tried to express my own views. Since, however, it is our fortune to be still debating a point on which they have often spoken before, I can safely claim your indulgence if I am the first to rise and address you. For if in the past their advice had been sound, there would be no need for deliberation today. [2] Now in the first place, Athenians, there is no need to despair of our present position, however hopeless it may seem. For that which is worst in the days that are past and gone is just what affords the best assurance for the future. And what is that? It is that your affairs are in this evil plight just because you, men of Athens, utterly fail to do your duty; since surely, were you so placed in spite of every effort on your part, it would be hopeless to look for improvement" (*see* Invective).

Picaresque novel is derived from the Spanish 'picaro' (rogue). It deals with the life, adventures and escapades of a scoundrel. Influenced perhaps by Roman writer Petronius's *Saryricon* (c. AD 50), the picaresque novel originated in Spain in the sixteenth century with *Lazarillo de Tormes* (1553) by an anonymous author. It is an autobiography of a miller's son who steals a blind man's money by his wit and fraud. He is employed by many and finally becomes the town-crier of Toledo. Other popular Spanish picaresque novels include *Guzman de Alfarache* by Mateo Aleman and *La vida del Buscon* by Francisco Quevedo. Such novels are episodic with the hero or heroine from the low strata of society who is known for his/her wit, trickery and cunning. The picaro lives by his roguery than by honesty and hard work. The protagonist wanders from place to place and meets different classes of people. Such characters are flat as they do not grow. It consists of first person narration with satiric overtones. Fonger de Haan called such writings the autobiography of a *picaro* or a rogue. In form it became a satire upon the conditions and persons of the time as well. The term is understood today as Walter Allen opines "any novel in which the hero takes a journey whose course plunges him into all sorts, condition and classes of men." These novels constitute the confessions of a liar or a realistic portrayal of criminal's life. Thomas Nashe's *The Unfortunate traveller* or *The Life of Jack Wilton* (1594) introduced the genre in English. Other known picaresque novels include Daniel Defoe's *Moll Flanders* (1722), Fielding's *Tom Jones*

(1749), Smollett's *Roderick Random* (1748), Charles Dickens's *The Great Expectations* (1862), Mark Twain's *The Adventures of Huckleberry Finn* (1884), Saul Bellow's *Henderson the Rain King* (1959) and John Kennedy Toole's *A Confederacy of Dunces* (1980).

The first chapter of *The Adventures of Huckleberry Finn* reads: "You don't know about me, without you have read a book by the name of *The Adventures of Tom Sawyer*, but that ain't no matter. That book was made by Mr. Mark Twain, and he told the truth, mainly. There was things which he stretched, but mainly he told the truth. That is nothing. I never seen anybody but lied, one time or another, without it was Aunt Polly, or the widow, or maybe Mary. Aunt Polly— Tom's Aunt Polly, she is—and Mary, and the Widow Douglas, is all told about in that book—which is mostly a true book; with some stretchers, as I said before.

"Now the way that the book winds up, is this: Tom and me found the money that the robbers hid in the cave, and it made us rich. We got six thousand dollars apiece—all gold. It was an awful sight of money when it was piled up. Well, Judge Thatcher, he took it and put it out at interest, and it fetched us a dollar a day apiece, all the year round—more than a body could tell what to do with. The Widow Douglas, she took me for her son, and allowed she would civilize me; but it was rough living in the house all the time, considering how dismal regular and decent the widow was in all her ways; and so when I couldn't stand it no longer, I lit out. I got into my old rags, and my sugar-hogshead again, and was free and satisfied. But Tom Sawyer, he hunted me up and said he was going to start a band of robbers and I might join if I would go back to the widow and be respectable. So I went back."

Picaresque is derived from the Spanish *picaro* who is a scheming trickster. Based on such a character a kind of novel appeared in the sixteenth century known as 'picaresque' such as *Lazarillo de Tormes* (Anonymous) and Aleman's *Guzman* *de Alfarache*. These are stories of rogues who are depicted as servants of several masters. They continue their wily tricks and finally repent of their misdeed. In English such picaresque writings appear with Daniel Defoe's *Moll Flanders,* Henry Fielding's *Tom Jones,* Mark Twain's *Huckleberry Finn,* etc. Episodes in the life of such a *picaro* (rogue) has been turned into episodic plays, e.g., Dale Wasserman's *Man of La Mancha* is based Cervantes's *Don Quixote*; Roger Miller's musical play *Big River* is an adaptation of Mark Twain's *Huckleberry Finn.*

Plagiarism is a literary theft by which a writer copies the ideas of another and presents as his own.

Platitude is a routine type of statement which has come to be quite dull in exprĕssion. Some idioms and proverbs have become platitudes in course of time, e.g., "You can't have butter and jam on both sides...."

Pleonasm is derived from Greek meaning 'superfluity' and refers to redundant use of words in writing or speaking, e.g., '*In the modern scientific world of nowadays*' instead of '*In today's scientific world.*'

Plot is the pattern of events in a poem, drama or a work of fiction. The literary artist places the incidents and characters in such a way as to arouse the interest and curiosity of the readers and audience. An ideal plot arouses questions in the readers and audience regarding the past, present and the future: Why did it happen? Why does it happen now? What will happen next? Most plots develop due to a conflict which could be internal or external (*see* Conflict). Plot is the centre of Aristotle's discussion of tragedy in *Poetics*. His word 'mythos' is used for 'legend' or 'story' and is translated into 'Plot'. A plot according to him consists of a beginning, middle and end. 'Beginning' initiates action which looks forward to something else. 'Middle' presumes what has gone before. 'End' follows from what has gone before and requires nothing further. In Chapter V he speaks of plot as 'unified stories'.

In Chapter VI he calls plot 'the whole structure of the incidents,' and 'the soul of tragedy'. The end of tragedy is plot and it is not a mere arrangement of events. It is the way in which action proceeds. Aristotle gives more importance to plot than character. There is no tragedy without plot, but can be tragedy without character. A tragic plot should be whole and complete. It must have certain size (magnitude), neither too short nor long. It should be aesthetic and utilitarian. Plot should have a certain structure such as : Prologue, Episode, Exode, Parode (Choral song). A plot should have the elements of 'probability' and 'necessity'. The poet's concern is with the possible and not what has happened, but what might happen. A plot should follow unities of 'time', 'place', and 'action'. In the plot of a play characters come in conflict with rising action, crisis, climax, and falling action with resolution. The plot is something that the poet makes (*Poetics* Ch. IX); but with regard to a story it is immaterial if the poet makes it or not (*Poetics* Ch. XVII). When Aristotle says tragedy must have "a beginning, a middle and an end" he refers to the poet as a maker. The beginning and end are within the control of the poet. E.M. Forster in *Aspects of the Novel* defines the difference between story and plot. A story begins and ends arbitrarily as they are not governed by reason. The plot is something which the poet makes, e.g., The king died and then the queen died (story); The king died, then the queen died of grief (plot). A plot must have a meaning. The poet who makes the plot with a beginning and end has it within his control as he is the maker. "A beginning is that which is not itself necessarily after anything else" (Ch. VII). The emphasis is on the '*necessarily*' upon the logic of connection. But the poet may not have to refer to matters supposed to have happened earlier in the story. *King Oedipus* is a fine example. The play begins with the plague in Thebes and the need to release the city from it by discovery and the punishment of the guilty man. The play's process is the process of discovery; its end, the punishment. The initial situation of the plague, etc., is given immediately in dramatic terms. Each step Oedipus takes provides the occasion for revealing some part of the antecedent knowledge which is necessary for the process of discovery. The idea of wholeness of a plot is referred to when he says that it should be "with all the organic unity of a living creature" (Ch.XIII). Again the concept of order is brought out in Ch. VII : "...to be beautiful a living creature...and every whole made up of parts must present a certain order in its arrangement of parts." The idea of order, harmony, proportion and completeness are all present in the normal Greek idea of what is beautiful. But in fiction there are writers who do not subscribe to the traditional concept of a plot such as James Joyce, Graham Greene,` Michel Butor, Kafka, Arnold Bennett, Saul Bellow, V.S. Naipaul and others (*see* Sub-plot).

Poetic justice is a term coined by Thomas Rhymer (1641-1713) in his *book The Tragedies of the Last Age Considered* (1678) which critically attacked Elizabethan drama. He was of the view that evil ought to be punished and good rewarded. Hence, literature should reflect some moral purpose giving a sense of poetic justice. Poetic justice is done when the villain, while trying to kill the hero, is accidentally killed.

Point of view is the narrative method that establishes the angle from which the story is told in a fiction. It establishes the relationship between the narrator and the story. Points of view can be : (a) Omniscient, First person and Dramatic. (*see* Omniscient narrator, First person narrative, Dramatic narrator).

Polemic is a scathing written attack on political, philosophical or religious opinion. Known polemicists are Milton, Jonathan Swift, Cardinal Newman, H.D. Thoreau, Hilaire Belloc, G.K. Chesterton, etc., e.g., "People say to me, that it is but a dream to suppose that Christianity should regain the organic power in human society which once it possessed. I cannot help that; I never said it could. I am not a politician; I am proposing no measures, but exposing a fallacy, and resisting a pretence.

Let Benthamism reign, if men have no aspirations; but do not tell them to be romantic, and solace them with glory; do not attempt by philosophy what once was done by religion. The ascendancy of faith may be impracticable, but the reign of Knowledge is incomprehensible...." (*from* Cardinal Newman's *Secular Knowledge Not a Principle of Action*).

Polyphonic prose is a form of poetic prose attempted by American poet Amy Lowell (1874-1925) influenced by the *Balledes* of French poet Paul Fort. Such poetic prose is written like prose and is marked for its rhythm, rhyme, free verse, assonance and alliteration.

Polysyndeton is the repetition of conjunctions in poetry and prose. Often 'and' is used repeatedly by some authors like Hemingway, e.g., "A waiter wearing a blue apron came out with a bucket of water and a cloth, and commenced to tear down the notices, pulling the paper off in stripes and washing and rubbing away the paper that stuck to the stone" (*from* Hemingway's *The Sun Also Rises*).

Pop mythology is a method by which a writer creates his innovative text using materials from popular culture. William Seward Burroughs used the device in some of his novels such as *Junky* (1953), *The Wild Boys* (1971), *Ghosts of Chance* (1995) and the like.

Pornography is derived from Greek *porne* meaning *writing of prostitutes.* It was a practice in ancient times to hang an advertising sign outside a prostitute's home. Pornography in fiction refers to certain writings that arouse sexual excitement in readers through their coarse descriptions of sex. Pornography can be of two types *erotica* and *exotica. Erotica* concerns pure eroticism in which the writing concerns heterosexual love and sex, while *exotica* emphasises sexually perverse and abnormal activities leading to masochism, narcissism, sadism, fetishism and the like. Works such as Joyce's *Ulysses*, D.H. Lawrence's *Lady Chatterley's Lover,* and Durrell's *Black Book* have been considered pornographic.

Portmanteau word is a device by which two words are put together for humour. Colloquial speech has also helped in coining such words. James Joyce used such words in his novel *Finnegans Wake* such as *quitewhite, gigglesomes, waterloose.*

Postcolonialism is a term referring to the historical phase that many former colonies of the Europian empires have undergone. After their independence, many of the colonised Asian, African and Caribbean countries began to restore their cultures and national identity. In literature, the term is associated with the literatures of India, Canada, Australia, Ireland, Pakistan, New Zealand, Nigeria, Kenya, Jamaica, and other Commonwealth countries. It is a rapidly expanding discipline dealing with literary and cultural studies. Commonwealth literature is an antecedent of Postcolonial literature (*see* Commonwealth literature).

Postmodernism is a term applied to the twentieth century spirit of high modernism since 1950s with space research and communication revolution with Television and the visual media. In literature postmodernism deals with certain absurd and disconnected writings that have emerged since 1950. The Second World War brought about a division between modernism and postmodernism. The postmodern literature shook off the Victorian morality which continued till the end of the World War. People looked for a new cultural and moral independence. Crimes increased. Increased educational opportunities gave independence to youth. There is an increasing contempt of authority and revolt of the young demanding labour. Strong influence of journalism had its influence on literature too.

There is the 'Movement' in poetry, drama and fiction by 1956 as depicted in "The Angry Young Men". Rock'n roll music; the Skinheads and the punks had their impact on society. The 'Teddy Boys' culture prevailed among the working class youth who were riot makers in society. By the 1960s pop music became part and parcel of society. Television and film personalities drew attention of the public. There was a transformation in the moral attitudes and family life. In the postmodern period there is a marked loss of faith in the traditional positions leading to scepticism and perplexity. It was an era of dilemma and writers reflect the anger of the generation like John Osborne in *Look Back in Anger* (1956). The traditional values of family, patriotism and conformity to social manners looked absurd. Many characters in the novels of the period undergo torture as in Graham Greene's characters; John Fowles's *The Collector* (1963), *The French Lieutenant's Woman* (1969); and Iris Murdoch's *A Severed Head* (1961), *and An Accidental Man* (1971). Writers find it difficult to embody human values and a mood of perplexity runs through literature. The loss of family ties predominates the period as seen in Philip Larkin's *A Girl in Winter* (1957).

Postmodernism in novel deals with certain absurd and disconnected writings that have emerged since 1950. Postmodern novel makes use of myth and fantasy. Writers such as Angela Carter, V.S. Naipaul, and Salman Rushdie are unique in their fictional techniques. Angela Carter (1940-1992) in her much feminist writing makes use of magic realism and fantasy. Her prominent works are *Shadow Dance* (1965), *The Magic Toyshop* (1967), *Heroes and Villains* (1969), *Nights at the Circus* (1984), and *Wise Children* (1991). V.S. Naipaul (1932-) is another of the postmodernist who writes satirically about political violence, alienation and conflict of values in society. His novels are *A House for Mr. Biswas* (1961), *In a Free State* (1971), *Guerrillas* (1975), *A Bend in the River* (1979), and *A Way in the World* (1994). Salman Rushdie (1947-) writes in surrealist style and makes use of fantasy and magic realism in his fiction. Some of his novels are *Grimus* (1974), *Midnight's Children* (1981), *Shame* (1983), *The Satanic Verses* (1988), *The Moor's Last Sigh* (1995), and *The Ground Beneath Her Feet* (1999). Today we are in a new era of high-tech and communication super-highway ushered in by the cyber-revolution in computer networking and inter-netting which gives a new twist to postmodernism.

Potboiler refers to a work written and published purely for financial survival. Johnson wrote his novel *Rasselas* (1759) to pay his debts and the bills of his mother's funeral.

Power literature is a term associated with Thomas de Quincey (1785-1859) who in his essay *The Poetry of Pope* distinguished between literature of knowledge and literature of power. He writes : "What is it that we mean literature?.... There is, first, the Literature of knowledge; and secondly, the Literature of Power. The function of the first is – to teach; the function of the second is – to move; the first is a rudder; the second, an oar or a sail. The first speaks to the mere discursive understanding; the second speaks ultimately, it may happen, to the higher understanding or reason, but always through affections of pleasure and sympathy. Remotely, it may travel towards an object seated in what Lord Byron calls dry light; but proximately, it does and must operate—else it ceases to be Literature of Power – on and through that humid light which clothes itself in the mists and glittering iris of human passions, desires and genial emotions."

Preface is an introduction to a work of literature presenting the circumstances and motive of writing, e.g., Charles Dickens's preface to *A Tale of Two Cities* reads: "When I was acting, with my children and friends, in Mr. Wilkie Collins's drama of *The Frozen Deep,* I first conceived the main idea of this story. The strong desire was upon me then, to embody it in my own person; and I traced out in my fancy, the state of mind of which it would necessitate the presentation to an observant spectator, with particular care and interest.

"As the idea became familiar to me, it gradually shaped itself into its present form. Throughout its execution, it has had complete possession of me; I have so far verified what is done and suffered in these pages, as that I have certainly done and suffered it all myself.

"Whenever any reference (however slight) is made here to the condition of the French people before or during the revolution, it is truly made on the faith of the most trustworthy witnesses. It has been one of my hopes to add something to the popular and picturesque means of understanding that terrible time, though no one can hope to add anything to the philosophy of Mr. Carlyle's wonderful book."

Prelude is a short independent composition to a work. A work can also be developed out of a prelude. Wordsworth's *The Prelude* is an autobiographical poem on the growth of his poetic mind in 13 books. In fiction some writers have written preludes to their works, e.g., George Eliot wrote in her Prelude to *Middlemarch*: "Who that cares much to know the history of man, and how the mysterious mixture behaves under the varying experiments of Time, has not dwelt, at least briefly, on the life of Saint Theresa,... Theresa's passionate, ideal nature demanded an epic life: what were many-volumed romances of chivalry and the social conquests of a brilliant girl to her? Her flame quickly burned up that light fuel; and, fed from within, soared after some illimitable satisfaction, some object which would never justify weariness, which would reconcile self-despair with the rapturous consciousness of life beyond self. She found her epos in the reform of a religious order.... Some have felt that these blundering lives are due to the inconvenient indefiniteness with which the Supreme Power has fashioned the natures of women. ...Here and there is born a Saint Theresa, foundress of nothing, whose loving heart-beats and sobs after an unattained goodness tremble off and are dispersed among hindrances, instead of centring in some long-recognizable deed."

Primer is a prayer book for the laity in the medieval church before the Reformation. It consisted of prayers from the Breviary (Daily Prayer of the Church consisting of psalms and readings). After the Reformation it consisted of daily prayers for people taken from the *Book of Common Prayer*. Later from the eighteenth century the term came to be applied to the little prayer book for children.

Primitivism is an eighteenth century doctrine that believed in the cult of the noble savage. It believes in nature than culture as the best educator of man. Primitivism had its origin from the classical concept of the Golden Age. Horace in his writings had extolled the past and had a nostalgia for the primitive lifestyle. In the eighteenth century the doctrine emerged as a reaction to the rationalistic neoclassicism. It glorifies the past. Every period looks to an uncorrupted earlier time. For instance, the *Bible* refers to the lost paradise; *Iliad* speaks of the great warriors; Aristotle spoke of the past glory and simplicity of Athens, etc. Renaissance spirit is a return to the Greek and Roman past. Primitivism speaks of the noble savage living close to nature. He has not been corrupted by modern civilisation. Philosophers such as A.S. Cooper, the third Earl of Shaftsbury (1671 –1713) and Jean Jacques Rousseau (1712-78) were the proponents of the doctrine. Earl of Shatsbury argued that since God exists in nature, primitive people living in nature are closest to God. They are better than civilised men. Rousseau even went to the extend of preferring man 'walk on all fours' in his revolt against the evils of modern civilisation. Wordsworth's Romantic movement being a return to nature was a return to the noble savage in the form of peasants and children. Realism in American literature has similar sensibility. Primitivism can be of two types : Chronological or Cultural Primitivism. Chronological Primitivism considers the past better than the present, e.g., ancient feudal life better than modern industrial civilisation. Cultural Primitivism glorifies the natural and rejects the artificial. Primitivism in literature is found in Philip Sidney's *Arcadia*, Shakerpeare's *As You Like It,* Goldsmith's *The Deserted Village*, Rousseau's *Emile,* Wordsworth's poems, Coleridge's *Rime of the Ancient Mariner*, Melville's *Moby-Dick,* T.S. Eliot's *The Waste Land*, Yeats's poems, D.H. Lawrence's *The Rainbow*, Conrad's *Lord Jim*, Joyce's *Ulysses*, Faulkner's novels, Saul Bellow's *Henderson, The Rain King*, William Golding's *Lord of the Flies*, Patrick White's *Voss* and others.

Problem novel presents conflicts in an unjust society. Such novelists delve deep into the socio-political situations and project their political opinion. It is a kind of propaganda novel, e.g., *In Uncle Tom's Cabin or Life Among the Lowly* (1852), Harriet Beecher Stove powerfully brings out her anti-slavery views. It depicts the story of Uncle Tom who is a noble Christian black slave who is sold over and over again. In the Preface to *Uncle Tom's Cabin* Stowe writes: "The object of these sketches is to awaken sympathy and feeling for the African race, as they exist among us; to show their wrongs and sorrows, under a system so necessarily cruel and unjust as to defeat and do away the good effects of all that can be attempted for them, by their best friends, under it" (*see* Propaganda).

Proletarian novel is a kind of sociological fiction dealing with the working classes. This genre has often the purpose of propaganda and to highlight the poor economic and social conditions of the working class, e.g., Walter Greenwood's *Love on the Dole* (1933) (*see* Propaganda).

Proletarskaya kul'tura is a Russian term meaning 'proletarian culture'. It is abbreviated *proletkult*. It was a movement by a group of writers led by Bogdanov in 1917 who wanted to evolve a proletarian culture and art. It was a movement by proletarians for proletarians and would be free of all vestiges of bourgeois culture. Though the movement received support from the state, it was free from the control of the Communist Party. The *Proletkult* organised workshops and classes throughout the Soviet Union to teach the workers to take to reading and writing plays, novels, and poems. But the writers that emerged mostly wrote in imitation of their predecessors. In course of time Lenin found the futility of trying to force this new proletarian culture on the working classes. The movement was closed down in 1923.

Prologue is the opening section of a work. It is a forward which consists of a speech before the dramatic action begins in a play, presented by one of the actors. Sometimes prologues are found in novels as well. In Greek tragedy 'prologue' was an early action before the chorus made its entry. Euripides presented a monologue as a prologue to his plays. In the medieval drama a prologue was presented by the master of ceremonies. The practice continued during the Elizabethan and Restoration plays, e.g., The Prologue to Sheridan's *School for Scandal* was written by the great actor David Garrick and refers to scandal mongering. Chaucer has a General Prologue to his *Canterbury Tales* which describes the meeting of 29 pilgrims in the Tabard Inn on a pilgrimage to Canterbury:

When April with his showers sweet with fruit
The drought of March has pierced unto the root
And bathed each vein with liquor that has power
To generate therein and sire the flower; ...
Then do folk long to go on pilgrimage,
And palmers to go seeking out strange strands,
To distant shrines well known in sundry lands.
And specially from every shire's end

Of England they to Canterbury wend,
The holy blessed martyr there to seek
Who helped them when they lay so ill and weal
Befell that, in that season, on a day
In Southwark, at the Tabard, as I lay
Ready to start upon my pilgrimage...

(from *Prologue to the Canterbury Tales*)

Propaganda literature is meant to persuade people on public opinion concerning social, political, or religious issues. Writers in this genre include Bunyan, Charles Dickens, Bernard Shaw and others, e.g., *In Uncle Tom's Cabin or Life Among the Lowly* (1852), Harriet Beecher Stove powerfully brings out her anti-slavery views. Dickens in *David Copperfield* writes about the social injustice meted out to children: "I was born with a caul, which was advertised for sale, in the newspapers, at the low price of fifteen guineas. Whether sea-going people were short of money about that time, or were short of faith and preferred cork jackets, I don't know; all I know is, that there was but one solitary bidding, and that was from an attorney connected with the bill-broking business, who offered two pounds in cash, and the balance in sherry, but declined to be guaranteed from drowning on any higher bargain. Consequently, the advertisement was withdrawn at a dead loss for as to sherry, my poor dear mother's own sherry was in the market then and ten years afterwards the caul was put up in a raffle down in our part of the country, to fifty members at half a crown a head, the winner to spend five shillings. I was present myself, and I remember to have felt quite uncomfortable and confused, at a part of myself being disposed of in that way. The caul was won, I recollect, by an old lady..." (*see* Problem novel, Thesis novel).

Propriety in literature refers to good taste and correctness of expression. In the eighteenth century a writer was expected to write in an appropriate style in accordance with the subject matter and form.

Prose comes from Latin 'prosa' which means 'direct discourse'. It is plain statement of daily speech distinct from verse or poetry. It is the language of essays, short stories and novels. Prose is structured different from verse. Poetry is arranged in lines and stanzas while prose is structured in sentences and paragraphs. Prose writings can consist of description, dialogue, narrative and commentary. Prose styles vary from writer to writer. Prose can be classified into Narrative, Argumentative, Dramatic, Informative, and Contemplative types (*see* Narrative prose, Argumentative prose, Dramatic prose, Informative prose, and Contemplative prose).

Prose poem is a form of verse in prose form which originated in France in the nineteenth century. It employs free verse and is printed like prose without regular line break. It has elements of poetry such as images and figures of speech, rhythms, rhyme, assonance, consonance and internal rhyme. Prominent writers of prose poems include Aloysius Bertrand,

Baudelaire, Rimbaud, Oscar Wilde, Amy Lowell and T.S. Eliot.

Prose rhythm is as old as the ancient Greek Sophist Thrasymachus. Rhythm is derived from Greek meaning 'flow'. It is the measured flow of aural or visual movement consisting of beat, accent, rise and fall, etc. Rhythm is a basic feature of all the arts, particularly music, poetry, and dance. In prose rhythm gives a balance of sentences by an orderly arrangement of words. There was a kind of rhythm used in prose writing by the Greeks. Aristotle accepted the practice as a help to structural order of prose. He spoke of a paeonic pattern. It is a metrical foot made up of one long syllable and three short ones. In accordance with the position of the long syllable paeon is called first paeon (- u u u) , second paeon (u -u u), third paeon (uu - u) and fourth paeon (u u u-). Aristotle recommended for prose first and fourth paeon: first paeon is best at the beginning of a period and fourth paeon at the end. Cicero used cretic (- u -) and some variation of trochee (- u). Rhythm varies from language to language. French has a staccato (detached) rhythm while English has a legato (smooth) pattern. In English prose there is no tendency to restrict the rhythmic pattern. Monosyllabic nouns are stressed while other nouns are stressed according to the word rhythm. Adjectives and adverbs are usually stressed. Verbs are usually stressed except auxiliary verbs. Conjunctions and propositicns are unstressed unless they come in pairs or come at the end of a sentence. Pronouns are unstressed unless for emphasis. Prose is presented in a continuous flow until paragraphs breaks it. Mark the rhythm in the following passage from Katherine Mansfield.

\- - - - - - -

On the other side of the beach, close down to the water, two

\- - - - - - - - -

little boys, their knickers rolled up, twinkled like spiders. One

\- - - - - - -

was digging, the other pattered in and out of the water, filling a

\- -

small bucket.

Protagonist is the principal character of a literary work such as drama, novel or short story. The term is derived from 'protos' in Greek. In ancient Greek drama it meant 'first combatant' or 'the principal character' around whom the action revolves. In Greek tragedy characters were divided into Protagonist (first actor), Deuteragonist (second actor) and Tritagonist (third actor). The concept of the protagonist as first actor began with Thepsis in the sixth century B.C. Aeschylus and Sophocles added second and third actors. The conflict in the drama centres around the protagonist. Some literary works are named after the protagonist such as Shakespeare's *Macbeth, Othello, Hamlet, King Lear, Julius Caesar,* Hardy's *Tess of the D'Urbervilles*, Dickens's *David Copperfield,* etc.

Protest literature deals with social and political injustices. In the twentieth century there are several such works protesting the apartheid policy in South Africa. Solomon Tshekisho Plaatje, (1876-1932), in his *Native Life in South Africa* (1916) brings out reasons for black opposition to the Land Act in South Africa under the apartheid system. Alan Paton (1903-1988) is another South African writer and social reformer who took keen interest in the social and racial problems of his country. His novel, *Cry, the Beloved Country* (1948) presents the struggle of those caught up in the racial conflicts. His other novels *Too Late the Phalarope* (1953), *Ah, But Your Land Is Beautiful* (1982), also speak of racial tensions. *The Long View* (1968) is a non-fictional writing that condemns apartheid. South African Nobel laureate Nadine Gordimer (1923-) condemns rigid racial segregation in her novels such as *A World of Strangers* (1958), *Occasion for Loving* (1963), and *The Late Bourgeois World* (1966).

Proverb is derived from Greek 'paroimia' meaning a short pithy familiar saying expressing a supposed truth or moral lesson. It is common to most cultures, nations and peoples, e.g., "Charity begins at home," "Death pays all debts," "Easier said than done," "God sends fortune to fools," "History repeats itself." The Book of Proverbs in the *Bible* is a very popular collection of moral and religious teachings in the form of practical sayings of everyday concerns, e.g., " A fool does not care whether he understands a thing or not; all he wants to do is to show how clever he is," "Intelligent people are always eager and ready to learn," "Better to live on the roof than share the house with a nagging wife."

Pseudepigrapaha is a term to describe books with false title or authorship.

Pseudonym in Greek means false name. It is the pen-name taken by an author, e.g., Samuel Langhorne Clemens used the pseudonym Mark Twain. Mary Ann Evans took the name George Eliot. Works by such authors are called Pseudonymous literature.

Psychoanalysis is a system of psychology associated with Sigmund Freud (1856-1939) who developed psychoanalytic psychotherapy. His study of the neurotic ailments led him to evolve his theories of normal and abnormal minds. He made inroads into the study of human sexual instincts, interpretation of dreams, working of the unconscious mind, and repression. Freud spoke of the unconscious in man which is kept in repression. These unconscious thoughts, feelings and images can be kept as abstract concepts or images. Dreams can bring out some of these kept in the unconscious. Psychoanalysis deals with these unconscious part of mental life. Freud also refers to the 'pleasure principle' by which man avoids pain from childhood. Psychoanalysis states that human thoughts, feelings and impulses are unconsciously linked and can give clues to an individual's past and present. He divided the mental functions into the *id*, *the ego*, and *the superego*. The *id* is the instinctive and illogical drive which is unconscious, yet seeks pleasure principle. *Ego* is a stage between the *id* and external reality being partly unconscious and partly preconscious. It applies defence mechanisms in dangerous situations. The *ego* stage weighs situations by logical thinking and perception to be realistic. The *superego* deals with the individual's internalisation of social norms implanted by parents in the form of conscience, morals and ethics. This stage is partly unconscious and partly conscious. By defence mechanism the *ego* attempts to reconcile the *id* and the *superego* and reality. Freud is associated with terms such as Oedipus complex, death wish, penis envy, etc. D.H. Lawrence's *Sons and Lovers* is considered a novel on Oedipus complex.

Psychological novel focuses on the mental life of its characters with their emotions, feelings and motives. It concerns itself with character studies than with the development of plot and action. Psychoanalytical study by Freud has influenced modern novelists to look beyond the conscious to the unconscious. In such novels the characters speak in the first person or through letters. Richardson is considered the first psychological novelist with his *Clarissa*. George Eliot used a third person analysis of characters in her works. By the end of nineteenth century the omniscient narrator begins to disappear from fiction. Instead we find introspection by main characters in works like that of Henry James such as *The Portrait of a Lady, The Wings of the Dove, The Ambassadors.* In the twentieth century Stream of Consciousness and Interior Monologues in the novels of writers like James Joyce, Virginia Woolf, and William Faulkner make the psychological novels excel in 'soul studies.'

Pulitzer Prizes are a series of 21 awards for outstanding contributions in drama, music, letters, and journalism. It was established in 1917 by the will of Joseph Pulitzer, publisher of the *New York World.* His legacy of $ 2,000,000 to found the Columbia University School of Journalism and $ 500,000 of that amount to be given as annual prizes "for the encouragement of public service, public morals, American literature, and the advancement of education." Originally four categories of American literature, namely, novel, play, US history and American biography were given the award. The awards are given annually by Columbia University at the recommendation of the Pulitzer Prize Board. The Board appointed annually its juries for each of the categories.

Pun or **quibble** is a play on words that are alike in sound but different in meaning. It is a figure of speech used in humour, e.g., The *grave* man died and went to his *grave*. It is an ambiguous statement that is intended to be humorous. Puns get their effect by using one of the thousands of word pairs in English called homonyms that are identical in sound and spelling but differ in meaning, e.g., If a lady says : "I know nothing of labour", it can mean either 'pain of childbirth' or 'employment'. A pun that is sexually suggestive is called *double entendre* (A French expression meaning 'to understand in two ways').

Purple patch is verbose expressions in a passage which renders it ornate. The phrase was used by Horace in *Ars Poctica* "purpureus...panus" to refer to grandiloquent passages which are excessively figurative with heightened rhythm and diction. Purple passages are used in a disparaging manner. Walter Pater used such a language in his description of Mona Lisa in his essay on Leonardo da Vinci in *The Renaissance*.

Q

Quadrivium refers to the four branches of education in the mediaeval times. It consists of the four liberal arts belonging to mathematical sciences. These were arithmetic, geometry, astronomy and music. Education in the middle ages comprised seven liberal arts divided into the *quadrivium* and the *trivium*. The *trivium* comprised grammar, logic and rhetoric.

Quibble is a verbal device by which one evasively turns away from the point in question into irrelevant matters. This is done through puns, word play or petty conceits.

Quotation titles occur when certain books derive titles from a famous quotation. Titles thus given can be thought provoking for the readers. Thackeray's *Vanity Fair* is derived from Bunyan's *The Pilgrim's Progress*. Hardy's *Far From the Madding Crowd* is taken from Gray's Elegy *Written in a Country Churchyard*. Shakespeare's phrase "brave new world' in *The Tempest* V, i, 26 inspired Aldous Huxley's title of *Brave New World*. Hemingway's *For Whom the Bell Tolls* is taken from John Donne's *Meditation 17*. Graham Green's *The Power and the Glory* is derived from the Gospel of St. Mathew 6:13.

Quoted monologue is the opposite of an autonomous monologue. In it there is word for word quoting of a character's thoughts by the narrator. In *Wuthering Heights*

Emily Bronte lets her narrator present the quoted monologue of Heathcliff at the death of Catherine : "May she wake in torment!' he cried, with frightful vehemence, stamping his foot, and groaning in a sudden paroxysm of ungovernable passion. 'Why, she's a liar to the end! Where is she? Not there – not in heaven – not perished – where? Oh! You said you cared nothing for my sufferings! And I pray one prayer – I repeat it till my tongue stiffens – Catherine Earnshaw, may you not rest as long as I am living! You said I killed you – haunt me, then! The murdered do haunt their murderers. I believe – I know that ghosts have wandered on earth. Be with me always – take any form – drive me mad! only do not leave me in this abyss, where I cannot find you! Oh, God! it is unutterable! I cannot live without my life! I cannot live without my soul!"

R

Rabelaisian is derived from French writer Rabelais Francois (c. 1493-1553), who is known for his boisterous satirical humour. The term is applied to coarse humour with incredible and exaggerated writing. Rabelais emphasised sensual enjoyment of life and propagated Renaissance humanism. His popular works of satirical entertainment are *Pantagruel* (1532), the story of a young giant of great strength and appetites, and *La Vie très Horrificque du Grand Gargantua* (1534) *(The Very Frightful Life of the Grand Gargantua)*, the story of Pantagruel's father. Both these works are humorous social and political satires like Jonathan Swift's *Gulliver's Travels.* Rabelaisian influence is found in the work of writers such as Swift, Sterne, Peacock, James Joyce and Henry Miller.

Rahmenerzahlung is a German term meaning 'frame story' in reference to story within a story found in certain works, e.g., Boccaccio's *Decameron*, Chaucer's *Canterbury Tales, Arabian Nights.*

Rationalism is derived from Latin *ratio* (reason). In Philosophy it is a system of thought that emphasizes the role of reason in acquiring knowledge. This comes in contrast to empiricism which gives emphasis to experience. Rationalism is identified with the seventeenth century French philosopher René Descartes. Descartes believed that by means of reason alone, certain universal, self-evident truths could be discovered, from which the remaining content of philosophy and the sciences could be deductively derived. He assumed that these self-evident truths were innate, not derived from sense experience. This type of rationalism was developed by Spinoza and Leibniz. It was opposed by the British empiricists like John Locke who believed that all ideas are derived from the senses. In England Rationalism had its influence on religion and literature of the eighteenth century.

Realism is a term loosely applied to the observed facts of life and an attempt to describe human behaviour and surroundings as they are. It is generally restricted to a movement that began in the mid nineteenth century, in reaction to the highly subjective approach of romanticism. The difference between realism and naturalism is harder to define, however, the two terms are often used interchangeably. Naturalism is a cruder form of realism that emerged by the end of nineteenth century and is associated with French novelist Emile Zola. The distinction between the two lies in the fact that realism is concerned directly with what is observed by the senses while naturalism attempts to apply scientific theories to art. Realism comes in contrast with Impressionism and Expressionism. Realism is a dominant trend in the 19th century French, British and American novel attempting to reflect the simple life of ordinary people. Noted novelists who wrote in this genre include Daniel Defoe, Samuel Richardson, Henry Fielding, Tobias Smollett, Lawrence Sterne, Jane Austen, Charlotte Bronte, W.M. Thackeray, George Eliot, Mark Twain, Henry James, Thomas Hardy, D.H. Lawrence, E.M. Forster and Anthony Trollope. Writing about the middle class these novelists had a wide readership. The readers could identify themselves with the characters in their situations, and the novelists merely reported events as though from real life replete with dialogue. These writers emphasised psychological analysis of characters than construction of a perfect plot. This eventually led to the psychological and stream of consciousness novels. Realism in fiction should not be taken as presentation of real life. Instead it presents such a credible picture with its texture. For example, Jane Austen through her novels such as *Sense and Sensibility* or *Pride and Prejudice* presents social concerns of young women puzzled by the problem of marriage. In presenting her story the novelist uses powerful description, dialogue and landscapes, rendering it realistic. There is also an element of moralising by such novelists commenting on good conduct and living.

George Eliot's *Middlemarch* begins with a realistic portrayal of Miss Brook: "Miss Brooke had that kind of beauty which seems to be thrown into relief by poor dress. Her hand and wrist were so finely formed that she could wear sleeves not less bare of style than those in which the Blessed Virgin appeared to Italian painters; and her profile as well as her stature and bearing seemed to gain the more dignity from her plain garments, which by the side of provincial fashion gave her the impressiveness of a fine quotation from the *Bible*—or from one of our elder poets—in a paragraph of to-day's newspaper. She was usually spoken of as being remarkably clever, but with the addition that her sister Celia had more common-sense. Nevertheless, Celia wore scarcely more trimmings; and it was only to close observers that her dress differed from her sister's, and had a shade of coquetry in its arrangements; for Miss Brooke's plain dressing was due to mixed conditions, in most of which her sister shared."

Reflexive novel is a genre by which the author draws the attention of the readers to his/her writing it. It is a self-referential form of fiction. Typical example is Lawrence Sterne's *Tristram Shandy* (1760-67). Sterne claimed that his concern is to produce a 'civil, nonsensical, good humoured *Shandean* book'. The narration is erratic with digressions. It is considered the precursor of the stream of consciousness novel. The novel consists of blank pages, asterisks, dashes and diagrams. He parodies the contemporary novelists and speaks of himself trying the novel form. The narrator himself is the main character of the novel. It is through his observations and thoughts that the readers enter into the characters and events presented. He is concerned with the predicament of human life, sex and death and the absurdity of writing about these. He writes: " "I do entreat the candid reader to believe me, that it was from the humblest conviction of what a beast man is—that I asked the question; and that I would not have let fallen an unseasonable pleasantry in the venerable presence of misery, to be entitled to all the wit that ever Rebelais scattered – and yet I own my heart smote me, and that I so smarted at the very idea of it, that I swore I would set up for wisdom, and utter grave sentences the rest of my days – and never—never attempt again to commit mirth with man, woman, or child, the longest day I had to live. As for writing nonsense to them – I believe, there was a reserve – but that I leave to the world" (From *Volume IX, Chapter XXIV*). *Tristram Shandy* has inspired the form of Fielding's *Joseph Andrews* and *Tom Jones*. John Fowles' *The French Lieutenant's Woman* (1969) is a modern reflective novel.

Regional novel is a genre in which the novelist writes in the bacxground of a particular region and its people. It will have the local setting and customs with folks speaking their language. Maria Edgeworth (1767-1849) is considered the first to regional as well as historical novelist of England with her *Castle Rackrent* based on Irish life. Hardy with his 'Wessex' and Faulkner with his 'Yoknapatwpha' county are popular with their regional setting. Others novelists who wrote in this genre include Charlotte Bronte, Emily Bronte, Anne Bronte, Mrs. Gaskell, George Eliot and others. Hardy in *The Mayor of Casterbridge* sets his locale : " Casterbridge was a place deposited in the block upon a cornfield. There was no suburb in the modern sense, or transitional intermixture of town and down. It stood, with regard to the wild fertile land adjoining, clean-cut and distinct, like a chessboard on a green tablecloth. The farmer's boy could sit under his barely-mow and pitch a stone into the office-window of the town-clerk; reapers at work among the sheaves nodded to acquaintances standing on the pavement-corner...."

Repetition is a rhetorical device to give emphasis or emotional effect to speech or writing. From the middle ages repetition has been used as a rhetorical device. Abraham France classifies them into (i) *Epizeuxis,* the simple repetition of words or phrases, e.g., The time is changed, my lute, the time is changed. (ii) *Anadiplosis,* the repetition of an important word or phrases. (iii) *Epistrophe,* the repetition of successive clauses with the same word, e.g., "Are they Hebrews? So am I. Are they Abraham's descendants? So am I" (2 Cor. xi.22). (iv) *Symploce,* the repetition of a word at the beginning and another at the end of successive clauses. (v) *Epanalepsis,* the repetition of the same word or phrase repeated at the end and the beginning of the same sentence. (vi) *Epanodos,* by which the same word is repeated in the beginning, middle and end of a sentence. (vi) *Epanadiplosis,* by which a sentence begins and ends with the same word, e.g., "Rejoice in the Lord always; I say it again: rejoice" (Phil. iv.4).

Resolution is the denouement or conclusion by which conflicts and discords are resolved in a plot. Denouement means unknotting. According to Aristotle in his *Poetics* "Every tragedy is in part Complication and in part Denouement. The complication consists of incidents that have taken place before the opening of the play and some of that occur within it; the remainder form the denouement. By complication I mean everything from the beginning of the story up to the point where the hero suffers a change of fortune; by denouement, everything from the latter point to the end." The same can be applied to a novel when all the issues are brought to a conclusion. In *Great Expectations* Dickens ends the novel bringing together Pip and Estella standing hand in hand. "I have been bent and broken, but—I hope – into a better shape. Be as considerate and good to me as you were, and tell me we are friends. 'We are friends,' said I, rising and bending over her, as she rose from the bench. 'And will continue friends apart,' said Estella. I took her hand in mine, and we went out of the ruined place; and, as the morning mists had risen long ago when I first left the forge, so, the evening mists were rising now, and in all the broad expanse of tranquil light they showed to me, I saw no shadow of another parting from her" (*see* Denouement).

Retrospective narration is based on retrospection of the past mostly done in first person narration, e.g., Nelly Dean's narration in Emily Bronte's *Wuthering Heights* looks back into the past. Retrospection helps the narrator and the reader make a comparative study of the events of the past and now.

Rhetoric derived from Greek *rhetor* means 'speaker in the assembly.' In the broad sense it is the theory and practice of spoken or written eloquence. It refers to the techniques of persuasive public speech in a logical and convincing manner. Spoken rhetoric is oratory. Classical theories of rhetoric were presented by Aristotle's *Rhetoric*, Quintilian's *Institutio Oratoria* and Cicero's *De Inventione,* etc. The classical tradition of rhetoric continued up to the nineteenth century. It required logical order in invention, arrangement, style, memory and delivery. It is concerned with beauty or forcefulness of style with appropriate figures of speech. In the Medieval period Rhetoric was one of the seven liberal arts (arithmetic, astronomy, geometry, music, grammar, logic, and rhetoric) taught at the universities. rhetoric was applied to three "artes": letter writing, preaching, and the composition of poetry. In the eighteenth century Rhetoric declined in its importance. However, there is a revival of studies in rhetoric by the first half of the twentieth century due to the rising interest in Linguistics and Semiotics. Critics like I.A. Richards, Kenneth Duva Burke and John Crowe Ransom and Cleanth Brooks stressed the important role of rhetoric.

Rhetorical irony is a device by which an author writes exactly the opposite of what he or she expresses. Example of such irony is found in the writings of Jonathan Swift and Samuel Butler. Swift in his tract "A Modest Proposal" makes a concise and fiercely ironic attack on England's exploitation of Ireland: "Sixthly, this would be a great inducement to marriage, which all wise nations have either encouraged by rewards, or enforced by laws and penalties. It would increase the care and tenderness of mothers towards their children, when they were sure of a settlement for life to the poor babes, provided in some sort by the public, to their annual profit instead of expense. We should soon see an honest emulation among the married women, which of them could bring the fattest child to the market. Men would become as fond of their wives during the time of their pregnancy, as they are now of their mares in foal, their cows in calf, or sows when they are ready to farrow; nor offer to beat or kick them (as is too frequent a practice) for fear of a miscarriage."

Rhythm is the measured flow of aural or visual movement consisting of beat, accent, rise and fall, etc. Rhythm is a basic feature of all the arts, particularly music, poetry, and dance. In prose rhythm gives a balance of sentences by an orderly arrangement of words. In poetry rhythm is maintained by proper succession of long and short syllables.

Riddle is a puzzling question intended to make a person use his wits. This is an ancient form of literature found in all cultures. The earliest collection of riddles in English is found in the *Exeter Book* of the eighth century. Riddles are found in the *Bible*, the *Quran*, Greek mythology, and Sanskrit manuscripts. Many cultures have riddles passed on from generations to generation by oral tradition. According to Greek tradition Homer failed to solve a riddle presented by fishermen: "What we caught, we threw away: what we could not catch, we kept." The answer is "fleas". In Greek mythology the riddle of the Sphinx is very popular. Sphinx, the mythical monster with the head and breasts of a woman, the body of a lion, and the wings of a bird asked a riddle to everyone entering the city of Thebes. Those who failed to answer the riddle were killed by her. The riddle was: "What is it that has four feet in the morning, two at noon, and three at night?" It was only Oedipus who solved it saying, "Man, who crawls on four limbs as a baby, walks upright on two as an adult, and walks with the aid of a stick in old age". The sphinx killed herself as the riddle was solved. The Thebans in gratitude made Oedipus their king.

Rising action is based on the pyramid principle of Freytag by which a drama develops during the first half with some inciting incident and when the hero makes his plans clear. This leads to intensity, excitement and climax. For example, in Shakespeare's *Macbeth* bewitched by the witches and their prophesies, Macbeth plans the murder of the king after the banquet. The same principle is applicable in the case of a novel (*see* Complication).

Rococo is an architectural term derived from the French rocaille,"rock-work". It is a debased style of architecture prevalent during the reign of Louis XV of France. It consisted of decoration with rock works, shells, asymmetry and broken curves. Rococo is widely applied to any art form that is frivolous in spirit. In painting it consists of works in sparkling colours on light-hearted subject matter. In literature the term is applied to anything written in a light hearted manner with wit and elegance. Pope's *Rape of the Lock* or Sterne's *Tristram Shandy* belong to rococo form of literature, e.g., "Oh my uncle!.. is it fit, good-natured man! Thou should'st sit up, with the wound upon thy groin, whole nights baking thy blood with hectic watchings? – Alas! 'twill exasperate thy symptoms—check thy perspirations—evaporate thy spirits—waste thy animal strength—dry up thy radical moisture—bring thee into a costive habit of body, impair thy health—and hasten all the infirmities of thy old age—O my uncle! My uncle Toby!" (from *Tristram Shandy*)

Roman a clef is derived from French meaning 'novel with a key'. It is a type of novel in which actual persons are presented in a disguised manner. Only well informed readers are able to know the true identity of these characters presented fictitiously. French writers who began this novel form are Madeleine Scudery (1607-91) and Jean de la

Bruyere (1645-96). In English such novels include Thomas Love Peacock's *Nightmare Abbey* on Coleridge; Nathaniel Hawthorne's *Blithedale Romance* on Margaret Fuller; Aldous Huxley's *Point Counter Point*; Somerset Maugham's *Cake and Ale*; Saul Bellow's *Humboldt's Gift*.

Roman a these in French is a thesis novel in which a novelist propounds his arguments on certain social, political or philosophical issues. Jean-Paul Sartre's novel *La Nausee* presents his existentialism (1938) (*see* Thesis novel).

Roman a tiroirs is a French term for a novel form which consists of a number of episodes which are not linked to one another. French novelist Alain-Rene Lesage (1668-1747) is noted for writing in this literary form. His picaresque novel *Histoire de Gil Blas de Santillane* is the tale of the adventures of a rogue. It is written like the Spanish picaresque romances of the sixteenth and seventeenth centuries. One of the earliest important realistic novels in European fiction is *Gil Blas*. Being one of the first realistic novels, it has influenced to a great extend the English novelists Tobias Smollet and Henry Fielding.

Romance is derived from old Latin *Romanice* meaning 'in the Roman Language'. It is a literary form popular in the Middle Ages from fifth century to fifteenth century concerned with tales of knights, chivalry, and courtly love. These were verse or prose written in the Latin vernaculars, namely, French, Provencal, Italian, Spanish, Portuguese, Romanian, Romansch with their different dialects. A romance had a legendary subject matter with supernatural and amorous elements. The romance is similar to an epic except for the fact that an epic is longer and less concerned with courtly love. Romances are found in Europe since twelfth century and continued to be popular till the Renaissance. Originally they were orally transmitted by troubadours and trouvères. Later, they were written by court musicians to entertain and edify the aristocracy. In England Romances have evolved around King Arthur and the knights of the Round Table.

Some of the Arthurian romances are *Sir Gawain and the Green Knight, Tristan und Isolt, Percival*, or *The Story of the Grail,* etc. In Rome there were romances around the stories of Alexander the Great and in France they were built around the adventures of Charlemagne and his knights. In Renaissance England Spenser's *Faerie Queene* and Sydney's *Arcadia* were examples of poetic and prose romances. The term 'romance' is applied to a novel that is fanciful, adventurous and extraordinary than realistic, e.g., Cervantes's *Don Quixote*, Emile Bronte's *Wuthering Heights*, Walter Scott's *Waverly*, Mark Twain's *The Adventures of Huckleberry Finn*, Herman Melville's *Moby Dick*, Joseph Conrad's *Heart of Darkness*, Scott Fitzgerald's *The Great Gatsby*, and Henry James's *The Portrait of a Lady*.

Roman-feuilleton is a novel that is serialised in newspapers. It is the anonymous Spanish picaresque novel *Lazarillo de Tormes* is considered the first to be serialised in the paper *Le Siecle*. It recounts the autobiography of a miller's son who lived beside the river Tormes in Salamanca. From nineteenth century such serialisation became popular.

Roman-fleuve is a French term for a series of novels. It presents a story of a character or a set of characters in sequence from one book to the next. Such novels can render vividly a comprehensive account of a particular period. Roman-fleuve is found since nineteenth century. French novelist Honoré de Balzac (1799-1850) had an innovative idea of giving life and continuity to his characters in his novels. He brought out a huge work entitled *La Comédie Humaine* (The Human Comedy) giving a panoramic view of his society from the time of French Revolution. Emile Zola (1840-1902) wrote *Les Rougon-Macquart,* a 21-volume serial which he called 'the natural and social history of a family under the Second Empire'. In English such novels include Galsworthy's *The Forsyte Saga* (1922) which accounts for the fortunes of three generations of the Forsyte family; C.P. Snow's *Strangers and Brothers,* later re-titled *George Passant,* traces the life of its barrister narrator Lewis Eliot; Henry Williamson's *A*

Chronicle of Ancient Sunlight in 15 volumes; and Anthony Powell's *A Dance to the Music of Time* in 12 volumes.

Romanticism or **Romantic Movement** took place in England and Europe between 1770 and 1848. By the late eighteenth century in France and Germany there is a shift in literary taste from classical and neoclassical conventions. The spirit of Romanticism initially came from French philosopher Jean Jacques Rousseau and German writer Goethe. Rousseau established the cult of the individual and championed the freedom of the human spirit. Goethe and his friends extolled the romantic spirit of the German folk songs, Gothic architecture, and the plays of English playwright William Shakespeare. The term romantic first appeared in eighteenth century English and originally meant "romance-like", resembling the fanciful character of medieval romances. According to Lacelles Abercrombie Romanticism is "the opposite not of Classicism but of Realism – a withdrawal from outer experience to concrete upon inner." For Victor Hugo Romanticism is "liberalism in literature". Theodore Watts Dunton called it "the Renaissance of Wonder". For Walter Pater it was "the addition of strangeness to beauty". Romantics sought to do away with the neoclassical stress on intellect and reason. Hence, it was a revolt against the neoclassicism of the previous period. It insisted on spontaneity with variety and stress on individualism. The movement took its inspiration from Spenser, Shakespeare and Milton. It was a revival of these great poets with a return to Nature and simple country life. The Romantics were inspired by the ideals of French Revolution: Liberty, Equality and Fraternity. They revolted against everything traditional. Romanticism is a broad term applied to philosophy, politics and arts which emphasise the subjective experience and imagination.

English Romanticism began with the publication of *Lyrical Ballads* in 1798 by Coleridge and Wordsworth. In the Preface to the second edition of *Lyrical Ballads* (1800), they present their manifesto of literary romanticism. Wordsworth wrote in the Preface, "...poetry is the spontaneous overflow of powerful feelings: it takes its origin from emotions recollected in tranquillity." The subject matter of poetry is " to choose incidents and situations from common life... a selection of language really used by men.... Humble and rustic life was generally chosen, because, in that condition, the essential passions of the heart find a better soil in which they can attain their maturity." The watchword of Romanticism was 'Imagination'. The movement was characterised by reliance on the imagination and subjectivity of approach, freedom of thought and expression, and an idealisation of nature. They affirmed the importance of feeling and imagination to poetic creation and disclaimed conventional literary forms and subjects. Imagination was praised over reason, emotions over logic, and intuition over science. This led to a literature of great sensibility and passion. They emphasized a new flexibility of form and freer style. There is an increasing demand for spontaneity and lyricism found in folk poetry and in medieval romance. They rejected regular meters, strict forms, and other conventions of the classical tradition. In English poetry, for example, blank verse largely superseded the rhymed couplet that dominated eighteenth century poetry. Wordsworth believed in a mystic communion with nature and simplicity of life. It was taking shelter in the lap of nature from the onslaught of industrialism. Since there was a decline in traditional religious beliefs, they made a religion of their own experience. Coleridge emphasised the supernatural and the function of imagination in poetry. Romantic movement believed in the inherent worth of the individual and pantheism. English romanticism has two phases. The first phase is a reaction against the revolutionary ideals of France. There is the trace of mysticism in the poetry of Wordsworth and Coleridge till 1815. Wordsworth, Coleridge and Southey, are known as Lake Poets (since they lived in the Lake District) with Burns and Blake form the first generation of English Romantics. The second generation of romantics (Shelley, Byron and

Keats) present a moral revolt and they believed in independence and justice.

In fiction there is the emergence of the tale of terror and suspense as in the Gothic novels of Horace Walpole's *The Castle of Otranto : A Gothic Story* (1764); Thomas Leland's *Longsword* (1762); Clara Reeve's *The Old English Baron* (1778); William Beckford's *Vathek* (1786); Anne Radcliffe's *The Mysteries of Udolpho* (1794); Lewis's *The Monk* (1796); C.R. Maturin's *The Fatal Revenge* (1807); Mary Shelley's *Frankenstein* (1818); Dickens's *Bleak House* (1853); Charlette Bronte's *Jane Eyre* (1847) and Emily Bronte's *Wuthering Heights* (1847) (*see* Gothic novel). Historical novels emerged with Sir Walter Scott's *Waverley* (1814), *Rob Roy* (1817), *Ivanhoe* (1819), and *Kenilworth* (1821) and W.M. Thackeray's *The Luck of Barry Lyndon* (1844) *(see* Historical novel).

Romantic prose began to emerge in the romantic period with Coleridge's *Biographia Literaria* (1817). Prose is defined as plain, simple, commonplace writing in contrast to poetry. In the Romantic period prose came to be concerned not only with practical things but "the expression or embodiment of beautiful or elevated thought, imagination, or feeling in language adapted to stir the imagination and emotions." Wordsworth in his *Preface to Lyrical Ballads* opined that between the language of prose and poetry there was no essential difference and that prose could be as poetical as poetry. Walter Pater in his essay *Style* refers to "imaginative prose" as a "special art of the modern world". Such prose writing is found in the writing of Hazlitt, Lamb and De Quincey. These writers had some kinship with the prose masters of the seventeenth century and were influenced by the style of Milton, Jeremy Taylor and Sir Thomas Browne. Excellent examples to the Romantic prose are: Charles Lamb's *Specimens of English Dramatic Poets who lived about the Time of Shakespeare* (1808); *Essays of Elia* (1823, 1833); William Hazlitt's *Characters of Shakespeare's Plays,* 1817; and Thomas De Quincey's *Confessions of an English Opium-Eater* (1821), e.g., "However, as some people, in spite of all laws to the contrary, will persist in asking what became of the opium-eater, and in what state he now is, I answer for him thus: the reader is aware that opium had long ceased to found its empire on spells of pleasure; it was solely by the tortures connected with the attempt to abjure it, that it kept its hold. Yet, as other tortures, no less it may be thought, attended the non-abjuration of such a tyrant, a choice only of evils was left; and that might as well have been adopted, which, however terrific in itself, held out a prospect of final restoration to happiness. This appears true; but good logic gave the author no strength to act upon it..." (from *Confessions of an English Opium-Eater*).

Romans d' adventure were verse or prose fictional narratives prevalent in the twelfth and thirteenth centuries. These, as the term implies, were on adventures of love and chivalry meant to entertain especially women. Prominent among such works are *Ipomadon,* a Middle English romance taken from the French *Huon de Rotelande* (c.1190), which narrates the adventurous story of prince Ipomadon who wins in disguise the love of the Duchess of Calabria. Others include *Guillaume de Dole, Partenopeu, Le Chatelain de Coucy, Guillaume de Palerme,* etc.

Romantic irony is a term associated with Friedrich von Schlegel (1772-1829) who expounded the theory of romantic irony which is the consciousness on the part of the writer who finds that his work is not taken seriously and which he does not expect either. Schlegel did this by contrasting classical and romantic works. Through the device the author tells the readers what he does at the time of that action. It often consists of his comments on his composition or on other literary works, e.g., Fielding in *Tom Jones* and *Joseph Andrews* comments on the author. Romantic irony is found in the writings of Chaucer, Cervantes, Sterne, Henry James, Thomas Mann, etc.

Romantic novel is a form of fiction in which action is given prominence than characters. Such novels revolve around amorous and adventurous episodes that are very legendary and idealistic (*see* Romance).

S

Sadism is a term derived from the name of the French philosopher and writer Marquis de Sade (1740-1814). According to psychiatrists it is a kind of neurosis by which sexual satisfaction is gained by the inflicting of pain on others by whipping, beating and wrecking psychologically. In some cases sadism can lead to mutilation of organs and eventual murder. Psychologically one becomes a sadist due to inferiority complex and low self-esteem from childhood. Such a person in inflicting pain on others tries to prove his superiority. Sade practised sadism in his life and considered such sexual perversions natural in his works such as *Juliette* (1797) and *Le Philosophie dans le boudoir* (1795) (*see* Masochism).

Saga in Old Norse means 'story.' It refers to prose tale about legendary or historical heroes in the old literature of Iceland. Old Norse and Icelandic are practically the same language. Medieval Icelandic literature is also known as Old Norse literature. There were several popular sagas in Iceland between the twelfth and fourteenth centuries. Most of these were prose narratives by anonymous authors and were recited by storytellers. These sagas can be classified as 'family sagas' concerning the early Icelandic settlers, 'King's sagas' concerning the rulers and 'heroic sagas' on the legendary heroes and their adventures, e.g., *Njals saga* is a family saga about a brave man named Gunnarr who marries a beautiful immoral woman who makes him fight feuds and is slain. *Snorri Sturluson's Heimskringla* is a King's Saga on the rulers of Norway from legendary times. Among the heroic sagas are *Egil's Saga* on the warrior-poet Egill Skallagrímsson; *Gísla Saga* on a heroic outlaw, etc.

Saga novel is a term derived from the Icelandic sagas like Njals saga which has influenced the development of novel sequence like Galsworthy's *The Forsyte Saga* (1922) which was written over a long period of time. It consists of the three novels, *The Man of Property* (1906), *In Chancery* (1920), *To Let* (1921); the interludes 'Indian Summer of a Forsyte' (1918) and *Awakening* (1920). All these different novels are connected to each other by the Forsyte family. The sequence presents the story concerning the fortunes of three generations of the family. D.H. Lawrence's *The Rainbow* (1915) is a saga novel which is a chronicle of the Brangwen family of March Farm.

Salon in French means a 'reception room.' The term referred to a French cultural institution of men of letters who met together on a weekly basis in the house of a noble lady for informal discussions. It was rather popular in the seventeenth and eighteenth centuries. Scudery and Recamier organised such salons. The English coffee houses and clubs are similar to the salon.

Samizdat in Russian means 'self-publication' referring to underground writing prevalent in Soviet Union from the late 1950s up to 1980s when President Mikhail Gorbachev introduced the policy of *glasnost* which stood for openness. It lasted Due to curtailment of freedom of press and opinion. Many books and articles were published without the knowledge and permission of the Communist regime. These were typewritten with carbon copies or cyclostyled and circulated by hand between trusted friends. The practice was also prevalent in Poland, Czechoslovakia, and Hungary. Eventually during the Khrushchev regime some journals of poetry by students appeared in public. They held poetry reading in Moscow. Aleksandr Ginzburg edited Sintaksis and Yuri Galanskov Phoenix. Both of them were imprisoned or harassed in different manner by 1960. In 1965 Andrei Sinyavsky and Yuli Daniel were arrested for anti-soviet activities which led them to publish their works outside USSR. This turned samizdat very political in nature. Efforts began in the West to broadcast these antisoviet views through Russian language stations. Eventually a *journal of the Chronicles of Current Events* was published in April 1968, voicing the rising democratic views and human rights abuses within USSR. The KGB tried to suppress the journal with massive arrests. The journal carried articles by human rights activists like the physicist Andrei Sakharov and the writer Alexander Solzhenitsyn. Solzhenitsyn's novels *The First Circle, Cancer Ward* and *The Gulag Archipelago* still continued publication through *samizdat*. These publications had led to his arrest and deportation from USSR in 1974. Other publications in this genre include Nadezhda Mandelstam's *Hope Against Hope,* Evgeniya Ginzburg's *Journey Into the Whirlwind* and Varlam Sharlamov's *Kolyma Tales*. Samizdat ceased to exist only during Gorbachev's regime.

Satire is a literary art of diminishing a subject by making it ridiculous and evoking amusement and scorn. It uses laughter as a weapon against a butt. A butt may be an individual or a society. Dryden wrote: "The true end of satyre is the amendment of vices by correction." Satire evokes laughter using wit in the form of irony or derision to expose human folly and evil. The Roman poet, Horace, was the first great satirist who commented with a smile on follies especially in sexual matters and ill-mannered behaviour. Juvenal, a contemporary of Horace, exposed the vices of Roman society in his satires. In imitation of Juvenal, Samuel Johnson wrote *London,* (1739), and *The Vanity of Human Wishes* (1749). Beast fables and dream allegories like the thirteenth century *Le Roman de la Rose* and the fourteenth century *Piers Plowman* of William Langland are satires. Chaucer used satire in *The Canterbury Tales. Don Quixote* of Cervantes is a great satire on knight-errantry. Satires in English include Ben Jonson's *Volpone, Alchemist*; Samuel Butler's *Hudibras*; Dryden's *Absalom and Achitophel;* Pope's *The Rape of the Lock,* and *Dunciad.* Swift, Addison, Steele, Fielding, Shaw, Galsworthy Bennett, Huxley and Orwell are also known satirists. Orwell's *Animal Farm* is a satire on Russian revolution. The satire presents the animal revolt in Mr. Jone's farm where the pigs become leaders. The final slogan is "All animals are equal but some animals are more equal than others."

S&F is an abbreviation used in modern fiction for a kind of romance in the 1980s written by women for women. These deal with matters concerning rich women such as expensive clothes, jewellery, perfumes and the like. Such novels also narrate certain sexual encounters in details, e.g., Judith Krantz's *Scruples* (1978).

Science fiction creates a make believe world of fantasy. It concerns with the scientific and technological advancement and is set in a future world or another planet. It takes us to a fantasy world of the future with space explorations and travels to alien planets. Traces of Scientific fiction is found in The Babylonian *Gilgamesh Epic* which a search for ultimate knowledge and immortality. Similarly the Greek *Daedalus myth* narrates the story of Dedalus who made waxen wings to escape from his imprisonment in a labyrinth in Crete. He flew up to the sun and fell into the sea as his wings melted. Sir John Mandeville in the fourteenth century compiled some of the Greek and Roman fantasy stories. In the seventeenth century, fictional narratives of man's journey to the moon have been written by British writer Francis Godwin and the French writer Cyrano de Bergerac. However, Mary Shelley with her *Frankenstein* (1818) is considered the first writer in this genre. French author Jules

Verne is credited to have contributed to a great extent to science fiction with his works such as *Journey to the Centre of the Earth* (1864), *From the Earth to the Moon* (1865), *Off on a Comet* (1877), and *Twenty Thousand Leagues Under the Sea* (1870). The writers who attempted this genre include Edward Bellamy, Edgar Allan Poe, Nathaniel Hawthorne, Mark Twain, Sir Arthur Conan Doyle's and Rudyard Kipling. H.G. Wells may be considered the founder of modern science fiction with his ironic stories of science. *The Time Machine* (1895), *The Island of Dr Moreau* (1896), *The Invisible Man* (1897), *The War of the Worlds* (1898), *When the Sleeper Wakes* (1899), and *The First Men in the Moon* (1901). *The Time Machine* is a social allegory of the future year 802701 : " 'Would you like to see the Time Machine itself?' asked the Time Traveller. And therewith, taking the lamp in his hand, he led the way down the long, draughty corridor to his laboratory. I remember vividly the flickering light, his queer, broad head in silhouette, the dance of the shadows, how we all followed him, puzzled but incredulous, and how there in the laboratory we beheld a larger edition of the little mechanism which we had seen vanish from before our eyes. Parts were of nickel, parts of ivory, parts had certainly been filed or sawn out of rock crystal. The thing was generally complete, but the twisted crystalline bars lay unfinished upon the bench beside some sheets of drawings, and I took one up for a better look at it. Quartz it seemed to be" (From *The Time Machine*). Some of the other science fiction novels are Matthew Phipps Shiel's *The Purple Cloud* (1901), C.S. Lewis's *Out of the Silent Planet* (1938). Jack London's *The Iron Heel* (1907), Aldous Huxley's *Brave New World* (1932), George Orwell's *Nineteen Eighty-four* (1949), Arthur C. Clarke's *Childhood's End* (1953), Robert Heinlein's *The Green Hills of Earth* (1951), Isaac Asimov's *The Caves of Steel* (1953), Philip K. Dick's *The Man in the High Castle* (1962), etc. Science fiction films have been very successful like *Destination Moon* (1950), *The War of the Worlds* (1953), *Forbidden Planet* (1956), *Invasion of the Body Snatchers*

(1956), *The Time Machine* (1960), *Planet of the Apes* (1968), *A Space Odyssey* (1968), *The Andromeda Strain* (1971), *The Man Who Fell to Earth* (1976), *Close Encounters of the Third Kind* (1977), *Star Wars* (1977), *Star Trek, E.T., the Extra-Terrestrial* (1982), *The Terminator* (1984) and *Judgment Day* (1991). Science fiction got recognition as a relevant literary form after the explosion of the atomic bomb in 1945 and the moon landing in July 1969. Science fiction world turned reality further with the space vehicle landing on Mars in July 1976 and the spacecraft Voyager I got photographs of Saturn in November 1980.

Scriptures are sacred books of any religion giving rules, liturgies, spiritual guidance and codes of conduct, e.g., *The Bible* (The Old Testament and the New Testament), *the Vedas, Brahmanas and Upanishads,* the *Quran,* the *Talmud,* etc.

Self-help book is a book with tips for readers regarding better living and self-improvement. The genre has been in vogue since nineteenth century in America. The tradition of "self-help" is found in the books of Horatio Alger (1832-1899) such as *Ragged Dick* (1867) and *From Farm Boy to Senator* (1882). These are books meant for young people to seek success through hard work and struggle against poverty. William Taylor Adams (1822-1897) wrote his series of adventure stories "*Onward and Upward*" in this genre. The New Age Movement began in the 1960s with the purpose of changing the lives of people through self-help and an eclectic spirituality. This movement has published several books. The trend has been to reject materialism for a holistic health through spirituality, retreats, meditation, yoga, occult, astrology, psychic healing, Zen, transpersonal psychology and the like.

Self-reflexive novel (*see* Reflexive novel, Metafiction).

Sensibility is an eighteenth century term to refer to a susceptibility to tender feelings, especially involving the feelings and sorrows of others in contrast to the neoclassical rejection of emotions. It is the capacity to feel and respond. Sensibility is related to Primitivism, Sentimentalism and Naturalism which are offshoots of Romanticism. T.S. Eliot spoke of "dissociation of sensibility" to imply the split between the sensuous and the intellectual faculties. By mid-eighteenth century external expressions of feelings was accepted as part of good manners. Hence, there are poems of sensibility such as Gray's *Elegy*, Goldsmith's *The Deserted Village* and the like. Sensibility is a concept prevalent in the eighteenth century to show sentiment with true virtues. A true man or woman of sentiment was expected to uphold morality and honour at the same time express true feelings and sentiments. Sterne's *A Sentimental Journey* (1768) is a work of fiction in this genre. It presents Parson Yorick, a man of sensibility who is moved to tears and feelings during his travels in France and Italy. It is meant to teach us to love the world and our fellow men. In Mackenzie's *Man of Feeling* (1771) the hero Harley is a man of feelings and assist the downtrodden to the extent of his failure in worldly pursuits. Other works in this genre are H. Brooke's *The Fool of Quality*, Lamb's *The Tale of Rosamund Gray,* etc. Jane Austen mocked the exaggerated sentiments expressed in the novel of sensibility in *Northanger Abbey* and her *Sense and Sensibility* is a kind of warning to those who are befooled by sentiments.

Sensational novel presents sensational events involving secret. It is the precursor of the detective novel, e.g., Wilkie Collins's *The Woman in White* (1860), Braddon's *Lady Audley's Secret* (1862) (*see* Detective story).

Sense is a popular eighteenth century concept by which a man is to acquire a balanced personality according to neoclassical tradition with high reason, decorum, correctness of taste and sensibility. A person with such a balance is called a man of good sense, e.g., Jane Austen brings this concept very powerfully in her novel *Sense and Sensibility*. She calls for a balanced sensibility and warns those who are befooled by their overt sentiments. Note her description of the three daughters of Mrs. Henry Dashwood namely, "Marianne's abilities were, in many respects, quite equal to Elinor's. She was sensible and clever; but eager in everything: her sorrows, her joys, could have no moderation. She was generous, amiable, interesting: she was everything but prudent. The resemblance between her and her mother was strikingly great. Elinor saw, with concern, the excess of her sister's sensibility; but by Mrs. Dashwood it was valued and cherished. They encouraged each other now in the violence of their affliction. The agony of grief which overpowered them at first was voluntarily renewed, was sought for, was created again and again. They gave themselves up wholly to their sorrow, seeking increase of wretchedness in every reflection that could afford it, and resolved against ever admitting consolation in future. Elinor, too, was deeply afflicted; but still she could struggle, she could exert herself.... Margaret, the other sister, was a good-humoured, well-disposed girl; but as she had already imbibed a good deal of Marianne's romance, without having much of her sense, she did not, at thirteen, bid fair to equal her sisters at a more advanced period of life."

Sentimentality is a strong emotional response which an author can arouse in the readers and the audience. The eighteenth century melodrama had much romantic plot, sensationalism and sentimentality.

Sentimental novel is a kind of fiction popular in the eighteenth century. It can be understood better in the context of sentimental comedy which began to develop in the middle of the eighteenth century as the stereotyped comedy of manners was getting exhausted and neoclassical tragedy had practically disappeared. This ushered in sentimental comedy, panoramas, and musical comedies. The comedies of this period are of two types, namely, the old fashioned witty plays provoking laughter and the sentimental Comedies. The

Sentimental Comedies grew in the eighteenth century due to the rise of the middle classes and the reaction against the licentious comedies of the Restoration. According to Goldsmith it arose since "the virtues of private life are exhibited, rather than the vices exposed, and the distresses rather than the frailty of mankind." These were meant to refine manners and improve morals, hence, lacked humour. These plays praised virtue and the cultivation of sentiment. This genre began with the sentimental comedies by Richard Steele such as *The Tender Husband* and *The Conscious Lovers*. The characters in these plays are middle class. The lovers are not frivolous and they consciously deal with serious domestic problems. The treatment of marriage is a proper affair of love rather than of sentiments. The play is replete with sentimental ideas. Men are waiting to destroy women and the extraordinary services they render women are only with self-interest. The sentimental comedy revolves around much moralising and sermonising. The characters were mostly caricatures and were very good or very bad. The features of Sentimental Comedies can be summed up: (i) They are mawkish and sentimental, (ii) the dialogue is full of moralistic cliches, (iii) there is often a sudden transformation in the villain, (iv) there is much praising of virtue rather than ridiculing folly, (v) virtue always triumphed, (vi) these plays attempted to improve society with tears.

Similar in sensibility is the fiction that began to be written during this period highlighting morality, virtue and honour which were duly rewarded. Such fiction include Richardson's *Pamela* or *Virtue Rewarded* (1740), Goldsmith's *The Vicar of Wakefield* (1766) and Maria Edgeworth's *Castle Rackrent* (1800). In *Pamela* or *Virtue Rewarded* in the form of letter Richardson narrates the story of a young maid servant's defence of her honour. She is a beautiful young girl of 15 who is wooed by her dead employer's son. She resists his advances to preserve her chastity. The novel consists of her letters expressing her feelings as well as her pride and imprudent behaviours.

Serapion brothers (Serapionovy bratya) is a Russian literary movement began in 1921 by a group of young non-conformist writers. They did not adhere to any political ideology. They were inspired by Zamyatin (1884-1937). The members included Tikhonov, Fedin, Ivanov, Slonimski, and Zoshchenko.

Sermon is a discourse delivered from the pulpit on Biblical themes to instruct and to edify. Often it is in the form of explanations to Biblical texts. It was a practice in the Church from the Apostolic times. In course of time sermons evolved to be a work of art in the hands of many Fathers of the Church (early Christian writers especially of the first five centuries) such as Origen, Clement of Alexandria, Cyprian, Athanasius, Basil the Great, Gregory Nazianzen, John Chrysostom, Tertullian, Jerome, Bernard, Ambrose and Augustine. In 1485 John Bromyard published his collection of sermons entitled *Summa Praedicantium*. Noted preachers of sermons include Lancelot Andrews, John Donne, Jeremy Taylor, Wesley Cardinal Newman, and Cardinal Manning. The following is an extract from John Donne's Sermon preached at St. Paul's for Easter day 1628: " 'For now we see through a glass darkly, but then face to face; now I know in part, but then I shall know even as also I am known" (I Corinthians 13:12). These two terms in our text, *nunc* and *tunc*, now and then, now in a glass, then face to face, now in part, then in perfection, these two secular terms, of which one designs the whole age of this world from the creation to the dissolution thereof, for all that is comprehended in this word *now*, and the other designs the everlastingness of the next world, for that incomprehensibleness is comprehended in the other word *then* – these two words that design two such ages are now met in one day, in this day in which we celebrate all resurrections in the root in the resurrection of our Lord and Saviour Christ Jesus blest forever...."

Setting in a novel refers to the scenes and verbal pictures presented in it consisting of the places, social contexts, customs and practices, and the atmosphere. For example, Mark Twain in *The Adventures of Huckleberry Finn* makes Huck describe elaborately on the river setting: "It was a monstrous big river here, with the tallest and the thickest kind of timber on both banks; just a solid wall, as well as I could see, by the stars. I looked away down the stream, and seen a black speck on the water. I took out after it....."

Seven deadly sins are those according to the medieval theology of the Church led to damnation. They are also known as capital or mortal sins. These are pride, covetousness, lust, anger, gluttony, envy and sloth. These sins occur in the literature of the time such as Langland's *Piers the Ploughman*, Chaucer's *Canterbury Tales, Everyman,* etc. God speaks to Everyman about how men have fallen victims of the seven deadly sins: "And now I see the people do clean forsake me / They use the seven deadly sins damnable; /As pride, covetise, wrath, and lechery...."

Shaggy dog story is one with incredible elements and which ends in a quasi witty manner, e.g., Joseph Heller's *Catch-22* (1961) which is a comical and surreal novel with apocalyptic and satirical overtones. Pilot Orr is described in a comical manner thus: "Orr was crazy and could be grounded. All he had to do was ask; and as soon as he did, he would no longer be crazy and would have to fly more missions. Orr would be crazy to fly more missions and sane if he didn't, but if he was sane he had to fly them. If he flew them he was crazy and didn't have to; but if he didn't want to he was sane and had to."

Short novel is one that is longer than a short story and shorter than a novel (*see* Novella, Novelette).

Short story is a fictional prose narrative written in about 500 to 15,000 words. Such a story focuses on a single theme unlike a novel. It is easily readable within a short time.

Usually it involves a few characters set in a single action. The purpose of a short story is meant to arouse thrill and interest in the reader. Chaucer's *Canterbury Tales* with its several characters narrating their stories is considered the prototype of this genre. It is in the nineteenth century that the short story form became popular. According to Edgar Allen Poe a short story has a length "requiring from half hour to one or two hours in its perusal." Poe is considered the father of short stories in modern times with his stories such as *The Murders in the Rue Morgue*, *The Fall of the House of Usher*, *Berenice*, *The Pit and the Pendulum*, *The Gold Bug*, etc. Some distinguished short story writers are Nathaniel Hawthorne, Balzac, Anton Chekhov, Tolstoy, Maupassant, O. Henry, Rudyard Kipling, Katherine Mansfield, Somerset Maugham, Hemingway, Faulkner, D.H. Lawrence, James Joyce, Doris Lessing, R.K. Narayan, V.S. Naipaul and others.

Silver fork novel is a type of fiction on the manners of upper class society prevalent during 1825 to 1850. The silver-fork school admired the wealthy and the fashionable. Theodore Edward Hook (1788-1841) was the most prominent writer of the fashionable novels such as *Sayings and Doings*, *Maxwell*, *Jack Brag*, and *Gurney Married*. Others in the school include T.H. Lister, P. Ward, Francis Trollope, Catherine Gore and Benjamine Disraeli. Hazzlitt called it 'the Dandy School' as it admired the follies and superficialities of the upper class. Thackeray's *Vanity Fair* is an excellent depiction of the school.

Simple and compound plots are found in fiction. A simple plot has a single story while a compound plot has two or more stories with sub-plots, e.g., Jane Austen's *Pride and Prejudice* has compound plots.

Sketch is a brief prose narrative simpler than a short story. The term is also applied to character sketches without development of plot. It is often found in newspapers and magazines. In drama the term is used to refer to a curtain raiser. Joseph Addison and Sir Richard Steele are known for many fictional stories in the form of sketches which appeared in *Spectator*. These concerned with contemporary character types. Washington Irving has similar sketches on his society, e.g., Steele's sketch on 'The Hours of London' which begins: "It is an inexpressible pleasure to know a little of the world, and be of no character or significancy in it. To be ever unconcerned, and ever looking on new objects with an endless curiosity, is a delight known only to those who are turned for speculation: nay, they who enjoy it must value things only as they are the objects of speculation, without drawing any worldly advantage to themselves from them, but just as they are what contribute to their amusement, or the improvement of the mind...."

Slang is the informal words and phrases used in ordinary colloquial speech. Slang can be contrasted with jargon and argot or cant. A jargon is a technical language used in a profession. An argot is a secret vocabulary of underworld groups. Slang has its origin in subcultures within a society like the police, computer specialists, armed forces, teenagers, racial minorities and the like. Slang used to indicate the attitudes and values of a particular group. The listener can know about the speaker's background from his/her slang expressions. For example, the Black Harlem district of New York has slang expressions such as *cool* for stylish, *The Man* for the law, *Uncle Tom* for a gentle black. Some slang expressions can be widely used such as *big cog* for an important person; *big noise, big wheel, big wig* for a powerful person; *blow one's cool* for to lose control; *button one's lip* for to be quiet; *cock movie* for pornographic film; *egg* for a henpecked husband; *grass* for marijuana; *half baked* for inadequate; *nutty* for foolish; *pencil-pusher* for clerk; *snake* for spy.

Slice of life is a French phrase '*tranche de vie*' used by playwright Jean Jullieng, referring to realistic part of life presented in literary art. It is a naturalistic presentation of life as it is lived with minute details devoid of the idealised. It was the French writer Émile Zola (1840-1902) who introduced the device by which he exposed social ills in his novels. Such fiction or drama focussed on the sordid and dingy side of life than the ideal or beautiful. Naturalistic writers such as Frank Norris (1870-1902), Theodore Dreiser (1871-1945) and Don Passos (1896-1970) present slice of life in their novels, e.g., Theodore Dreiser in his novel *Genius* presents social realism through a study of the artistic temperament in a mercenary society (*see* Naturalism).

Slave narrative is form of fiction that has emerged as a part of the abolitionist literature in the United States preceding the Civil War. It consists of account of slavery given by a freed slave or a runaway. American abolitionist Frederick Douglass (1817-1895) who escaped from slavery encouraged the blacks fight for their freedom. Douglass wrote Narrative of the *Life of Frederick Douglass, an American Slave* (1845) to convince his detractors that he was a liberated slave himself. The book appeared in its final form in 1882 entitled *Life and Times of Frederick Douglass.* A work in this genre in the modern times include the Cuban anthropologist Miguel Barnet's *The Autobiography of a Runaway Slave* (1968) which is the story of a 104-year-old former slave Esteban Montejo. He recounts his story in the form of interviews.

Socialist realism is a theory of art and literature that developed in Russia in the 1920s and 1930s with the purpose of spreading the Marxist doctrines. The artist became a tool in the hands of the socialist system and was tagged 'the engineer of human souls' by Stalin. The term was used by Lunacharski and Gorki. Nikolay Ostrovsky's *How the Steel Was Tempered* (1934) is considered the best work of socialist realism presenting the new Soviet man according to the Marxist ideology. Later Socialist realism turned more propagandist portraying working classes. Writers like Pasternak and Solzhenitsyn revolted against such an artistic credo. In America, Theodore Dreiser (1871-1945) was acclaimed the leader of Social Realism. His first novel *Sister Carrie* (1900) was banned for its realistic treatment of sexual problems. His later works such as *Genius* (1915), and *An American Tragedy* (1925) had great popular success in this genre. *The American Tragedy* is based on an actual murder case in New York. It recounts the story and murder of a young man who rose from extreme poverty to be a member of the worldly society. Earnest Hemingway wrote his *Old Man and the Sea* inspired by the life of Gregorio Fuentes who was the captain of Hemingway's boat in Cuba. Fuentes died in January 2002 at the age of 104.

Social criticism in literature deals with social situations and depicts critically problems afflicting society. It is often presented through prose fiction or essay, e.g., Sir Thomas More's (1477-1535) *Utopia* is a fictional work in this genre. It is a search for the ideal form of government in the island called 'nowhere land'. Winifred Holtby's (1898-1935) *South Riding* (1936) depicts the society of Yorkshire and evils that thrive in it. Harriet Beecher Stowe (1811-1896) in *Uncle Tom's Cabin* brings powerfully her social criticism of slavery in America. John Steinbeck's (1902-1968) *The Grapes of Wrath* accounts for the struggle of emigrant farmers. Alan Paton's *Cry, the Beloved Country* is on racial reconciliation.

Sociological novel is a genre in fiction that concerns itself with social issues. Besides pointing out social problems such novels also suggest certain amendments for social transformation, e.g., George Eliot's *Middlemarch*, Charles Dickens's *Hard Times*, Harriet Beecher Stowe's *Uncle Tom's Cabin*, John Steinbeck's *The Grapes of Wrath*, Ralph Ellison's *Invisible Man*, Alen Patton's *Cry, the Beloved Country*, etc. Under the general frame of sociological novel falls other forms such as proletarian novel, novel of the soil, problem novel and the like. Dickens's *Hard Times* is a novel of the Industrial Revolution with its squalor and struggle of children, men and women. The novel begins very vividly presenting Gradgrind philosophy : "Now, what I want is, Facts. Teach these boys and girls nothing but Facts. Facts alone are wanted in life. Plant nothing else, and root out everything else. You can only form the minds of reasoning animals upon Facts: nothing else will ever be any service to them. This is the principle on which I bring up my own children, and this is the principle on which I bring up these children. Stick to Facts, sir!" (*see* Proletarian novel, Novel of the soil, Problem novel, Thesis novel).

Socratic method is the philosophical method of the Greek Philosopher Socrates (469-399BC) found in the *Dialogues* of Plato. His mission was as he claimed "searching into myself and other men". He followed the dialectic method by asking questions pretending to be ignorant of the subject matter. In the process a proposition is made and a series of questions are asked to test the validity of the proposition. By trying to elicit answers from the opponents he proved their ignorance of the subject matter. Such a method of debate was called 'Socratic irony' by his friends as he was the most knowledgeable person in the discussion resplendent with humour and rhetoric. By Dialectic method Socrates was able to arrive at truth with regard to beauty, justice and good by dialogue and debate which led to contradictions by his opponents. Aristotle applied the term dialectic to the science of logic.

Spoof is a light-hearted humorous piece of prose or verse on any subject matter. It is purely meant to provide laughter, e.g., Cervantes (1547-1616) in his *Don Quixote* presents a spoof on the romantic literature of the time and making fun of the Spanish society. Bernard Shaw's (1856-1950) *The Devil's Disciple* is a spoof of nineteenth century sentimental melodrama. James Grover Thurber (1894-1961), American cartoonist and writer, in his *Is Sex Necessary?* (1929), presents a spoof on the pseudo-scientific investigation of sex.

Static characters are those characters that do not change essentially in course of a novel, narrative or a play. Either they are evil or good throughout the story. In contrast to static characters there are the dynamic characters that change in course of the story. Static characters are mostly seen in the eighteenth century classical literature. With the Romantic revival, the writers replaced the static universal types with more complex and idiosyncratic characters (*see* Dynamic characters, Flat and round characters).

Stereotype is a type of character who appears in works of literature such as a cunning servant, a foolish old man, an innocent heroine, or a calculating villain. Such stereotypes are characters from particular social or religious groups. There can be also stereotype situations, gestures and linguistic jargon employed in fiction and drama.

Stock character in fiction represents a universally recognised type. Such a character represents a particular personality type representing a stereotype. These include character types such as the Harlequin the buffoon and servant, the braggart soldier, the Pantaloon the cuckold, the nagging wife, etc. The private eye in detective stories is a stock character, e.g., Erle Stanley Gardner's (1889-1970) Perry Mason, the lawyer-detective, is a central stock character in works such as *The Case of the Velvet Claws* (1933), *The Case of the Sulky Girl* (1933). Dashiell Hammett (1894-1961) has created his stock character detectives in Nick Charles and Sam Spade who appear in his works *Red Harvest* (1929), *The Maltese Falcon* (1930), *The Thin Man* (1932). Raymond Chandler's (1888-1959) detective Philip Marlowe is a stock character who appears in his fiction such as *The Big Sleep* (1939), *Farewell, My Lovely* (1940), *The High Window* (1942), *The Lady in the Lake* (1943) and *The Long Goodbye* (1953).

Stock situation is the usual recurrent pattern of relationships or events in fiction or drama such as an old uncle or aunt blocking young lovers or a husband and wife separated by misunderstanding, e.g., in Congreve's *The Way of the World* Lady Wishfort wishes to block the love of her niece Millamant for Mirabell.

Story and plot: E.M. Forster in *Aspects of the Novel* defines the difference between story and plot. A story begins and ends arbitrarily as it is not governed by reason. The Plot is something which the poet makes, e.g., The king died and then the queen died (story); The king died, then the queen died of grief (plot). A story is episodic as the events are simply linked to one another by 'and'. But the plot gives the reason why? And it moves back and forth to give emphasis to certain events. A plot must have a meaning. The poet who makes the plot with a beginning and end has it within his control as he is the maker. In the opinion of Forster Brecht's plays are mere stories and they are episodic as the scenes are connected by 'and'. Instead, in the plays of Ibsen, the scenes develop a plot as they are linked by 'because'. However, both the dramatists are concerned with causality which is a relationship of a cause to its effect. It is through the sequence of events arranged in such a way that a cause-and-effect relationship seems probable, (*see* Plot).

Story within a story occurs when another story enters into the main story as a digression. It is a pattern found in the long romances such as the *Arabian Nights, Decameron, The Canterbury Tales,* etc.

Straightforward prose is the everyday prose of a writer. It is also known as utilitarian prose. It depends on the skill and experience with which the author handles the language. Such everyday prose does not employ literary devices and the readers do not look for literary style. Such prose is used purely for communicating information as in everyday life. The following example is from Sir John Gielgud's essay on the production of Wilde's *The Importance of being Earnest.* He writes in a practical and simple manner on the 'pace' in the production of a comedy of manners. "The pace of the comedy must be leisurely, mannered; and everybody must, of course, speak beautifully – but the wit must appear spontaneous, though self-conscious. The text must be studied and spoken so as to arouse a cumulative effect of laughter from the audience. That is to say it may be sometimes necessary to sacrifice laughs on certain witty lines in order that a big laugh may come at the end of a passage, rather than to extract two or three small ones in between, which may dissipate the sense and retard the progress of the dialogue. There are, if anything, too many funny lines, and the actor may easily ruin a passage by allowing the audience to laugh in the middle...."

Stream of consciousness is a literary technique applied in fiction since the late nineteenth century. It is a psychological device by which subjective and objective reality can be presented. Through the method a character's random expressions, feelings, thoughts, and actions are recorded which are more at the pre-conscious level before being organised in the mind. It describes the unspoken thoughts and feelings. It is not to be confused with interior monologue which is expressed inwardly. Stream of consciousness often consists of rambling dialogue without logical order. It was William James (1842-1910) who used the term in his book *Principles of Psychology* (1890) to express the flow of inner experiences. The technique is applied in narrative fiction to depict the continuous chain of thoughts, feelings and emotions that pass through human minds. There are the layers of the conscious, unconscious and the subconscious in human consciousness. These are powerfully brought out in stream of consciousness fiction in which the characters speak in the first person through interior monologues. Such analysis of the human mind is found in the writings of Bergson, Freud, William James, Alder and Jung. Stream of consciousness novel came as a reaction to the well made nineteenth century fiction with clear plot and characterisation. In the opinion of Robert Humphry in such fiction "the basic emphasis is placed on exploration of the pre-speech levels of consciousness for the purposes primarily of revealing the psychic being of the characters." Known novels of stream of consciousness include Dorothy

Richardson's *Pilgrimage,* James Joyce's *Ulysses*, Virginia Woolf's *Mrs Dalloway*, and William Faulkner's *The Sound and the Fury,* e.g., "Wonder how is she feeling in that region. Shame all put on before third person. More put out about a hole in her stocking. Molly, her underjaw stuck out head back, about the farmer in the ridingboots and spurs at the horse show.... Wait. Hm. Hm. Yes. That's her perfume. Why she waved her hand. I leave you this to think of me when I'm far away on the pillow. What is it? Heliotrope? No Hyacinth? Hm. Roses, I think. She'd like scent of that kind. Sweet and cheap: soon sour. Why Molly likes opoponax. Suits her with a little jessamine mixed. Her high notes and her low notes. At the dance night she met him, dance of the hours. Heat brought it out. She was wearing her black and it had the perfume of the time before" (from Joyce's *Ulysses*).

Style in literature consists of the writer's particular literary manner and expression. Style and taste can be in the background of the period, its customs, language, sensibilities, etc. It is style that distinguishes a writer from others. It can make the reader identify a passage attributing it to the particular author. Styles have been categorised according to periods such as Classical, Medieval, Elizabethan, Jacobean, Restoration etc. At times styles are known by individual authors like Chaucerian, Shakespearean, Miltonic, Lawrentian, Hardian and the like. An author's style reveals his or her attitudes and background. For example, Hardy's style is pastoral as he wrote in the Wessex background, e.g., "One evening of late summer, before the nineteenth century had reached one third of its span, a young man and woman, the latter carrying a child, were approaching the large village of Weydon-Priors, in Upper Wessex, on foot. They were plainly but not ill clad, though the thick hoar of dust which had accumulated on their shoes and garments from an obviously long journey lent a disadvantageous shabbiness to their appearance just now" (from Hardy's *The Mayor of Casterbridge*).

Subjectivity is the quality of presenting characters and plot in a literary work influenced by one's personal sentiments and opinions. It comes in contrast to objectivity as these do not maintain the aesthetic distance from their characters and situations. The readers can identify the writer who presents himself as the protagonist. Subjectivity is found in autobiographical fiction such as James Joyce's *Portrait of the Artist as a Young Man*, Samuel Butler's *The Way of all Flesh*, Thomas Wolfe's *Look Homeward, Angel*, and Somerset Maugham's *Of Human Bondage*, e.g., Stephen Dedalus's story in Joyce's *Portrait of the Artist as a Young Man* is Joyce's own development from childhood to adulthood.

Sub-plot is a subsidiary plot in a play, story or novel that coincides with the main one. It is a story within a story to add more action and thrill in the complication of the main plot. It is usually involving a group of minor or subordinate characters. The subplot either reinforces the main plot or comes as a contrast to it. It was a practice in the Tudor and Jacobean drama. Shakespeare's *King Lear* has the 'Gloucester' as subplot involving Gloucester, Edmund and Edgar. 'Gloucester' subplot becomes a link between King Lear and the audience. The use of subplot became rare after the seventeenth century. Dickens in *David Copperfield* has the subplot of Steerforth alluring the pretty little Em'ly. He persuades her to run away with him causing intense misery to Peggotty household. Finally after a long search Mr. Peggotty finds her abandoned by Steerforth.

Supernatural element is brought in by some poets, dramatists and novelists to add seriousness to their writings with out-of-the-ordinary situations that bring about fatal consequences. For example, Coleridge adds supernatural element in *The Rime of the Ancient Mariner*. Shakespeare used ghosts and witches. In *Macbeth,* Macbeth and Banquo, while returning from military campaigns encounter the three witches who prophesy, that Macbeth shall be thane of Cawdor and king. As a consequence Macbeth is led to his ambition and evil designs to murder the king. In *Hamlet* supernatural element is presented in the form of the ghost of Hamlet's father. Hamlet is commanded by the ghost to avenge his father's death by killing Claudius. In Golding's *Lord of the Flies* the novelist presents supernatural elements. Melville's *Moby Dick* is a symbolic account of conflict in man with supernatural associations. In Emily Bronte's *Wuthering Heights* after the death of Heathcliff his spirit has been seen by people: " But the country folks, if you asked them would swear on their bible that he walks. There are those who speak of having met him near the church, and on the moor, and even within this house. Idle tales, you'll say, and so say I. Yet the old man by the kitchen fire affirms he has seen two on 'em looking out of his chamber window, on every rainy night since his death..."

Surfiction is a postmodernist trend in fiction by which a writer sets aside realism and writes in the manner of metafiction that speaks about itself. It was a concept developed by the American writer Raymond Federman in 1973 in his essay "Surfiction – A Position." In the essay he proposes his theory of future fiction that will turn away from realistic presentation (*see* Metafiction).

Surprise ending is a device by which there is an unexpected ending of a sentence for emphasis, e.g., "*Bartholomew Fair* is chiefly remarkable for the exhibition of odd humours and tumbler's tricks. And is on that account amusing to read once" (from Hazlitt's "Lectures on the English Comic Writers").

Surrealism is a literary and artistic movement which developed out of symbolism and dadaism in the 1920s. It fought against realism and concerned itself with the world of dreams and the unconscious mind. Its impact on theatre is found in movements such as the theatre of cruelty and the absurd theatre. It was founded by the French poet and critic André Breton. Breton published his *Surrealist Manifesto* in Paris in 1924 and held the view that the irrational is the best mode of perceiving and representing reality. Surrealism emphasized the role of the unconscious in creative activity and employed the psychic unconscious in a more orderly and serious manner. It was a movement in painting, sculpture and literature. Surrealists stressed hallucination, psychotic utterance, automatic writing and free associations. By using automatism they wrote whatever words came into their conscious mind and regarded these words as inviolable. The authors felt that this free flow of thought would establish a rapport with the subconscious mind of their readers. This purely psychic automatism was modified later by the conscious use of symbols derived from Freudian psychology. For example, a surrealistic proverb by Paul Éluard reads : "Elephants are contagious." In its simple form surrealism is present in modern literature as whatever is visionary and dreamlike. French playwright Alfred Jarry (1873-1907) with his *Ubu Roi* is the first to attempt Surrealism in drama. *Ubu Roi* derides traditional views of authority by presenting the rise to power of a grotesque and pompous king Ubu. He is a personification of greed, ignorance, and the bourgeois attitudes. The farce is considered the first work of the theatre of the absurd. Jean Cocteau (1889-1963), the French author, is a leading member of the surrealist movement, which emphasized the role of the unconscious in artistic creation. His works *Orpheus*, an adaptation of the Greek myth of Orpheus and *The Infernal Machine* are excellent surrealistic plays. American playwright Sam Shepard is known for his oblique story lines with mysterious characters. He uses surreal elements with images of popular culture. There is a movement from surreal to the realistic in treating people and situations. Some of his known plays include *Operation Sidewinder* (1970), *Curse of the Starving Class* (1977), *Buried Child* (1978, *True West* (1980), *Fool for Love* (1983), *A Lie of the Mind* (1985), and *Simpatico* (1994). In fiction William Burroughs, Sir Herbert Edward Read, and Gabriel Garcia Marquez are known for their surrealistic writings. Read's novel *The Green Child* (1935) is an allegorical fantasy on innocence. Colombian novelist and Nobel laureate Gabriel Garcia is known for his magic realism in his novel *Cien años de soledad* (1967; *One Hundred Years of Solitude*, 1970) which narrates the story of a Colombian family (*see* Magic Realism)

Suspense is the state of uncertainty which keeps the reader or audience wait in curiosity with regard to the outcome of the story or play. Suspense can be one of uncertainty or of anticipation. Suspense can turn sympathetic when the audience identifies itself with the painful situation of a character. Such a suspense turns intense due to dramatic irony when the audience knows what is going to happen to the protagonist who is unaware of it. Suspense is also maintained due to ignorance of what is going to happen. Shakespeare is a master craftsman who sustains suspense in his plays. In fiction especially in detective stories suspense grips a reader with a sudden disappearance of a character or a clue that is received.

Suspension of disbelief is a phrase derived from Coleridge's *Biographia Literaria* Chapter XIV where he writes : "... that my endeavours should be directed to persons and characters supernatural, or at least romantic; yet so as to transfer from our inward nature a human interest and a semblance of truth sufficient to procure for these shadows of imagination that willing suspension of disbelief for the moment, which constitute poetic faith." According to Coleridge there needs to be a temporary acceptance of the truth of a story presented in a drama or a fiction in poetic faith. Hence, one part of the mind accepts the story in faith, while the other part of the mind is aware that the story is fictional. For example, while watching the scene of the strangling of Desdemona in *Othello*, the audience is aware that it is in a world of play-acting and yet the audience temporarily accepts it in poetic faith. While reading the story of Orwell's *Aminal Farm* the reader believes in the supreme position of the pigs in the social order in poetic faith.

Symbol is derived from Greek 'symbolon' meaning 'mark' or 'sign'. Hence it refers to anything animate or inanimate that represents something beyond what is perceived. It implies something more complex. Symbols are used in poetry, drama and fiction. Coleridge's "The Rime of the Ancient Mariner" is a symbolic poem. In expressionist and surrealist drama, symbols play a very dominant role. In Shakespeare's *Macbeth,* when Lady Macbeth in her sleep walk, washes her hands it is a symbol of her guilt being washed. Ibsen very powerfully brings the meaning of the symbolic title he gives to his play *Ghosts* when he lets his protagonist Mrs. Alving utter, "Ghostlike. When I heard Regina and Oswald in there, it was as if I saw ghosts. I almost think we are all ghosts .... It isn't just what we have inherited from our father and mother that walks in us. It is all kind of dead ideas and all sorts of old and obsolete beliefs. They are not alive in us; but they remain in us none the less, and we can never rid ourselves of them." Ghosts become a symbol of incest and syphilis in the play. Symbols are used in fiction too, e.g., Hemingway's *The Old Man and the Se*a is a full of symbols as it portrays the parable of man's struggle, courage and endurance. At the end of the novel there is a symbolic description of the old man as a Christ-like figure: ""It was quiet in the harbour though and he sailed up onto the little patch of shingle below the rocks. There was no one to help him so he pulled the boat up as far as he could. Then he stepped out and made her fast to a rock. He unstepped the mast and furled the sail and tied it. Then he shouldered the mast and started to climb. It was then he knew the depth of his tiredness. He stopped for a moment and looked back and saw in the reflection from the street light the great tail of the fish standing up well behind the skiff's stern." Willian Golding in *The Lord of the Flies* presents Simon's death symbolically like Christ's death when "the sun stopped shining and darkness covered the whole country until three o'clock; and the curtain hanging in the Temple was torn in two" (Luke 23:44-45). Golding writes: "Then the clouds opened and let down the rain like a waterfall. The water bounded from the mountain-top, tore leaves and branches from the trees, poured like a cold shower over the struggling heap on the sand. Presently the heap broke up and figures staggered away. Only the beast lay still, a few yards from the sea. Even in the rain they could see how small a beast it was; and already its blood was staining the sand."

Symbolist movement in literature and the visual arts originated in France in the late nineteenth century. Symbolism in literature is expressing ideas, feelings, and values by means of symbols or suggestions rather than by direct statements. It was a reaction against the dominant realist and naturalist tendencies in literature. For symbolists imagination is the true interpreter of reality. They discarded rigid rules of versification and Parnassian. The symbolist movement had its beginning in the poetry of Charles Baudelaire. Symbolist writers attempted to explore the musical qualities of language through sound relationships. Others in the movement include Stéphane Mallarmé Paul Verlaine, Swedenborg, Poe and Arthur Rimbaud. In English literature symbolism is found in Blake, Coleridge, W.B. Yeats, Ezra Pound, T.S. Eliot, D.H. Lawrence and others (*see* Symbol).

Symposium is derived from Greek meaning 'drinking together' while gathering for a philosophic conversation. It is found in Plato's Dialogues *The Symposium*. By modern connotation the term refers to a collection of essays by scholars on a particular topic or the presentation of the same in a conference.

T

Table talk is a literary device by which a person's sayings and opinions are compiled. Ancient Greek *Deipnosopistai* is a collection of the dinner talks of the Sophists. Some known works in this genre are James First's *Proverbs and Aphorisms*; Worcester's *Apophthegms*; John Selden's *Table talk: Being the Discourses of John Selden Esq*; Joseph Spence's *Anecdotes*; Sheridan's *Sheridaniana*; Thomas More's *Memoirs, Journal and Correspondence*; Leigh Hunt's *Table-Talk,* etc.

Taboo is a prohibition in primitive societies which calls for certain type of behaviour socially or religiously. In religious taboos certain items are forbidden and are considered unclean or sacred. Such items have taboo attached to them for protection against their power. Since drama originated from ancient rituals, taboo is often infringed in them. An example of behavioural taboo is the prohibition against incest. In the case of Oedipus he breaks the taboo of incest in marrying his mother after patricide. Infringement of taboo is often presented in Greek, Jacobean and Neo-classical tragedies such as regicide, patricide, matricide, incest, etc.

Tale is a written or spoken prose or verse narrative loosely constructed for the sake of entertainment. It is a striking story with mysterious, bizarre or supernatural elements in it. Though a tale is similar to a story they are distinct in so far as a tale stresses action while a story focuses on the character. A tale is casual in structure while the story is more carefully constructed. Some of the traditionally known tales are: Chaucer's *Canterbury Tales*; *The Arabian Nights*; Swift's *A Tale of a Tub*; C. Day Lewis's *The Nabara*; Thomas Parnell's *The Hermit*; William Cowper's *John Gilpin*; Wordsworth's *Michael*; Coleridge's *Ancient Mariner*; Keats's *Eve of St. Agnes*; Tennyson's *Morte d' Arthur*, Dickens's *A Tale of Two Cities*; Poe's *Tales of the Grotesque*; Arnold's *Sohrab and Rustum*; Hardy's *The Sacrilege*; R.L. Stevenson's *Ticonderoga*; Kipling's *Tomlinson*; Mansfield's *The Rider at the Gate*; Alfred Noyes's *The Highwayman*; Patrick Kavanagh's *The Great Hunger*; Margaret Atwood's *The Handmaid's Tale* and the like.

Tall tale is a highly exaggerated and impossible account of the heroic and superhuman feats of a hero, e.g., Expliots of Odusseus and Beowulf; *Vision of Tundale* has several tall tales; Sir. John Mandeville's *Book of Travels*; Rabelais's *Pantagrue;* Voltaire's *Zadig*. Writers such as Mark Twain, O. Henry and Faulkner also wrote tall tales.

Tautology is derived from Greek meaning 'the same saying' and refers to repetition of words or concepts in different words, e.g., I myself personally shall see and look after your problem and case.

Techno-criticism is a new literary theory that has emerged in the wake of electronic mediated hypertext. There is a shift in aesthetics from linear and authoritative criticism to a non-linear form which calls for an active encounter between the reader and the text. Techno-criticism liberates the reader from passivity and gives a new thrust to writers, critics and readers.

Tension is the suspense created in a poem, drama or fiction which arouse excitement and grips the attention of the readers or audience. Allen Tate used the term to refer to 'extension' and 'intention' referring to the abstract and the concrete meaning in a work which has an interplay of the literal and the figurative.

Ten-year test is a term used to refer to a work that is in circulation as one of literary merit ten years after its first publication, e.g., R.K. Narayan's *The Guide* (1958), Salman Rushdie's *Midnight's Children* (1981), Vikram Seth's *Golden Gate* (1981).

Testament is derived from Latin meaning 'witnessing'. It refers to a document that affirms a belief. For example, the *Bible* is divided into New Testament and the Old Testament. The following are some examples of literature in this genre. Augustine's *Confessions* (c.400); Thomas Usk's *The Testament of Love* (1387); Villon's *Grand Testament*(1461); Humphry Powell's *Wyll of the Devil* (1550); Newman's *Apologia Pro Vita Sua* (1864); Bridges's *The Testament of Beauty* (1929), etc. Newman writes in his *Apologia Pro Vita Sua*: "From the time that I became a Catholic, of course I have no further history of my religious opinions to narrate. In saying this, I do not mean to say that my mind has been idle, or that I have given up thinking on theological subjects; but that I have had no variations to record, and have had no anxiety of heart whatever. I have been in perfect peace and contentment; I never have had one doubt. I was not conscious to myself, on my conversion, of any change, intellectual or moral, wrought in my mind. I was not conscious of firmer faith in the fundamental truths of revelation, or of more self-command; I had not more fervour; but it was like coming into port after a rough sea; and my happiness on that score remains to this day without interruption."

Theme is the central idea of a literary work with its subject matter, concerns and preoccupations. It unifies and controls the whole work. Through it the author comments on the subject matter and the various issues and shares his ideas with the readers. A theme is related to the organic unity of the whole work. In some works meant for pure entertainment like adventure stories or detective novels, the theme may not be so clearly defined. Sometimes the theme presented by the writer may not be in accordance with the beliefs of the reader. However, it presents another point of view to the reader in a world of free ideas. The reader should be careful to avoid confusing the theme of a work with its subject matter. At times the title of a work can be indicative of its theme, e.g., Jane Austen's *Pride and Prejudice* presents the theme of Darcy's pride and Elizabeth Bennet's prejudice.

Thesis novel deals with social, political or religious struggle in society with the purpose drawing public attention to social anomalies (*see* Problem novel, Sociological novel).

Third person narrative is a device in storytelling by which the narrator is not a character involved in the events but stands outside. Such a narrator is omniscient and is able to recount the events and enter into the mind of the characters and reveal their feelings and thoughts. Most stories are written in this genre, e.g., D.H. Lawrence's *Sons and Lovers*. " Paul had been many times up to Willey Farm during the autumn. He was friends with the two youngest boys. Edgar, the eldest, would not condescend at first. And Miriam also refused to be approached. She was afraid of being set at nought, as by her own brothers. The girl was romantic in her soul. Everywhere was a Walter Scott heroine being loved by men with helmets or with plumes in their caps."

Thriller is a term to refer to sensational novel, play or film in which there is intense action and suspense such as detective stories, spy stories, adventure stories, horror stories, war stories and crime stories. It has its origin from the German 'shudder novel' during the Romantic period as well as the Victorian 'tale of terror' and 'sensational novel'. Thrillers are meant to excite and frighten the readers or the audience with violence, crime and suspense. Often heroes and villains in thrillers reoccur in the novels of the same author. Elements of thriller is found in Edgar Allen Poe's *Tales of the Grotesque* *and Arabesque* (1840) and Wilkie Collins's *Woman in White* (1860). However, Edgar Wallace is said to have pioneered thrillers in English with his *The Four Just Men* (1905). He is considered the king of the genre with *Sanders of the River, The Angel of Terror, The Crimson Circle, The Green Archer, The Fellowship of the Frog, The Dark Eyes,* etc. Others noted thriller writers are Dornford Yates (1885-1960) who introduced his crime-buster Chandos and his friend Mansel in thrillers such as *Blind Corner* (1927); Ian Fleming (1908-64) popular with his James Bond thrillers like *Casino Royale, Live and Let Die, Diamonds for Ever, On Her Majesty's Secret Service,* etc.; John Buchan (1875-1940) with his thrillers such as *The Thirty-nine Steps, Greenmantle, Mr. Standfast,* etc. Agatha Christie, Dorothy L. Sayers, G.K. Chesterton Frederick Forsyth, Mickey Spillane, Raymond Le Queux, Nathaniel Gould, Raymond Chandler, Graham Greene, James Barlow, Francis Clifford, Lionel Davidson, and Adam Hall wrote in this genre. Among the movie thrillers are Mario Puzo's crime epic *The Godfather* (1969); the 'techno-thrillers' of Michael Crichton and Tom Clancy are replete with science and technology.

Time shift is a technique used in fiction by which a writer through flashbacks goes back and forth in time sequence, e.g., Emily Bronte in *Wuthering Heights* lets the story be narrated by Lockwood and Nelly Dean who is also a witness to many events.

Time novel is a stream of consciousness type of fiction in which time is central to its theme and movement, e.g., James Joyce's *Ulysses*, Dorothy Richard's *Pilgrimage*, Thomas Mann's *The Magic Mountain.* Dorothy Richardson's novel *Pilgrimage* (1911-1938) is a study of the growth and development of a young woman in which time plays a vital role as the novel is a 12-volume sequence. Joyce's *Ulysses* (1922) presents the theme of time as the action takes place in the course of a single day in modern Dublin and the mental lives of the characters are revealed through stream of consciousness technique.

Title of a novel can often give the central theme in it, e.g., Dickens *Great Expectations* is a study of the growth of Pip and fulfilment of his expectations; Austen in her *Pride and Prejudice* comment on Darcy's pride and Elizabeth's prejudice; Hemingway's *The Old Man and the Sea* is a study of human courage and endurance of the old man Santiago.

Tone reflects the attitude of a writer. By it he/she expresses his/her outlook and mood. Sometimes the author talks to himself/herself in a piece of work.

Tour de force is derived from French meaning 'turn of force' to refer to an author's exceptional mastery and skill, e.g., Orwell's *Animal Farm*. However the tem is also applied in a disparaging manner to works which are highly intellectual but lacking sincerity of expression.

Tract is pamphlet or leaflet of religious or political nature presenting a view-point with the purpose of propaganda, e,g., A series of 90 pamphlets entitled *Tracts for the Times* (1833-1841), were published in 1833 by Keble, Newman, Richard Hurrell Froude, and Isaac Williams explaining their religious views. The term Tractarianism is derived from this. Newman was a key writer of tracts and contributed 29 pamphlets including the famous final Tract 90 which opined that the Thirty-Nine Articles of the Church of England were pointers to the abuses in the Roman Catholic Church and not concerned with her dogmas of faith (*see* Oxford Movement).

Tractarian movement *(see* Oxford movement).

Tradition is a term referring to certain beliefs, practices, customs, works and conventions passed on from one generation to the next. In literature too such a tradition exists. T.S. Eliot in his essay "Tradition and the Individual Talent" brings out powerfully his concept of tradition when he says " It (tradition) cannot be inherited, and if you want it you must obtain it by great labour. It involves, in the first place, the historical sense...; and the historical sense involves a perception, not only of the pastness of the past, but of its presence; the historical sense compels a man to write not merely with his own generation in his bones, but with a feeling that the whole of the literature of Europe from Homer and within it the whole literature of his own country has a simultaneous existence.... This historical sense, which is a sense of the timeless as well as of the temporal and of the timeless and of the temporal together..." For example the Orestes story of Aeschylus reappears in Sophocles's *Electra*; T.S. Eliot's *The Family reunion;* O' Neill's *Mourning Becomes Electra* and Sartre's *Les Mouches.* In English literature we may speak of native traditions presented in the writings of Chaucer, the Scottish Chaucerians, Wyatt, Shakespeare and his contemporaries, Donne and some of the seventeenth century poets, Burns, Blake, Browning, Hopkins, Yeats, Pound, Eliot, W.H. Auden, Dylan Thomas, Ted Hughes and others. The Italian tradition is found in the writings of English poets such as Surrey, Sidney, Spenser, Milton, Keats, Shelley, Tennyson, Arnold, Francis Thompson, etc. In between these two traditions we find the neoclassical tradition from the Renaissance to the eighteenth century as represented by Dryden, Pope, Johnson, Crabbe and others.

In fiction and prose there is less of such classification under a particular tradition. F.R. Leavis in his *The Great Tradition* brings together novelists such as George Eliot, Henry James and Joseph Conrad as belonging to a great tradition of novels. He also speaks of a tradition in Jane Austen, Mrs. Gaskell, Scott, the Brontes, Dickens, Thackeray, George Eliot, Trollope, etc. F.R. Leavis writes: "Fielding made Jane Austen possible by opening the central tradition of English fiction. In fact, to say that the English novel began with him is as reasonable as such propositions ever are. He completed the work begun by the *Tatler* and the *Spectator*, in the pages of which we see the drama turning into the novel." However several great writers like James Joyce, Virginia Woolf, William Faulkner and others cannot be classified as belonging to any tradition.

Transcendentalism is a belief in a higher reality than that found in sense experience. The movement believed in the all embracing mystical power of nature to which materialistic man can attune himself by shedding all social restraints. It is a philosophy of a superior intuitive knowledge than the power of human reason. It divides reality into a realm of spirit and a realm of matter and emphasises the ethical power of man. Transcendentalism grew out of the Unitarianism and Romanticism of the 1830s among some American writers under the leadership of R.W. Emerson. In his essay *Nature* (1836) Emerson presented the manifesto of the movement which was further strengthened by the writing of Thoreau's *Walden.* The Transcendental club had other members such as Margaret Fuller, A.B. Alcott and W.E. Channing who wrote regularly in their magazine *The Dial* (1840-44). The movement influenced the writings of Herman Melville, Nathaniel Hawthorne and Walt Whitman.

Travel book is a non-fictional narrative which has been in vogue from ancient times recounting the travels, explorations, observations and adventures of people like travellers, explorers, sailors, soldiers, missionaries, diplomats and the like. The Classical Greek prototype is Homer's *Odyssey* which describes the adventures of Odysseus while returning to his kingdom of Ithaca after the Trojan Wars. Marco Polo's (1254-1324) account of his travels in the thirteenth century was a popular travel account of the Far East and China. Travel writing in Britain became popular in the Colonial period in the nineteenth century. Known works include Charles Darwin's *Voyage of the Beagle* (1839), Thackeray's *Cornhill to Grand Cairo* (1846), David Livingstone's *Missionary Travels in S. Africa* (1857), Richard Burton's *First Footsteps in Africa* (1856), and Henry Morton Stanley's *In Darkest Africa* (1890). Tourism industry has made people travel around the world and more and more travel books are read to know of various lands, people and cultures. Some of the popular travel books in the last century include Norman Douglas's *In Siren Land* (1911), Peter Fleming's *Brazilian Adventure* (1933), Graham Greene's *Lawless Roads* (1939), Evelyn Waugh's *When the Going was Good* (1946), Thor Heyerdahl's *The Kon-Tiki Expedition* (1950), Norman Lewis's *A Dragon Apparent* (1951), Robert Byron's *Reflections on a Marine Venus* (1953), Wilfred Thesiger's *Arabian Sands* (1959), R.K. Narayan's *My Dateless Diary* (1960), V.S. Naipaul's *An Area of Darkness* (1964), Patrick Leigh Fermor's *Roumeli* (1966), Eric Newby's *Slowly Down The Ganges* (1966), Wally Herbert's *Across the Top of the World* (1969), Paul Theroux's *The Happy Isles of Oceania* (1992) and others.

Travesty is a kind of parody in which a serious subject is ridiculed and treated frivolously, e.g., *Don Quixote* of Cervantes is a travesty of chivalry in which the protagonist imagines himself a knight-errant doing great feats as recounted in medieval romances (*see* Burlesque).

Treatise is a formal written work which investigates systematically a particular subject. Such treatises are usually undertaken in philosophy, theology, literature, science and so on, e.g., Aristotle's *Poetics*, Philip Sidney's *Apologie for Poetrie*, Francis Bacon's *Novum Organum*, Isaac Newton's *Principia Mathematica*, Locke's *Essay Concerning Human Understanding*, David Hume's *Treatise of Human Nature*, Darwin's *Origin of Species*, etc. *Origin of Species* begins: "When we compare the individuals of the same variety or sub-variety of our older cultivated plants and animals, one of the first points which strikes us is, that they generally differ more from each other than do the individuals of any one species or variety in a state of nature. And if we reflect on the vast diversity of the plants and animals which have been cultivated, and which have varied during all ages under the most different climates and treatment, we are driven to conclude that this great variability is due to our domestic productions having been raised under conditions of life not so uniform as, and somewhat different from, those to which the parent species had been exposed under nature."

Turning point in a story, novel or a drama refers to something that brings it to a crisis point such as an event, a recognition, or a choice that leads to a sudden change in the development of the plot. Such a turning point precedes a rising and falling action. It consists of an incident when there is a movement towards final resolution. Such a turning point is a climax. In a tragedy it is a fulcrum point from where the reversal of action begins leading to its catastrophe. Sometimes a play or a story may have more than one turning points, however there will be one central to all. In *Othello* the event of the handkerchief that falls by chance in Act III, iii becomes a turning point in the play that will lead to the strangling of the innocent Desdemona. Aristotle describes it as *peripeteia* or reversal. Thomas Hardy in *Far From the Madding Crowd* uses the device. The incident of the valentine letter with "Marry Me" sent to Boldwood by Bathsheba turns out to be a turning point leading to murderous consequences: "At dusk on the evening of St. Valentine's Day Boldwood sat down to supper as usual, by a beaming fire of aged logs. Upon the mantel-shelf before him was a time-piece, surmounted by a spread eagle, and upon the eagle's wings was the letter Bathsheba had sent. Here the bachelor's gaze was continually fastening itself, till the large red seal became as a blot of blood on the retina of his eye; and as he ate and drank he still read in fancy the words thereon, although they were too remote for his sight – 'MARRY ME.'"

Type is literary character who represents a particular class in behaviour (*see* Flat and round characters).

U

Ultraism is a radical attitude in literature by which certain authors make use of expressionism, surrealism absurd expressions. It also characterises the age of confusion, hopelessness and bitterness after the Great Wars, e.g., James Joyce in his *Finnegan's Wake* uses very strange expressions in a unique style resorting to puns and portmanteau words. The story narrated is that of a Dublin tavern keeper who has strange dream sequences with mythical and historical connotations. "I apologuise, Shaun began, but I would rather spinooze you one from the grimm gests of Jacko and Esaup, fable one, feeble too. Let us here consider the casus, my dear little cousis, (husstenhasstencaffincoffintusse... mtossemdamandamnnacosaghcusaghhobixhatouxpeswchbechoscashlcarcarcaract) of the Ondt and the Gracehoper" (from *Finnegan's Wake*).

Universality is the quality of literature by which it appeals to people irrespective of their particular situations in time and place. Longinus in his *On the Sublime* states that "lofty and true greatness in art pleases all men in all ages." A writer who aims at universal appeal ought to write primarily on human nature and behaviour. We have such writers of universal appeal such as Aristophanes, Juvenal, Ben Jonson, Dryden, Moliere, Pope, etc., who wrote on human behaviour. In fiction universality is found in making a story appeal to all men in all ages as for example the story of the old man Santiago as portrayed by Hemingway in *The Old Man and* *the Sea.* The courage and endurance of the old man is of universal significance.

Unitarianism is a form of Christianity that denies the doctrines of the Trinity (Father, Son and the Holy Spirit). They believe that God exists in one person only. It began in the first century and continued in the teachings of Monarchians. At the time of the Reformation, theologians all over Europe began questioning Unitarian beliefs. In nineteenth century England the Unitarians were legally classed with other dissenters. In the nineteenth century America, it became popular in the New England region and many left the Episcopalian church to become Unitarians. Unitarianism provided the theological background to the nineteenth century American Transcendentalism. They deny the doctrines of the Trinity, the vicarious atonement, the divinity of Jesus Christ, original sin, and everlasting punishment. They celebrate the Eucharist, not as a sacrament, but as a commemoration of Jesus' death.

Utopia is a word derived from Greek 'outopos' meaning 'not place' and refers to an imaginary state of perfection described by Sir Thomas More in his Latin political satire *Utopia* (1516). It is an account of the evils of his day and speaks of an ideal ordered hierarchy to be kept from the God-fearing King downward. In the second book he describes the island state a traveller named Raphael Hythlodaeus found in his voyages. In that state he found perfect order according to reason and people do what they say. It is a 'nowhere land'. Thomas More finds the virtuous pagans of Utopia living in harmony. They all work together for six-hours daily to raise crops. The society is patriarchal with family units and slaves who performed menial duties. Everything was held in common and people were not greedy for money, gold, silver and precious stones. Everything is well ordered with Communism as the general law. In the Utopian society there is religious freedom, education for men and women and marriage customs. They hate war and minimise it by all means. The Utopians do what is morally good to bring maximum happiness to all. They need no laws and lawyers. They love knowledge and worship a single God. They believe in the immortality of soul and happy life after death. More's thesis is that such a world of nowhere land remains an ideal and we can only wish for such a state of life. "But I am of a contrary opinion (quoth I) for me thinketh that men shall never there live wealthily, where all things be common. For how can there be abundance of goods, or of anything, where every man withdraweth his hand from labour? Whom the regard of his own gains driveth not to work, and the hope that he hath in other men's travails maketh him slothful. Then when they be pricked with poverty, and yet no man can by any law or right defend that for his own, which he hath gotten with the labour of his own hands, shall not there of necessity be continual sedition and bloodshed? Specially the authority and reverence of magistrates being taken away, which, what place it may have with such men among whom is no difference, I cannot devise..." (From *Utopia* Book I). Other works of similar nature are Francis Bacon's *New Atlantis* (1627), Samuel Gott's *New Jerusalem* (1648), Hobbes's *Leviathan* (1651), Bulwer Lytton's *The Coming Race* (1871), William Morris's *News from Nowhere* (1890), H.H. Wells's A *Modern Utopia* (1905), Aldous Huxley's *Island* (1962) and the like.

Utopian novel deals with ideal and perfectly ordered society where men live in peace and harmony devoid of problems. Such fiction is a reflection of the social problems than mere day dreaming, e.g., William Morris's *News from Nowhere* (1891) (*see* Utopia).

V

Vade mecum is a term derived from Latin meaning 'go with me' and refers to a handbook or pocket companion for reference like guides for birds, animals, plants, insects, etc.

Variorum is the short form in Latin for *'editio cum notis variorum'* which means 'an edition with notes of various editors.' It is a complete works of a particular author with notes of commentators and editors in course of different editions.

Vedanta is derived from Sanskrit *veda* meaning 'knowledge', and *anta*, meaning 'end'. Hence it is concerned with the six orthodox philosophies of Hinduism concerned with knowledge of Brahman who is the universal supreme being. It is the speculative part of Late Vedic literature especially *Aranyakas* and *Upanishads.*

Verisimilitude is a very important Renaissance concept which called for the appearance of truth or reality in a literary work. In a fictional work a writer of quality is able to present it with an element of truth. For example, Daniel Defoe's presentation of Robinson Crusoe is so realistic that the readers are led to believe that the novelist is presenting a first hand observation of reality. "Contented with this discovery, I came back to my raft, and fell to work to bring my cargo on shore, which took me up the rest of that day;

and what to do with myself at night, I knew not, nor indeed where to rest; for I was afraid to lie down on the ground, not knowing but some wild beast might devour me, though, as I afterwards found, there was really no need for those fears. However, as well as I could, I barricaded myself round with the chests and boards that I had brought on shore, and made a kind of a hut for that night's lodging; as for food, I yet saw not which way to supply myself, except that I had seen two or three creatures like hares run out of the wood where I shot the fowl". (From *Robinson Crusoe*) (*see* Naturalism, Realism).

Victorian period is from 1837 to 1901 when Queen Victoria reigned. It was a time of great social and religious ferment. There was a fundamental conflict between faith and reason, religious beliefs and the growing scientific development. The evolutionary theory of Darwin's *Origin of Species* had challenged the Biblical truths. The Victorians became a poor, blind, complacent people lost in a troubled world. They were supposed to be unconcerned with eternal values, yet were excessively religious and nostalgic about the past. Their tragic flaw was a moral hypocrisy and social snobbery. It became an age of contrasts: authority with freedom, wealth with poverty, faith with doubt, culture with philistinism. In spite of these, the Victorian age is an age of compromise, a typical English virtue following the golden mean, avoiding both the extremes in politics, religion, morality, science and literature. Close links were established between the writer and the reader. Most Victorians faced the problem of child labour, poverty, prostitution, etc., and found difficult to write. Most were preachers: Tennyson spoke of orderly existence; Browning – of spiritual enlightenment; Arnold – on sweetness and light; Carlyle – on devotion to duty; Ruskin – on righteous living; Pater – on the cult of the beautiful. Significant writers of the period are Carlyle, Keble, Cardinal Newman, Darwin, Thackeray, Robert Browning, Tennyson, Dickens, Emily Bronte, George Eliot, Ruskin, Arnold,

Thomas Hardy, R.L. Stevenson, Oscar Wilde, Rudyard Kipling, Synge, Henry James and others.

Viewpoint is the stand of the writer in narrating a story. Narration could be by an omniscient author who knows all things as in the case of Fielding's *Tom Jones*. Another viewpoint is the third person narrative by which the author puts into the mouth of a third person to narrate the story as in the case of D.H. Lawrence's *Sons and Lovers*. Authors also take recourse to first person narrative by which the story is related by one of the characters as, for example, Joyce's *A Portrait of an Artist as a Young Man*. Authors shift from one viewpoint to the other as in the case of Tolstoy in his *War and Peace*. Some writers make use of minor characters in presenting a viewpoint, e.g., in *Wuthering Heights* Emily Bronte makes use of Lockwood who is a tenant and the servant Ellen Dean to narrate the story (*see* Omniscient narrator, Third person narrative, First person narrative).

Vignette is a kind of decoration at the beginning or end of a chapter. It can also mean a brief passage or sketch inserted into a work.

W

Weltanschauung in German means 'worldview' referring to one's philosophy of life. The world view of Thomas Hardy as depicted in his novels is based on fatalism. Man according to him is the victim of chance, 'hap' and circumstances.

Weltliteratur is a German term coined by Goethe (1749-1832) to refer to a kind of world literature bringing together ideas of various nations and peoples and thereby ushering in exchange of ideas.

Wertherism is a term derived from the semi-autobiographical epistolary novel of Goethe *Die Lieden des jungen Werthers* (*The Sorrows of Young Werther*, 1774). The story surrounds Werther desperately in love with Charlotte who is engaged to be married to someone else. Stung by love the hero commits suicide. This concept of suicide caused ripples in Europe and the term Wertherism was coined in English to refer to a self-indulgent man of melancholy. Young men dressed themselves in blue coat like that of Werther and several were led to commit suicide.

Wit is a word pregnant with meaning. In the Renaissance it meant intellectual keenness by which writers were inventive in the use of conceits and figures of speech. In the seventeenth century the term was applied to metaphysical poets to mean inspiration, originality and creative imagination. T.S. Eliot in his discussion of the metaphysical poets commented on the wit of Marvell as "tough reasonableness". For the neo-classicists, the term 'wit' meant new critical attitudes. It meant intellectual humour meant to delight and surprise. Later the word wit came to mean 'fancy'. Hobbes in *Leviathan* referred to judgement rather than fancy. "Judgement without fancy is wit, but fancy without judgement not." In the nineteenth century wit was considered artificial while imagination real. Arnold spoke of Chaucer 'lacking high seriousness' and he considered his wit pure light-heartedness. T.S. Eliot considered metaphysical poets great due to their combining wit and thought.

Writers Workshop was founded in 1958 in Calcutta by Prof. P. Lal with the purpose of encouraging creative writing in English and transcreation in India, the Commonwealth and other English using territories. Writers Workshop holds discussions on Sunday mornings at 162/92 Lake Gardens, Calcutta, India. Today it has become the largest publisher of creative writings in India with over 3000 publications to its credit. It has published works of prominent writers such as Mulk Raj Anand, Keki N. Daruwalla, Kamala Das, Sashi Deshpande, Nissim Ezekiel, K.R. Srinivasa Iyengar, Shiv K. Kumar, Jayanta Mahapatra and others.

Y

Yarn is a colloquial word for a spun out sailor's story having incredible elements. The word is derived from sailor's slang metaphorically meaning spinning a story like making rope. It is a loose-knit tale consisting of accounts of strange happenings. Yarn is narrated in casual and colloquial manner and is usually passed on by oral tradition. Some yarns can be like tall tales which are very improbable. It is popular during campfires, bar-room or club gatherings. Writers who attempt such improbable stories are called yarners. Writers in this genre include R.L. Stevenson, Joseph Conrad, Mark Twain, William Faulkner and others.

Year book is an annual publication with references to various topics of interest. In recent times such books are becoming popular as they are a kind of encyclopaedias of latest in general knowledge, e.g., *Manorama Year Book.*

Yellow journalism refers to sensational journalism that began in America in the 1880s. In order to increase circulation yellow journalism was developed by certain publishers. Joseph Pulitzer tried it successfully in the *New York World* with a child in yellow dress popularly known as 'The Yellow Kid'. William Randolph Hearst attempted the same in the *San Francisco Examiner* and the *New York Morning Journal.* Eventually it led to sensational and scandalous news coverage in these papers with drawings and comic strips.

Yellow-backs are cheap editions of novels in circulation towards the end of the nineteenth century. These were bound in yellow boards.

Z

Zeitgeist in German refers to the spirit of an age. It seeks to capture the thoughts and preoccupations of the period. For instance, neoclassicism stood for reason, judgement, decorum and correctness.

Zeugma is a rhetorical device by which a single word is related to two or more words. The relations between the words are grammatically incorrect, e.g., "I went to the lake and caught three fish and a cold."